LYNN Howells

Despite the Knock-backs

LYNN HOWELLS

Despite the Knock-backs

LYNN HOWELLS

WITH ROGER HUGHES

First impression: 2012

© Copyright Lynn Howells and Y Lolfa Cyf., 2012

The contents of this book are subject to copyright, and may
not be reproduced by any means, mechanical or electronic,
without the prior, written consent of the publishers.

The publishers wish to acknowledge the support of
Cyngor Llyfrau Cymru

Cover photograph: Emyr Young

ISBN: 978 184771 483 1

FSC

Published and printed in Wales
on paper from well maintained forests by
Y Lolfa Cyf., Talybont, Ceredigion SY24 5HE
website www.ylolfa.com
e-mail ylolfa@ylolfa.com
tel 01970 832 304
fax 832 782

I would like to dedicate this book:

To my wife Jeromin
Thanks for always being there for me,
for being my wife, my soul mate, and best friend

To my children Lee and Claire
who always make me proud

Not forgetting Lee and Claire's partners, Louise and Darren

To my grandchildren Caitlin, Dale, Kian and Kia
for all the happiness you bring into my life

To my Mam, Dad and sister Wendy
and all my family past and present
Thanks for everything

To my friends who have always supported me

To Rugby Football,
without which none of this would have been possible

Acknowledgement

I would like to thank Roger Hughes, without whom this book would not have been finished, for all the hours he has put in and the tireless work encouraging me and keeping me focused. We met to write a book and became friends. I would like to thank all the contributors to this book for being so kind, especially Graham Henry and Neil Jenkins, and thanks also to Huw Evans for his generosity in supplying many of the photographs.

Lynn Howells
October 2012

No one is perfect... if you'll not settle for anything less than best, you will be amazed at what you can do with your life. You will be amazed at how much you can achieve.

Vince Lombardi
American football coach

Contents

Forewords Graham Henry and Neil Jenkins   9

1 They Killed Valleys Rugby   17

2 A Year of Achievement   34

3 They Can't Take That Away from Me   58

4 The Darkest Day   93

5 Little Moscow   114

6 Playing Days   131

7 The Battle of Brive   155

8 Down the Road to Cardiff   164

9 The Comfort of Home   184

10 Making History with Wales   196

11 The World Cup   222

12 Leading the Nation   236

13 Foreign Lands   258

Foreword
by Graham Henry

LYNN HOWELLS MIGHT not be the biggest name in world rugby. As a player his name was never discussed along with the great heroes who graced the red shirt with the three feathers, but as a coach I put him up there with the best.

Let's try to get this into context. During the latter part of the southern hemisphere Super 12 season in 1998 while coaching the Blues in Auckland, I had a phone call from one Terry Cobner who was in charge of the professional game in Wales. Well that's probably a bit of a stretch. It was the Welsh Rugby Union Board who were really responsible but they had to answer to all clubs in Wales. Hundreds of them, one in every valley, one in every town and every village, and the clubs were happy continuing the traditions of one hundred years: beat each other up on a Saturday afternoon and then have a few pints and a few more pints after the game, just like Granddad and Dad used to do. They, the clubs, elected the board, so progress in the professional era was painfully slow. The amateur clubs controlled the professional game.

Back to the point. Terry rang me to discuss whether I would be interested in coaching the Wales national team. Surprise, surprise, as Welsh rugby fans will know, I already expected the call because the *Wales on Sunday* and my old mate Andy Howell from the *Western Mail* had called me the week before to tell me Terry would be calling. But I was still surprised and I felt honoured; a traditional and passionate rugby country like Wales wanted to talk to me about being their coach.

Unbelievable. I didn't think these things happened and perhaps they didn't before then!

But being a loyal man with New Zealand rugby in my blood I thought it best to discuss this opportunity with the New Zealand Rugby Union. I really wanted to stay and coach the All Blacks one day. After the phone call from Terry, I made an appointment to see David Moffett, a man, later to become very well known in Welsh rugby, who was then CEO of New Zealand Rugby. I gave him some warning re the agenda. Well! He just abused me, and abused me, I was astounded. I couldn't believe the language, both body and word. He was totally out of control. I was shocked. He told me even if I went to Wales to discuss the opportunity I would never coach in New Zealand again. But he also didn't give me any confidence that I would be in line to coach the All Blacks one day.

So I didn't go to Wales. I met Glanmor Griffiths (chairman), Dennis Gethin (secretary), and Terry (head of rugby), over a weekend in June 1998 in Sydney, Australia. It was an opportune time as these gentlemen had just flown in from South Africa, where they had been with the Welsh team which had been heavily defeated. We met at a restaurant in The Rocks – very cordial, very positive, all seemed very keen to make this happen. Then in entered Lynn Howells. Who's he? What's this all about?

Lynn, and Leigh Jones (doing a great job in rugby development in Hong Kong) happened to wander into the very same restaurant and spotted us. I obviously didn't know who they were, but the reaction of my meeting colleagues suggested this was not part of the agenda. The best kept secrets and all that!

These guys, as I found out, were among the young rugby leaders in Wales, and were on their way to New Zealand for some professional development. I had some time with them later in Auckland where they had been joined by Geraint John (now doing a great job in rugby development in Canada),

David Pickering (my mate – and now the Welsh Rugby Union boss). They were obviously enjoying the situation, asking me leading questions, like where I was intending living, east or west? Newport, Cardiff, Swansea, Llanelli or even Pontypridd? But I enjoyed their company and was impressed with their knowledge and passion for the game. The rest is history.

We were all to meet up again when I became Wales coach. Geraint was involved with Cardiff rugby and was the backs coach of the highly successful Wales development team that toured Canada. Leigh coached at Newport and was the forward coach of that development team. David was appointed manager of Wales while I was the coach, and Lynn became my assistant with responsibility for the forwards. So it all worked out well in the end with no bribery or corruption.

As the saying goes, first impressions are important and I was immediately impressed with Lynn Howells. Humble, understated, but passionate; hard-working and knowledgeable about the game. He related to people well and was above all a person I could trust totally, the very first criteria when you are working and coaching together at any level and particularly at international level. He was a man of integrity, and basically a good 'bugger'.

From my point of view, being a foreign coach of Wales, I thought initially it was important for the rest of the management/coaching team to be predominately Welsh. Lynn at this time was coach of Pontypridd and they were always knocking around the top of the Premier League. The club and the team had a good environment and culture and did a lot for rugby development in the area. It was one of the clubs that I enjoyed visiting, travelling up from my village of Castleton for training or games. Lynn was at home at Ponty; he was a Valleys boy and he did a top job. The team played quality attacking rugby; Lynn had the forwards humming and the team was superbly navigated by Neil Jenkins, a player who I had a ton of respect for. It was obvious to me that Lynn was my man; he ran a good 'ship'. The culture was positive and he had his boys enjoying the game and winning with less talent than some of the more fashionable clubs.

Later on, when Wales started to get to grips with professionalism, how one of the franchise teams was not based in Pontypridd has always been a mystery to me. That enormous passion for the game in Wales seemed to me to have its backbone in the Valleys, and Pontypridd lead that.

After some initial challenges, winning only one of our first four games and with John Leslie, a New Zealander, son of All Blacks captain Andy Leslie scoring within 20 seconds of our first Six Nations game at Murrayfield, things improved. During these early days there was a bit of tension. I even got a letter from one of the 'money men' from Ebbw Vale offering me a one-way first-class ticket back to New Zealand. He was obviously concerned about my ideas about regional/franchise rugby. It amazed me how some successful businessmen wanted to protect a rugby structure that had brought failure and pain to those involved in rugby in Wales for 30 years.

However it all worked out reasonably well in 1999. We won 11 Tests on the trot, including the first victory in Paris since 1976; England at Wembley (what a day!); two Tests in Argentina; and South Africa for the first time to open the Millennium Stadium.

Lynn worked with senior forwards David Young, Garin Jenkins and Scott Quinnell to establish a top quality pack. Their set piece gave a platform to play from and they showed remarkable improvement with the ball in attack and in defence on their one-on-one tackling. We went on to the RWC quarter-final and got beaten by Australia, who went on to be the world champions. From there in 2000 and 2001 we never produced the consistency of 1999 but that's a story for another day. During late 2001, I replaced Lynn with Steve Hansen. I thought a new voice with some new ideas may have helped to bring that consistency. It was no reflection on Lynn's ability.

My initial assessment of Lynn Howells never changed. He was a top bloke. He was a quality forwards coach. He bought the understanding of the Welsh mentality that I didn't have. He bought loyalty, total support, composure under pressure, and the ability to get on easily and well with both players and management.

Because of the trust and respect built doing the job well, Lynn and I became good mates and got close as people – and we still are, which is why I am writing this for his book. We would talk long and often about how we could improve individual players and the team – I loved it! We also enjoyed a pint or two and later in the night a 'top' red. One of my most enjoyable times in rugby was, after a huge Test, finding a small private bar later in the night, and my wife Raewyn and I having a sing song with the Welsh management. We were awful but they were outstanding.

Graham Henry

Foreword
by Neil Jenkins

Lynn Howells, a longtime friend

IT WASN'T QUITE an ordinary training night as two new coaches were about to arrive to take charge of Pontypridd. Dennis John I had heard of, but not the guy who was to be his assistant, Lynn Howells. It never went through my mind that evening back in 1992 that I would set up such a long-standing rugby relationship and friendship with Lynn from that evening to this very day.

I didn't have much experience of his coaching at that time as Dennis looked after the backs and Lynn did the forwards, but our paths crossed and it became clear to me that he was a good coach and a good guy.

Those two between them put Pontypridd on the rugby map. They got the best out of the players. If anyone got ahead of themselves then Lynn would soon bring them back down to earth.

Even though I was amongst the backs I could see what an important job Lynn was doing with the forwards, a great deal of the Ponty success was down to him.

Eventually Lynn's chance came to become a head coach, and there was no bigger or possibly more difficult job in Wales than Cardiff. It was progress for him and eventually I joined him on the journey down the A470. I had no hesitation as I knew that wherever Lynn was coaching the job would be well done. I knew how he operated and I knew how he went about things, so it made my decision to leave Pontypridd and go to Cardiff easier knowing Lynn was the coach.

All the teams I played with under Lynn had a very good grasp of the basics, and a very good work ethic which is something not every side around at the moment can say.

Lynn played a massive part in the success of Pontypridd on both the occasions he was there, with Cardiff and the Warriors. We had good packs and when we needed to be pointed in the right direction Lynn provided that leadership. His pre-match team talks were colourful, and passionate, although often not for the faint-hearted or those with delicate ears.

Not to forget, of course, that Lynn was also the Wales forwards coach under Graham Henry, and he made a considerable contribution to the success the team had at that time.

When I returned from the Lions tour in 2001 I was ready to finish. I had injuries and eventually it was discovered that I had arthritis so I would have retired from playing. It was Lynn who persuaded me to carry on for another season, which saw the start of the Warriors. I probably wouldn't have done it for anyone else.

Lynn gave us the freedom and the ability to play, and whatever we did he backed us to the hilt. Wherever it was, we won together and we lost together and that togetherness was fostered by Lynn. I always enjoyed playing in the teams he was coaching as we played an attractive style of rugby, but we enjoyed ourselves as well.

We had a good banter on the pitch and a good banter off it, but it was not always smooth sailing. I remember during the last season of Pontypridd as a first class club, we had lost players to the World Cup preparation, people were beginning to think about what was going to happen with regional rugby and things at Ponty were starting to go off the rails. I recall we played against Newport and it was a poor game which we lost. Lynn accused one or two of the boys of not putting in a full shift, something I disagreed with. I accused him of taking his eye off the ball on the coaching front, something he took exception to. He invited me outside to continue the discussion. And I remember saying, "I don't care if you fine me or drop me from the team, but you needed telling." He agreed but because I had said my piece in front of the boys I would have to suffer the consequences. "I'll have to fine you Jenks," he said. "I can't drop you, we don't have enough players." At which point we both collapsed laughing and that was the end of the matter.

We had a good few arguments, but it was all done and dusted afterwards and we were mates again. You don't meet many nicer people than Lynn Howells, and I am delighted that he has asked me to write something in his autobiography.

Neil Jenkins

1

They Killed Valleys Rugby

THE BASTARDS. THOSE were my thoughts as I slumped down in my chair at our training complex at Pencoed after I realised what had happened. Eating, sleeping, walking the hills, out in the garden, drinking a pint, on my own, with friends or with my wife, I could think of nothing else that summer of 2004. I had landed a job which made me proud; I was coach of the Warriors, one of just five regions in Welsh rugby. A dream job for me. True, my success had come at a heavy price. My beloved Pontypridd had been one of the sacrifices made in the name of regional rugby, and that hurt. It hurt badly. My joy at being the Warriors coach was tinged with sadness that Pontypridd rugby would never be the same again.

Also when the Warriors were being put together, there were one or two people who didn't want one or two other people to be involved, and one of the people they didn't want to be involved was me. Steve Hansen, who replaced Graham Henry as national coach, and his assistant Scott Johnson didn't like the way I put Pontypridd before their claims for the Wales team. I had my priorities, they had theirs. I had overcome them, but now after all I was on the losing side. To go through the interview process I had to go through knowing that even some of the people on the interview panel were also against me, and to stick two fingers up at them was pleasing. But now it meant nothing.

It was all about to be taken away from me, and my team. At least some of the players were to move on, but for rugby in the Valleys, the heartland of Welsh rugby, it was the final curtain. For us, the coaches and the backroom staff, no one, least of all the Welsh Rugby Union seemed to care. They had succeeded.

The idea of bringing the best players together was probably correct; the failure from my point of view was that it didn't take into any consideration at all anything outside the playing aspect. My beef was with David Moffett. The man had no concept of Welsh rugby as far as I could see; he had no consideration as to what happened to the Gwent Valleys, what happened to the Rhondda Valleys, what happened to the Cynon Valley, what happened to Bridgend, some of the traditional hotbeds of Welsh rugby. These were then some of the biggest nurturing areas where the game grew, was played, and was watched. He gave no thought to the communities. Just take Pontypridd because I know it well. He had no idea that there was a Cynon Valley, two Rhondda Valleys, and then when you came around the lower end of Pontypridd, there was Church Village, Beddau and those areas, all supporting Pontypridd. The people supported Pontypridd, and for me he never had a concept of that. His line at the time was, "We're bringing this thing to a head. They've been talking about it and fiddling around the edges for the last couple of years, and you can't go on like that. You've got to actually say, this is what we believe in. It's up to others to show us that we're wrong and not only that, recommend something better."

It was just a numbers game with him all the time. I felt bitter towards him, and I still feel bitter towards him because in the end he just washed his hands of it and just walked away from it. The only consideration in his mind was money. It was just a matter of dividing everything up and we are just going to put one side in and lump you all together.

Ideas had been put forward, decisions had been made, and the biggest decisions which had affected Welsh rugby for a long time had been made by people from the other side of the world.

True, the WRU had recognised that something had to be done, and had recognised that there would be difficulties putting them into practice, but the final decisions had been implemented by three men with no real affection for, or affiliation to, Welsh rugby. Those three men were Graham Henry, Steve Hansen and David Moffett, although by the time the real discussions on regional rugby started taking place Graham had gone. He resigned after the 54–10 defeat by Ireland in Dublin in February 2002. When people look at it, the decisions were made by people who were not part of the country, and when they had returned to wherever they came from, we would be left picking up the pieces. In Wales it is more than rugby. You only have to look at Pontypridd the town, and since it has not been part of the hotbed of rugby, people from the Valleys have nothing to support. OK, one or two go to support the Ospreys. They certainly do not go down to Cardiff. Look at the way Bridgend have fallen to the third tier of Welsh rugby. Pontypridd, Neath and Ebbw Vale are now small-part teams when once they were crucial to the foundation of the game in Wales.

For me, from a rugby point of view, it was never thought through. If rugby becomes a money game then you have to have the support. If you don't put the teams in the right places then you don't get the support. Those are the things in my opinion which were never given enough thought. Moffett for me was one of the most ignorant men I have ever met, because you couldn't have any discussions with him, it was his way or nothing. The man wouldn't take any criticism or just wouldn't talk. The first time I met him was at one of the Six Nations games. He didn't want to talk to the likes of me. He just about ignored me and only wanted to speak to Graham. I just think it was the wrong people putting the structure into place.

Even as early as the mid-1990s the Welsh Rugby Union director of rugby Terry Cobner had highlighted failings in the structure of Welsh rugby. The game had just gone professional and Wales were in danger of being left behind the nations who had grasped the nettle.

After those glorious days of the Sixties and Seventies, the Eighties and Nineties were barren periods for our national game. In the Five Nations championship as it was in those days, from 1989 to 1996 Wales had the embarrassment of five wooden spoons, and one shared championship in eight years. Wales then embarked, in the summer of 1996, on a tour to Australia. They were thrashed. They lost the two internationals 56–25 in Brisbane, and 42–3 in Sydney. Worse than that, they also lost the three provincial games, 69–30 to ACT Brumbies, 27–20 to New South Wales, and 51–41 to the Australian B side.

Terry Cobner, who had experienced the glory days having played for Wales and the British Lions, wasted no time in starting his examination of the problems facing our national sport. Discussions started on the flight home but it didn't need someone of Cobner's astute rugby brain and experience to work out that the players we were producing were not up to international standard. In what was to become the Rugby Charter, Cobner identified that there were three elements to the success of the game: talent, money and fixtures.

At this time there were 12 teams in Wales which could be called the premier clubs. Of all those sides the discussions identified that only something like 45 to 50 players were of international class, about four per team. It was also known that there were probably only about fifteen boys a year coming out of the schools and youth rugby. Of those, five or fewer had the potential to make the grade at international level. The talent and, importantly in the professional age, the money, was being spread too thinly. The idea was put forward to bring some of this scattered talent together to play in European competition, but the idea wasn't popular and it died in the water.

The fortunes of the Wales team didn't improve and the idea of bringing the talent together surfaced once more. This time the clubs were reduced from a dozen down to eight, nine if you include Caerphilly. Terry Cobner's idea of four regions was still a long, long way off, but at least the talent would be a little more concentrated. Academies were to feed quality players through to the top clubs and the number of foreign players, who had blocked the route forward for much of the home grown talent, it was hoped, would be controlled. That was as far as the clubs, who ran the game in Wales in those days, were prepared to go. The money too would be less spread out, important if the players were going to be paid enough to stop them flooding over the bridge to England, or across to Ireland and France where clubs could afford to pay more than those in Wales.

The third element identified by Cobner was the fixture list. If the clubs would ever agree to go down to four then they could not end up playing each other endless times in a season. Talks took place with the English clubs about an Anglo Welsh competition. They said quite bluntly that Wales brought nothing financially to the table. They weren't interested apart from accepting Cardiff and Swansea who they saw as the most attractive money-spinning opposition in the Principality. Both those clubs did flirt with their English counterparts for one season, much to the annoyance of the WRU. Having been rebuffed by the English, talks then started with the other Celtic nations, and a viable competition was put in place initially with teams from Wales and Scotland, with the Irish joining for the 2001/02 season. The Celtic League consisted of eight teams from Wales, two from Scotland and four from Ireland. Later would come the Heineken Cup and its subsidiary competition, the Parker Pen Shield.

That was what was in place when regional rugby came back onto the agenda during the time Graham Henry was Wales coach. At the time everything was going in the right direction for Graham. Graham was all-important. They were falling over each other at the WRU to please him. He was the one who was driving through the regional concept, but his idea was five regions, always five, never any other number. That was the number he thought was right.

He believed that with the nine clubs, a lot of quality players were missing out on the big European action, the Heineken

Cup. For Wales to be successful nationally the best players had to be playing at the highest level. To some extent he was right. There was not the number of quality players to justify the number of teams that were there. So it was a matter of bringing all the quality players together. That concept had my total support.

I don't know to this day whether Graham was right in his assumption that players were missing out on the big matches. Results like Pontypridd beating Leicester, Llanelli winning away at Sale, Newport beating London Irish, Swansea beating Bristol, and Bridgend overcoming Bath showed what could be done in the European competitions. I really do not think the idea was thought through. It was just a question of putting as many quality players into a group and then it becomes very easy for the national coach because you are only looking at four teams not nine. Nothing wrong with that. I think that all structures should be geared towards the national team anyway.

I'm not sure whether a report commissioned by the Rhondda Cynon Taf Substance Misuse Action Team had any bearing on matters, but it also showed that something had to be done to improve Welsh rugby. The report claimed that, 'The decline in Welsh rugby is partly to blame for the increase in domestic violence. Wife beating,' it said, 'doubles on international days, quadruples if Wales lose, and increases eight times if Wales lose to England!'

The man I will never forgive for the part he played in my life is David Moffett. I didn't know the man when he was appointed. I did some research on him and looked to see what he had done and he was a hatchet man out in Australia.

Although always referred to as an Australian, David Moffett was born in Doncaster – how ironic considering that I would spend time coaching there. After spending part of his childhood in East Africa, his family eventually moved to Brisbane, Australia. Here he set up his own business in cleaning and waste disposal, before becoming involved in sports administration. He had been executive director of the New South Wales Rugby Union, then chief executive of the New Zealand Rugby Union, followed by a spell in Australia as the chief executive of their National Rugby League. After ten years in those roles, he had oceans of experience of sports administration. He had also been instrumental in setting up the Super 12 tournament between Australia, New Zealand and South Africa. But he knew hardly anything about Wales.

His first sortie into the UK came when he applied for the post as chief executive of the Football Association, a position which went to Adam Crozier. He was successful though in January 2002 when he became chief executive of Sport England. He was a driven and determined character who lasted less than a year in his post before announcing in October 2002 that he was leaving for personal reasons. He said at the time, "Agents of change only have a certain shelf life." He did add that he was going to stay in his post until a successor could be appointed in the spring. That didn't happen. By the end of October chairman Glanmor Griffiths and David Pickering had appointed David Moffett group chief executive of the Welsh Rugby Union on a salary which varied from £120,000 to £200,000 a year depending on what you read. The Welsh Rugby Union needed a professional chief executive in the professional age, and the headhunters appointed by the Union came up with David Moffett.

He started work on the second of December 2002, and started to rattle cages as soon as he sat behind his desk in the Custom House, then the WRU headquarters. He announced three new appointments: that of chief executive of the Welsh Rugby Union, therefore making redundant another Ponty man, Dennis Gethin, who had been secretary. The Millennium Stadium was to have its own chief executive, and there was to be a marketing director. Again he was clearing out the amateur way Welsh rugby had been run, and replacing it with a more professional format. Take nothing away from the guy, he did get the Union financially sorted, but he had no idea of rugby.

He just went in and chopped everything. He was the one who shook it all up. He was a money man. He apparently once said that professional sport is all about money, and the only good decision is the tough decision.

He also announced that the pitch at the stadium which had come in for some criticism during the autumn internationals would be changed. They had been bringing in and taking the pitch out on pallets which were put together rather like a jigsaw. The problem was that the height of each pallet never matched with the one next to it, so the pitch was bumpy, a problem, especially as international soccer was now being played at the stadium as well. It was decided to lay an ordinary pitch even though the experts said this would have to be changed two or three times a year.

As early as 3 December Moffett gave the first hint that he was going to become involved in the regional rugby debate. He said that only the top 150 players in Wales should be paid. No one below that level should receive money for playing. A week later he put forward his first tentative proposal to the premier division clubs. He admitted that he was not surprised they rejected that plan for four regions, but expected them to come back with their own ideas "soon". He warned that he was "not prepared to wait years", but agreed that a decision by the clubs "appeared to be a long way off".

Whereas Moffett was looking towards four regions, the clubs were not prepared to entertain anything less than five, but where they did agree with him was that a new structure was essential and urgent. There did not appear to be total negativity towards change from the clubs. They were confident that the five new sides could attract sponsors and supporters, but the dangers were the deep rifts between some of the clubs. There were egos to be massaged, rivalries to be overcome, and in some cases jobs to be preserved by those doing the negotiating.

Bridgend and Neath had already taken the bull by the horns and announced that they were happy to form one of the new regions. Newport had started tentative discussions with Ebbw Vale, although feeling they were the team with history in Gwent, Newport would have preferred to have stood alone. Cardiff were quite happy to swallow up Caerphilly, but at the other end of the scale Llanelli and Swansea would not have joined at any price. Well they would have joined but only if Swansea agreed that they would play in red, play all the games at Stradey Park and the region would be called Llanelli! Likely? I think not. Even so it appeared that the clubs were not that far away from coming up with a very viable proposal which would have been Newport and Ebbw Vale, Bridgend and Neath, Cardiff would incorporate Caerphilly but retain the name Cardiff. The stumbling block was that Pontypridd, Llanelli, and Swansea also wanted to stand alone.

But Moffett was still insisting on four teams based in Newport, Cardiff, Swansea, and wait for it, Wrexham! He had this hankering to include north Wales which had never, with due respect to the few players who have come from that area, played a major part in Welsh rugby. "North Wales would be the equivalent of the Brumbies in the Super 12," he said. "They're already playing rugby there; there is an appetite for a strong rugby presence; there are a million people in that area, and the time is right to embrace the whole of Wales in this, not just south Wales."

Attempts had been made in the past to try to integrate north Wales, but because of a lack of any tradition, and travelling difficulties between north and south, these had always failed. The premier clubs had never considered north Wales in any of their discussions. It was another example of how naïve Moffett was about Wales and Welsh rugby. There was to be a lot of midnight oil to be burnt before any agreement was reached.

Whilst trying to establish his plan for regional rugby, David Moffett was also pushing ahead with his plans to cut the Welsh Rugby Union deficit. 'Slashing and burning' was what one newspaper called his plan to cut 50 members of staff who were to be laid off. On the playing side, the Wales A team, which some regarded as an important piece in the jigsaw making up the international progression, was to be axed. So too were the international teams at younger age group levels, and there would be a reduction in the funding of the women's game. Even the senior internationals were hit, with a reduction in their expenses and match bonuses. It appeared that David Moffett was upsetting just about everyone involved in Welsh rugby less than a month into his new job.

Suddenly, a day after an agreement on the regional picture seemed to be coming to some sort of resolution, the pieces of the jigsaw were thrown into the air and came down with a different picture. Bridgend would now go with Pontypridd, Neath with Swansea, Cardiff would swallow up Caerphilly, and Newport would merge with Ebbw Vale. The stand alone now was Llanelli. Newport, Cardiff, Pontypridd, Swansea and Llanelli, who were the architects of the plan, were to become known as the 'Gang of Five'. If anything agreement was further away now than it had been 24 hours earlier.

So far Moffett had only met with the chief executives of the Premier clubs. At this time Welsh club rugby was financed by a number of millionaire backers. Tony Brown at Newport who made his money from Bisley Office Furniture; Peter Thomas at Cardiff, who was into construction, as were Mike James and Robert Davies who were the backers of Swansea. Huw Evans of Llanelli was into computers; Leighton Samuel put money from his picture frame business into Bridgend; and Mike Cuddy at Neath ran a demolition and earth moving organization. Pontypridd were supported by Buy As You View, whilst Ebbw Vale boasted Marcus Russell, manager of pop groups such as Oasis.

They were dead against Moffett's four region plan, but the WRU boss could see that these men held the key and wanted to meet them "as a matter of urgency", he said. Early in the New Year the meeting with the benefactors took place. "I'm all ears to hear what they come back with," announced Moffett. The problem was, all they came back with was the news that Cardiff,

Swansea, Pontypridd and Llanelli wanted to stand alone. Apparently Cardiff chief executive Bob Norster kept reminding the meetings that Cardiff could in theory amalgamate with Pontypridd, but as it was in the Cardiff constitution that all home matches had to be played at the Arms Park, no games could be played at Sardis Road. Ponty clearly would never have gone along with that.

I never attended any of these meetings, either with the club benefactors, or the chief executives, but I am told that there were some pretty aggressive and feisty characters amongst them. There was plenty of fist banging on tables and finger pointing as each defended his own domain. It clearly wasn't a place for the faint-hearted and each was prepared to stand his corner.

Tony Brown came out with a rallying cry backing Moffett's call for four regions. He urged the other money men to follow Newport's lead in joining Ebbw Vale, "for the good of the game". Brown recognised that there was great loyalty to the clubs, but pleaded, "We must try to drive the game forward in Wales. It is essential that we reduce the number of fully professional clubs. The funding is inadequate for nine; the general opinion is that there is only room for four."

"Every premier club," continued the Newport benefactor, "could put forward a solid argument for standing alone. We have got to cut our suit according to the cloth we have available." Brown, though, did accuse the WRU of a "total lack of competence or leadership", claiming ominously that David Moffett seemed "like a guy who wants to get a job done and I think he will".

The pro-Moffett revolution was echoed by Bridgend benefactor Leighton Samuel. "We only have the players and the money for four in my opinion," he pointed out. Others too were starting to come around to the Australian's way of thinking, even if they were nowhere near agreeing with his method.

By 11 January a Cardiff–Pontypridd amalgamation was

being mooted. Tommy David, the former captain of Pontypridd who had pulled on the famous black and white shirt more than 400 times, prefixed his thoughts by saying that he personally wouldn't like to see union between the two bitter rivals. He added: "The reality is that if changes have to be made then we would simply have to accept the merger." He continued, "If we do that then we must get 100 per cent behind it, everyone, the players, the clubs, and the supporters. I think people would travel to Cardiff to support the team." As a counter to that one Pontypridd supporter came out with the quip that if his team joined Cardiff and happened to be playing on his back lawn, he still wouldn't draw back the curtains to watch them!

On 17 January Moffett got his meeting with the club benefactors. It didn't last long as the money men flatly refused to agree to the four-team scenario. Moffett stormed out, slammed the door of his car and drove back to Cardiff. "I'm wasting my time," was his take on the proceedings. The owners, though, had second thoughts, asking for a meeting with the group chief executive again that very night. Now it was agreed that two proposals should be put before the WRU committee. Proposal one: Cardiff joining Pontypridd, Llanelli with Swansea, Newport and Ebbw Vale and Neath with Bridgend. Proposal two: Cardiff and Llanelli standing alone, Bridgend joining with Pontypridd, Newport with Ebbw Vale and Swansea with Neath.

It appeared suddenly now that peace was about to break out. Whatever was going to happen, I was determined that Pontypridd was going to be part of it. I was fed up with the likes of Newport, Cardiff, Swansea and Llanelli being termed the so-called 'big clubs'. Pontypridd had been successful but never got the credit. I was determined that we had to make the club so successful that it was impossible for them to ditch us. We had to make sure the Welsh Rugby Union looked upon us as one of the big clubs.

Despite their willingness to join Neath from a very early stage, Bridgend were willing to join with Pontypridd as a second option. Neath, though, were not so enamoured about getting into bed with Swansea. It was another false dawn and another, this time potentially more damaging, prospect of legal threats. Leighton Samuel wanted more money for the Bridgend link-up with Pontypridd. Confusion reigned again.

Despite this the two proposals were put before the WRU and the plan for four was passed. That wasn't surprising as it was what the WRU had come up with after its original investigation in the rugby charter. That would now be put before an Extraordinary General Meeting of all the 239 member clubs in February. So confident was he of success that the group chief executive presented his proposals for four Welsh regions before the movers and shakers of the European Club Rugby (ERC), for inclusion in the Heineken Cup competition. Wales were given until 2 April to present their final plans to ERC.

Moffett was acting as if everything in the garden was smelling of roses, but the clubs were about to dig over the flower bed yet again. They were still not prepared to accept the WRU committee's vote for four regions, they were still split. Newport, Ebbw Vale, Bridgend and Neath were still arguing that there was only enough money for four, Llanelli, Cardiff, Pontypridd and Swansea still wanted five. Now came the absolute hammer blow to Moffett: if Cardiff and Llanelli were allowed to stand alone, Ponty and Swansea would sue the Union over the 10-year 'loyalty agreement' they had been forced to sign in 1997. When Cardiff and Swansea had decided to abandon Welsh club rugby and play the English clubs, the WRU persuaded the other major clubs to sign that agreement. In return the WRU agreed that those clubs would always play at the highest level of competition organised by the Welsh Rugby Union. In 2003 that was going to be the proposed regional rugby. It was clear to us that Llanelli were also prepared to use the 'loyalty agreement' in their bid to stand alone, and they actually issued a writ against the Union. By the time any court proceedings would have been heard it would have been too late for any Welsh clubs to gain entry into the European competitions.

So Moffett now turned to brinkmanship. He said that rather than risk an expensive legal battle in the courts he would leave things as they were with nine clubs. "I will not put the Union at risk financially if we are threatened with legal action from some clubs."

Llanelli said they were willing to take responsibility for north Wales, even playing some of their matches up there. Some cynics saw this as an attempt to get the support of the north Wales clubs. Moffett's ploy worked. With the prospect of having to go back to nine clubs with all the problems which regional rugby would have removed, the threats of legal action were withdrawn. Suddenly on 21 March hatchets were buried, old rivalries forgotten, and the feud came to an end. The nine clubs for the first time agreed on the formation of the five regions they had wanted. Cardiff and Llanelli would stand alone, getting less money from the Union than the amalgamated clubs. Newport and Ebbw Vale, Swansea and Neath, and importantly for me, Ponty would join with Bridgend. The clubs met with David Moffett, presented their plan, and he accepted.

There was one other major skirmish between Newport and Ebbw Vale which culminated in Tony Brown being barred from entering Eugene Cross Park one wet and windy night to watch Ebbw Vale and Newport in a premiership match, but it didn't blow the agreement apart.

On 1 April 2003 David Moffett called a press conference at the Millennium Stadium. The press gathered. Derek King, who had been the chairman of all the meetings between the chief executives, was also on the top table, having moments before witnessed the signing of the documents to put regional rugby in place for the start of the 2003 season. His face was a picture when the group chief executive announced to the press that the deal was off, all negotiations had broken down and that was the end of it. The press couldn't believe the words coming out of David Moffett's mouth either. Then he reminded them of the date: April Fool! It was a moment of light relief at the end of many battles, arguments and threats. Regional rugby was born.

No doubt somewhere in Wales that night there were people celebrating. It might have been Moffett, although with him wanting four sides, and possibly one in the north, he had hardly won. I doubt the benefactors raised a glass, and it was probably beyond many members of the WRU for them to understand what was going on. Certainly there were no celebrations where I was. How was it going to happen I wondered? The only celebration for me, and I would suggest many other Pontypridd faithful, was that we were not going in with Cardiff. That would never have worked.

I do not think that there was a problem from our point of view that we were going to amalgamate with Bridgend once the decision had been made. The side we were always naturally drawn towards was Neath. Even though they were further away than Bridgend, I think that had the supporters and the club had a preference, it would have been to join with Neath. There was always an allegiance between Pontypridd and the Welsh All Blacks; it was a rugby link and a mutual feeling between the supporters. Having said that, as the discussions developed the supporters still felt Pontypridd had done enough to warrant standing alone. They didn't want it to happen, but once the decisions on regional rugby had been made, I got the feeling that the fans were willing to get behind it – reluctantly.

I felt strongly about it, and that gave me something of a dilemma. I wanted to be part of the coaching set up in the new regional rugby, but I also didn't want to see Pontypridd disappear. I stuck my neck out a bit in speaking about Pontypridd's qualifications to stand alone, but the club had been good to me both as a player and a coach. It had been a successful club, and a successful club in developing young players who had gone on to play for Wales. I felt that it was the right thing to say that the club was strong enough to stand on its own. Yes, that might well have damaged my chances of landing one of the coaching jobs, but I felt that strongly about it. I was asked about the possibility of Valleys rugby disappearing after our defeat by Newport in January 2002 and I said, "There has to be Valleys rugby somewhere, be it Ebbw Vale, Merthyr – anywhere. Everyone has raped the Valleys for so many years that it is about time we put something back. It's certainly a place where the communities are close knit and offer something different. Valleys rugby adds something to the game in Wales. It has a culture of its own and it would be a terrible shame if we lose it. We must make the right decision, but it should be a rugby decision and not a financial one."

Saving Pontypridd was more important to me at that time than getting one of the jobs. Without a doubt, I would have gone as far as necessary to save the club. I would have done as much as it would have had taken, but eventually it was out of anybody's control.

I was in a strange position. At the time I was not against regional rugby, and I was part of Graham Henry's Wales's coaching team. When I was with Wales I could see why the national coach would want it. It was important to be able to see as many of the prospective Welsh international players as possible in the shortest possible time, and against the best opposition. Then, when I was with Pontypridd I just didn't want to lose the club game and all that went with it.

The players were also concerned and probably even more worried about their futures. All of a sudden there weren't going to be the same number of places for players. They certainly started discussing their futures at Pontypridd and Bridgend, and they certainly discussed it at Neath and Swansea. What people forget is that at Newport, Cardiff and Llanelli nothing would change. They just kept going the same way as they had always done, so it was the players at the four amalgamating clubs plus Ebbw Vale and Caerphilly which it affected. The players were fighting for their lives. They were fighting to be at one of the regions. Certainly at Sardis Road the players got disheartened, and the season fell apart for us. We were up there with a chance of winning the league, but things just faded away and Bridgend won the title on the very last day, beating us at Sardis Road.

Everyone could see what was going to happen and it was a difficult time. In my personal opinion we did not have to reduce the number of top sides. There were enough top quality players in Wales for us to keep going the way we were. Why do I say that? Well look at the situation now. If you lose a tight-head prop then you are scratching your head to find another one. You now have four tight-head props to choose from whereas before you might have had nine. Some of those props may not be Welsh, some may be past their international sell-by date, but at least you had a bigger choice.

My other big criticism of the system involves the number of players who are not actually playing. Teams are stacking up players in certain positions to strengthen the depth of their squads. You have to in the modern game. You have to have cover in all positions, but that doesn't help players in the national squad who might only be getting twenty minutes here and there. Coaches of the regions have to think of their region first and they have to have a big squad.

When the final agreement was reached we were about to embark on a radical change, and whether I agreed with it or not, I wanted to be part of it. Little did I or anyone else realise that within twelve months we would lose everything we had fought for, everything we had bought into, and everything we had worked hard to make a success.

2

A Year of Achievement

Now that regional rugby was going to happen, it must have been the ambition of every coach at the senior level of the game in Wales to land one of the five regions. It certainly was high on my agenda. Without believing for one moment that I was a certainty to get a job, or that because of my experience I was an obvious choice for one of the five regions, I thought I had a fair chance. You have to prove you are worthy of the job and that is why I wasn't taking anything for granted.

I said at the time to the newspaper guys that I was hopeful of landing one of the regional jobs and I thought I was in with a possibility of one of them. I had coached most of the top players at national level, and gained a lot of experience from my time at Cardiff and at Pontypridd, so I wouldn't be worried which of the regions I took on. At this time, early in 2003, there was still strong talk of four regions and of Pontypridd joining with Cardiff. Not wishing to burn any bridges I said that I wouldn't mind being involved with Cardiff again, I thought that was the right thing to say at the time. I would have gone back to coach at the Arms Park if certain people hadn't been at Cardiff, such as Peter Thomas and one or two of the senior players, such as Jonathan Humphreys and Rob Howley. I wouldn't have gone back to Cardiff with those people there for a gold clock after what had happened when I was coach.

By the time everything had been sorted out and there was to

be an amalgamation between Pontypridd and Bridgend, being the coach at Ponty, that was the natural one to go for, and that was my first choice. My second choice would have been the Swansea–Neath combination, and I made this known to the powers that be.

Other names were in the frame. Apparently the WRU wanted Mike Ruddock who was coach at Ebbw Vale and also the Wales A coach, to take over our region. Mike preferred to stay in Gwent and for him to take over the Newport–Ebbw Vale outfit. I think he could also see that his appointment at Pontypridd might cause a lot of friction with the locals. My good friend and Bridgend coach Allan Lewis pushed a case for the two of us to remain at the region saying, "I would like to be coaching the new team alongside Lynn because we would work well together in the interests of both our clubs. We have already begun some discussions about players and we know and respect each other's work. It is important for some sense of continuity and experience to remain."

Continuity would prevail at some of the other regions. Gareth Jenkins and Nigel Davies, who had done wonders with Llanelli, would be favourites to stay at Stradey, whilst Neath coach Lyn Jones was in line to get the Neath–Swansea region. Former Wales outside half Paul Turner, who was the backs coach at Harlequins, threw his hat into the ring, I think, by declaring that he was interested in coaching at Cardiff alongside Dai Young.

The owners and others were all pushing the case for their man to get the local position. Peter Thomas always said that Dai Young was going to be the Cardiff coach; Llanelli chairman Stuart Gallagher turned round and said that Gareth Jenkins was going to be the coach at Llanelli. Thankfully Allan Lewis and I got support from Pontypridd chief executive Gareth Thomas and Bridgend owner Leighton Samuel. They both said that they wanted the two of us to guide the regional side. Gareth is quoted as saying, "There has been a lot of hot air and speculation about the coaches. We want the best people for the job and in our view that's Allan and Lynn." Leighton, being Leighton, went a bit further, "We will employ the people we want to and nobody will tell us who our coaches will be. Mike Ruddock will not be coming to our region and Lynn Howells and Allan Lewis will be our coaches next season." For those two to come out and support us was a show of confidence, and it was important. I don't for one moment think it helped us get selected for the job in the end, but it was important to know that someone had enough faith in us to come out and bat for us as they did. Samuel went on to say that he thought the selection process was 'humiliating'. I didn't find the process humiliating, but what I did find humiliating was that the people who had put all the money into the clubs and kept them going for as long as they had, and were now being expected to put money into the regional team, were going to be told who they were going to have as their coaches.

As I recall each of the existing Premiership club coaches were asked if they were interested in the regional jobs, and their responses were passed onto the Welsh Rugby Union. Who else applied apart from those of us who were successful I don't know, other than Mark Ring, and I only know he was called because he came out from his grilling before I went in. Leigh Jones who was coaching Newport was also in the mix for the job as coach to the Newport–Ebbw Vale set-up.

As I have already suggested there was no way any of us could go into this interview process thinking that our records as coaches would get us selected. Who we were, what we had done, where we had been, was probably going to mean very little. Certainly in my case my reputation was not going to get me through a very tough challenge. Each of the candidates could lay claim to having coached at the highest level in Welsh club rugby. It was true that some of us had experienced more success than others, but in some cases that was down to the money which enabled us to have better players than other clubs. You could say that some of the other club coaches who had been at the less fashionable and less rich clubs had done a better job with inferior players than those of us lucky enough to have a squad of international names to call upon. Nothing could be taken for granted. I had to pull out all the stops. I knew that there were people like Leighton Samuel and Gareth Thomas and many others who were supporting me. I also realised that the likes of Steve Hansen and Scott Johnson were against me.

I was lucky enough at the time to be studying for a master's degree in Sports Science at the University of Wales Institute, Cardiff. So I was in the studying and dissertation mode. I was into researching a subject and writing essays. Studying therefore came a little easier for the boy from North Road School, Ferndale.

I really put a lot of work into preparing for the interview and it became apparent to me that it was not going to be a job of just coaching the team to go out and play. The job was going to be the director of rugby for everything within the region. There would be the first-team squad, but as well as that the remit would include the coaching staff, then the players and coaches from the premiership clubs within the region, the junior players, and setting up an academy. All of that had to feed through to the region. It was about educating coaches, educating players, it was about looking for the right type of player to bring through from the academy, only then would you be hands-on with the team. So the new posts were going to involve a much wider role than simply going onto the training ground and coaching Pontypridd or Cardiff.

No one, in Wales anyway, had experience of this type of job so I had to go and get help from the places where regional rugby was already up and running. Ireland already had their system well established, so my first port of call was to Michael Bradley who was coaching at Connacht. His advice was to push the loyalty button and get everyone on board. It would be difficult setting up the regions from scratch as there was a lot of club loyalty in Wales, and one day clubs like Neath, Pontypridd, Bridgend or Swansea would exist, and the next day they would be just part of history. Families had supported these clubs for generations, and they now had to be convinced that regional rugby was the way forward. They were going to be the lifeblood of the set-up. Their support would create the atmosphere on match days, and their money through the turnstiles and through the commercial aspects was going to be vital to the regions' survival. They had to identify with the new brand and feel part of it.

As for the coach, he had to be seen not to be representing one club, but all the clubs in the region. He had to be seen to be doing things in an even-handed way. A popular player with one of the clubs might not be offered a contract, but the coach had to balance the correct decision for the region as a whole with keeping that club's supporters on board. Emotions would run high but having to make unpopular decisions was the mark of a good leader.

Graham Henry was another I asked for advice. His take on the job was simple: produce a winning team. There were elements which he could see that went into that – concentrating on selection, and getting selection right; having a simple game plan which the players could understand. It would also need a good leadership group so that whatever you were trying to do as a coach would be transferred onto the field. Most important as well was to have the right people around you. The stronger the people you have around you, advised Henry, the better the job you will do. Wise words from the master.

It was a case of going around and asking questions of everybody, picking everyone's brains then pulling it all together and making the presentation. The main point that came out of all the chats I had was to make sure there were stepping stones for everything within the region. The presentation had to be professional and it took a long time to get the whole thing together. But Clive Jones, who was the director of rugby at Pontypridd, helped me with the development side of regional rugby. It was a good exercise for me, though, and going through that process did focus my career. It showed me what was required of a director of rugby not just in a club but also in a region. Being in at the beginning of a new existence gave me an overview of what was required to run it. At the clubs we'd never had to work for supporters. They were always there. Now we had to get them to buy into the regional team. I had to raise the standard of both the players and myself. We had to have better players than we had been satisfied with at Pontypridd or Bridgend, and my coaching had to be better as well. Everything would have to be organised from scratch, then we would have to show the Welsh supporters that we could play and win things. I say this focused my career because I carried those concepts with me to the roles later in my career in Italy, with Edinburgh, and with Doncaster.

So what did I come up with? Well I read the WRU's document 'Ideas For Regional Rugby', and lifted a number of ideas from that. After all if they had produced the document then I presumed they wanted the regional coaches to go along with it. I picked out the following bullet points:

- To achieve success in the Celtic/European competitions in order to breed confidence in our players when they take the international field; and to restore pride in our national game
- To remove the complacency that exists amongst current players by providing greater competition for places
- To reduce drastically the need for non-Welsh qualified players
- To provide a playing structure which will encourage 'exiled' players to return to Wales
- To create a pathway for coaches, players, and administrators
- To provide a stepping stone to breach the widening gap between club and international rugby
- To establish academies within each of the regions
- To underpin the regions with a semi-professional/ amateur game which is competitive and vibrant

None of this would happen unless we were all working together, from the structure to the success of the regional team and through to the development of the players and coaches. How would we achieve this? We would have to develop players from within the region; to remove complacency and have all players and coaches challenging for places in the region; have a playing style which would entice supporters and also playing role models that youngsters would want to emulate; seminars and practical coaching sessions with access for coaches who want to attend regional coaching sessions.

All this would be achieved through the identity, the players, and a community programme with grass roots development including player participation, and a media campaign using the local and national outlets.

I could see key elements for the success of each region. There had to be continuity between the players, the supporters and sponsors. We had to create an identity, a 'buzz'. This was the place to be; this is where it was happening. We were going to be Wales' answer to Auckland or ACT. We had to have the right structure. The structure needed to fit the needs of the region, rather than the region being fitted to a structure which was alien to it.

Finally I went into the way that all the regional management team would pass their skills down to their counterparts lower down the clubs, within their region, coaching, skills, fitness, development officers, etc.

The day of reckoning was Friday, 11 April. I cannot deny that the interview process was one of the most uncomfortable experiences of my life. I had to go to what was then the WRU headquarters in Golate House. I sat outside the interview room and the old ticker was going nineteen to the dozen, and I must have lost a few pounds that afternoon. This must have been exactly what they wanted because the whole process was very formal. One of the WRU staff came and called 'Mr Howells'. No 'Lynn'. No light relief. Very formal. Very unnerving. When I entered the room there were four men I knew very well sitting behind the table. When I sat in a chair in front of them I felt the whole set-up was intended to put a deliberate strain on the interviewees. If they wanted to get us out of our comfort zone, they certainly succeeded with me. I was nervous because of the differences between Hansen and myself. Also I was going into an interview not having any certainty as to what they were looking for, or what it really entailed. Strangely, though, I was confident because I knew I had covered most things I felt was needed for the position.

I had varying amounts of respect for all four of those conducting the interview. Firstly there was Steve Hansen, and I will have more to say about him in a later chapter. His rugby knowledge is without question, although I always find it difficult to understand a coach who says that the performance far outweighs the result. Enough to say at the moment that I was perfectly happy that he was on the panel in his position as national coach. The players we were going to be dealing with were part of the national set-up and the national coach would want to be involved in their development and informed of their progress. He was going to be coming to us and asking us to do certain things with the players, and asking us for the players for the national squad. The national coach, whoever he was, would have to get on with the regional coaches, so I suppose it was right that he should have some say in their selection.

Next was Bob Norster. This was difficult for me only because I had brought Bob in as team manager when I was coaching the Cardiff club. Now here he was interviewing me for a coaching job. The only thing you can say about Bob is that he had the necessary rugby credibility. He had played for the British Lions and represented Wales. He had been the national team manager. You could not ask for anyone better to talk rugby than Bob. It was strange to have a chief executive from a region on the panel, but the regions had wanted that, and Bob had the best credentials for the task.

Terry Cobner had every right to be on the panel. He came from a coaching background. He had done the spadework, following the defeats in Australia, on what was to become regional rugby. Terry had always had some very, very good ideas, but in my opinion he had never been given the opportunity to push those ideas forward as much as he wanted to. He knew what was needed and what the coaches would be required to do. He would be the man to identify whether the candidate had the technical and tactical knowledge required, also be able to spot the candidates with that little bit extra which put them above the herd. I felt comfortable in the knowledge that Terry would make the right decisions.

The one I had most problems with was Steve Lewis. Lewis, for me, has only ever done anything in Welsh rugby for Steve Lewis. It has never been for the betterment of clubs or players in Wales in my opinion. He was the WRU representative on the panel, but to my mind he didn't have any rugby credibility. What had he done in the game? He had never played for Wales; in fact he had an England trial. He had played a couple of seasons for Newport and for Ebbw Vale. He had been to Oxford University. Because he had been involved in rugby administration, David Moffett had brought him into the WRU as general manager. But on a panel to appoint a coach? I just wondered what part he had to play in it. The man did not have the knowledge of what was required to be part of the decision making for the setting up of regional rugby. Also there were skeletons in Steve Lewis's cupboard as well. To be answering questions put by someone like him, I wondered what sort of credibility there was to the whole process. I also got the impression that the panel were trying to find the right way forward for the regions. I don't think they assumed they had all the right answers.

The presentation had to be professional. I had the overhead projector, I had the flip charts, I had the hand-outs, so from that point of view I think I did put together a decent technical presentation. Thanks to the work I was doing at UWIC I didn't feel too far out of my comfort zone, but you never know in that sort of environment whether you are telling them what they want to hear. Once you get in front of a panel like that it certainly tests you. It is the uncertainty for anyone who goes for an interview: are you telling them what they want to know? Once I had done the presentation it became easier. They started asking me questions, but it was about things I had covered. The reassuring thing was that they asked me nothing which hadn't been in the presentation. It made me feel that at least I had covered everything. They did ask me if I could work with the national coach and I answered, "Yes". I didn't enthuse, but I was positive, which is what I thought they would want to hear.

I had done my best. Now it was just a matter of waiting and, sure enough, within a couple of days I had a call from Gareth Thomas, the chief executive of Pontypridd. It was good news. I had the job I wanted as coach of the Pontypridd–Bridgend region, but I had mixed emotions. There was excitement because I had the job, but disappointment because it was the end of Pontypridd. Incidentally, I have since found out that the interviews were all a bit of a con. There is no way that they planned to appoint anyone to a region against the wishes of the benefactors. So all the hype generated by the likes of Peter Thomas, Stuart Gallagher and the others was unnecessary. But, as I said earlier, it was nice of Leighton Samuel to come out fighting for myself and Allan Lewis as the coaching partnership for our region. Needless to say my first job, once it had been confirmed that I was to be the coach, was to ring Allan and ask him to be my assistant.

I had known Allan a long time. We had been coaching club sides against each other, and we had chatted after match as coaches do. I really got to know him better when we became part of the Wales set-up together. More recently, of course, he had been coaching successfully at Bridgend and the more there was talk of a link-up between Bridgend and Pontypridd the closer we worked together. His coaching ability was never in question, and his credibility as a person was never in doubt. You could hang your hat on Allan, and you knew he was always going to be there for you. It was more than that, though. We were friends, and when you have someone who is coming in to coach with you, that sort of relationship is big.

We then had to put together the rest of our coaching team before we could really start work, and that took longer. The conditioning coach was appointed by the WRU and the national conditioning coach, Andrew Hore. Andrew opted for Nick Johnson. We would have preferred Steve Richards, who had been my conditioning coach at Sardis Road, but Nick came with good recommendations and qualifications from the English Institute of Sport, so it wasn't worth rocking the boat. Anyway we did keep Steve as the academy conditioning coach. Clive Jones, who had been the director of rugby at Pontypridd, remained as the director of rugby development with the new region. Justin Burnell would develop the academy having previously done the same job for Pontypridd. More names would have to follow later.

The next task we had was getting the playing squad assembled. I remember saying at the time that the combining teams would generally choose their squads from both the former clubs. That is to say Swansea and Neath region would pick the best from those two clubs, whilst we would do the same picking the best from Pontypridd and Bridgend. Any players then left over who were of the right quality would go into a pool and would go to regions short of their particular position. For example, if we had a scrum half we didn't require then he could very well be picked up by one of the other regions. Likewise props, hookers, wings, full backs. After all, we were intending to distribute what had been nine squads into five. There would be an abundance of good players for some positions within a region, yet there might be a dearth of talent in another. On the other hand there would be a lot of players who were not going to make regional contracts.

We had two pretty strong squads to choose from. Bridgend had won the Premiership, pipping Pontypridd, so in theory we had the best group of players at our disposal. Some people might think that I would be biased towards the players I had coached with Pontypridd, but Allan and I had discussions about players, their strengths and weaknesses. In some cases we might not agree, so we would talk about a particular player, then go away and think about it a little longer before coming back and discussing him further. There were some good debates. At scrum half we had the decision to make between Huw Harries and Sililo Martens, who had both played at Bridgend, or Gareth Baber, who had played for Pontypridd. In the back row there would be a decision to make between Richard Bryant or Geraint Lewis. Who they had played for didn't matter. We discussed what type of personality they brought to the squad, plus of course their strengths and weaknesses as a player. It may have taken a bit of time before we came to a decision, but I cannot remember having a disagreement about the eventual player that we picked. It was never an argument; it was all about strengths and weaknesses; what would be best for the squad and the structure of the squad. Allan and I decided that we would meet the players from the club we were coaching to inform them whether they were in the regional squad or not. We felt that we owed that to the players. But telling someone that they were not going to be involved was not an easy task. It hurt to see players who had done a good job for us at club level being cast aside. It hurt Allan and me, and it certainly hurt the players, and it wouldn't be the last time we had the experience of seeing players discarded like pieces of meat.

Letters appeared in the newspapers suggesting that the ratio of former Bridgend players to former Pontypridd players was a political decision. Nothing can be further from the truth. I cannot tell you to this day off the top of my head what the ratio of former Pontypridd players to former Bridgend was, and it certainly never entered my thoughts at the time that I was picking more from Sardis Road than the Brewery Field or vice versa. It never ever came down with either Allan or me that because we had so many players from one club we had to balance that with the same number from the other. It was always what was best for the squad. Our futures depended on the squad so it would have been suicide to pick players to please other people, whoever they might have been. From my point of view if the best 20 players had come from Bridgend, and only five from Pontypridd, then that is the way it would have gone. Having said that I don't think it was far off being fifty-fifty. The unfortunate players who weren't selected all went into a pool to be available for the other regions if they wanted them. Unfortunately that decision ended most of their careers as players, but Dale McIntosh, 'The Chief' as he is known everywhere in Welsh rugby, is now part of the Pontypridd coaching team. Kingsley Jones went on to coach Sale in the Guinness Premiership and then become head coach of Russia. For the likes of Jason Lewis, Huw Harries and Gareth Cull it was the end of their first-class careers. Others did carry on with other teams. Brett Davey and Gareth Baber were picked up by the Dragons. Christian Loader and Geraint Lewis went to Rotherham whilst Duncan Bell crossed the bridge to Bath and a successful career which included five England caps.

There were examples of players we chose not just for their ability, their quality, or even their future prospects. There was also a bit of what they brought to the squad. We realised that it was a big step bringing two groups of players together and we realised that the changing room had to be right. We didn't in all cases pick someone because he was the best rugby player. Of course that was a big part of it, but another part of it had to be that the player would fit into the squad that we were trying to build. There was one player I wanted in particular, and that was Neil Jenkins. I needed a figurehead and Jenks could fit that role as he was certainly someone the players respected. I don't think people realised what it meant to the players to have Neil Jenkins around, as he was such a big influence on the squad. I had known Jenks for a long time at Pontypridd and he epitomised what we had been about at Ponty, and it was what I wanted at the Warriors. The problem for me was that Jenks had finished. When Pontypridd finished, Jenks intended to retire. He wanted to finish. He got through his last season on drugs, no not the type of drug which all sportsmen and women should avoid: he would never ever have touched them. The drugs Neil was using were for the arthritis he was suffering. I had to coax him to give me another year and help launch the region. To have Neil Jenkins in your team was awesome. His kicking was out of this world. You just knew if you got a penalty anywhere in the opposition half, Jenks would more or less be certain to land it. Apart from that, his quality and experience was second to none, especially when we were missing our World Cup players and we had a lot of young, inexperienced players in the team and he galvanised them. He played for that extra year because I asked him to, and I owe him so much for that season.

Steve Hansen had an influence on one player we kept and one player we lost. Allan met with the players from Bridgend to tell them their futures, which was only right, and one of his squad who wasn't at all in favour of the regional set-up was Gareth Thomas, or 'Alfie' as he is known by everyone. Gareth got his nickname from an American television programme in which the main character was a puppet called Alf. Apparently one of Gareth's friends thought that he looked like Alf, and gave him the nickname by which he is known throughout rugby.

Alfie wasn't keen to join the new combination of Bridgend and Pontypridd and was planning to move to join the Cardiff Blues. He told Allan Lewis that he didn't want a Warriors contract. Steve Hansen then stepped in and advised Gareth that with so many Wales players in his position at Cardiff, he would be better off staying with the Warriors. I offered him the captaincy of the region and with this added incentive he went back to Allan and joined us.

The only player we didn't keep whom we wanted to was Michael Owen. That decision was down to Hansen. He wanted Michael to play second row. I thought he was a better number eight. If he played for me it would be at eight. I would not have picked him in the second row. So Hansen decided he would be better off at Newport and Michael had to move to stay in contention for the Wales team.

We were very happy with the squad we assembled. We had a good mixture of established players and names for the future. Gareth Thomas, Maama Molitika, Kevin Morgan, Mefin Davies, Emyr Lewis, Richard Parks, Rob Sidoli, and Nathan Budgett were natural first-choice selections. Sonny Parker was another established name. Then we had fringe players who could well develop into the next crop of regional and national names. Players like Ryan Jones, Geraint Morris, Ian Evans and Matthew Rees were young players coming through, but they weren't established players as yet. We selected well, and we knew that because the squad came together really quickly as a group. The players knew each other. Many of them had obviously played together and against each other for Bridgend or Pontypridd, and in many cases they had played together for Wales.

Apart from the Michael Owen issue, the WRU left us alone to establish our squads and our regions. Their attitude seemed to be that there are five regions, we have selected the coaches, now we should let them get on with it. There was little interference from the governing body, but that is not to say they would not have liked to have dictated to us which players we used and when. I think there was an attempt by Steve Hansen to influence what went on. You cannot condemn a national coach for wanting to get the best for his players. Look at the problems the international football managers have in the club versus country argument. The clubs feel they have first call on a player because they pay his wages; on the other hand to play for your country should be the pinnacle for any player in any sport. Steve Hansen did not consider or grasp the idea that we had Celtic League and Heineken Cup matches to win, and these were the bread and butter for the regional sides. So, sorry Steve, I wasn't having any of it. There was quite a bit of conflict there, and certainly Lyn Jones and I think Gareth

Jenkins also went into battle to preserve what we all thought was best for our regions.

The rugby set-up then was going pretty well. Off the field marketing was taking shape, and we had a board of directors. The man who had kept Bridgend rugby solvent, Leighton Samuel, was the chairman of the new region, joined by his brother John and Bridgend chairman Derrick King, while regional chief executive Gareth Thomas, Richard Hope and Margaret Foster would represent the Sardis Road club. Still there were a couple of important questions to be answered, such as what we were to be called, and what our colours were going to be. Here the supporters became involved, which wasn't a bad thing. Making decisions like that would make them feel part of what was happening, and hopefully it would show that they were buying into the idea of this being their region. Bringing the players from two teams together was one thing. Getting two sets of supporters on side was another. Various names were put forward and were buried as quickly as they surfaced. Glamorgan Giants, Glamorgan Gladiators, Celtic Giants, Glamorgan Bowman, Glamorgan Celts, and so it went on, with names plucked from the atmosphere. Getting nearer to the eventual title, we had Valley Warriors, but nothing satisfied the supporters. There were attempts to include the names of the two clubs, Pontybont marrying Pontypridd and the Welsh name for Bridgend, Pen-y-bont. Ponty Ravens put together Pontypridd and the name for the Bridgend rugby team, the Ravens. Valley Ravens was a little nearer the mark as it kept the link with Valleys rugby. None of them met the approval of the supporters, especially the Pontypridd fans. Anything with Ravens in it smacked too much of the Bridgend connection to sit comfortably with the Valleys faithful.

At first every reference to the new amalgamation of Bridgend and Pontypridd was calling us the Rhondda Cynon Taf Ravens. Rhondda Cynon Taf is the unity authority for the Valleys which, it was thought, would keep the Valleys connection alive, and as I have mentioned it was hoped that the Ravens connection would placate the Bridgend support. But the marketing branch of the new region was already having an influence and they were trying to bring a commercial feel to the operation as well as a brand identity. At that time one of the top teams in Australia were the ACT Brumbies so it was felt that by abbreviating the name to RCT Ravens we were thinking along the right lines. No chance. Bridgend didn't fall within the Rhondda Cynon Taf area, and the Pontypridd faithful believed the name was the thin end of the wedge, especially as Leighton Samuel was about to confirm the title. They thought that Ponty would be eventually overwhelmed by the Bridgend half of the amalgamation. Some of them stated that they wouldn't go and watch the region because of the name which they thought had too much of a Bridgend feel to it.

Fair play to Leighton, even though the deadline for the launch of the region was fast approaching, he was prepared to meet the Pontypridd fans to discuss an alternative. As he said at the time both sets of supporters are proud of their clubs and want something that represents Pontypridd in the title like Ravens does for Bridgend. So the decision on the name was postponed for a month. One thing was certain: we would not be called the RCT Ravens. Leighton agreed the name was a dead duck. We weren't the only organization having problems with the name. The Swansea–Neath amalgamation was struggling as well, having ditched the name Celtic Ospreys, and Newport Tigers wasn't acceptable to the fans of Newport or Ebbw Vale. It was easy for Cardiff and Llanelli, the stand alone teams, to simply add something to their club name. They didn't have to worry about bringing together supporters from a couple of teams. Blues and Scarlets were their choices from an early date and they stuck.

By the middle of June the name Crusaders had emerged. This was one of the suggestions a group of Pontypridd fans came up with, others being Chieftains, Warriors and Gladiators, but Crusaders appeared to be the favourite, and looked like being announced at the region's launch a few days later. It wasn't, and we launched a ship without a name, although we did have an £800,000 sponsorship deal over two years with the old Pontypridd sponsors Buy As You View. We had a captain in Wales international wing Gareth Thomas, and we had a shirt in blue, black and white. Leighton Samuel also announced plans to build a brand new stadium in the next three to five years, somewhere between Sardis Road and the Brewery Field. Things were progressing at a rate, or so it seemed.

Less than a week after the launch, Crusaders was the latest name to be ditched. Fans were polled by newspapers, websites, and radio stations and it proved not to be the choice of so many after all. Also an objection came from the other side of the world when the New Zealand Super 12 team, Crusaders, would have taken issue with us copying their name, and it might even have ended up in legal action. Next up, Glamorgan Celts appeared on the agenda. It was dragging on and becoming a bit of a farce. We had more important things to worry about, and Leighton Samuel was beginning to lose patience with the whole naming process.

On 3 July he hit us with a bombshell. The problem of Leighton Samuel was always lurking in the background. He had a reputation for brinkmanship, often threatening to walk away from the regional rugby talks. He was always a reluctant recruit to the five region idea, believing that there was only enough money for four. Let me set the record straight with Leighton. For me as coach in charge of rugby matters he could not have been more helpful. Just about everything I asked for we got. Players, facilities especially, the training set-up at Pencoed; he put his hand in his pocket and it was there. Having said that, some of the decisions he made at the time proved in the long run to help bring about the death of the Warriors. We went way over budget. He signed up Gareth Thomas and Dafydd James, at the time probably the two highest paid players in Welsh rugby. Both were on well in excess of £100,000 a year. They were employed by his company Deco Frames, but those who needed to know at the Warriors never knew exactly how much they were being paid and how much came out of the region and what the extras on their contracts were.

By the beginning of July there were already financial problems looming large on the horizon. According to Leighton the WRU were due to pay the Warriors £137,500 every month. So far they had only paid £98,000. Apparently the shortfall was due to be made up in September after the WRU received the gate receipts from the World Cup warm-up internationals. That wasn't any good as someone had to make up the shortfall and meet the bills, including wages. Leighton had made up the shortfall in June, but said that he was not prepared to do it again and furthermore he was pulling out of regional rugby. He claimed that there would be four regions eventually as one of them would go bust within two or three years, and none of them would ever make a profit. He also had a dig at people like Gareth Thomas, chief executive Gareth Thomas that is, and some of the other board members, suggesting that their business knowledge was not good enough to run the region. This was a real problem for us now as quite rightly Leighton wanted to know who was going to make up the shortfall. There was no income coming into the region from gates, or even merchandise which was still being developed. The region at this time needed his support and he was taking his ball back to Bridgend whom, he said, he would continue to fund. Leighton was canny enough to stay on the board of the Warriors as chairman, but the burden now fell on Gareth Thomas to complete the preparations for the start of the season. Thankfully after a couple of meetings Gareth did manage to persuade Leighton to continue his financial commitment to the region, and was also hopeful that Leighton would return as chairman. There was even a personal plea for him to stay from David Moffett!

So we went into our launch at the Vale of Glamorgan Hotel. It came on the back of a humdinger of a violent argument between Gareth and Leighton over the name. Leighton was adamant we would be called the Crusaders, and because

Leighton wanted that name, he thought it would just happen because Leighton wanted it to happen. Gareth had been in touch with the Crusaders in New Zealand, and sure enough they weren't happy about us muscling in on their name. They also confirmed that if we had insisted on using that title they would have taken legal action. It was another step in the worsening relationship between the chairman and the chief executive. Off the field too there were still big gaps in our team. We didn't have a doctor, we didn't have a team manager, we didn't have a training facility nor a real base to work from. It was hard and someone asked me if I had a summer holiday that year. You must be joking.

Eventually a week after the launch it was announced we would be called the Warriors. Fans from both sides were happy as it had a ring about it, and as the chairman of the Pontypridd supporters' club said the name should either reflect both or neither of the amalgamated clubs. The fans agreed that this was a name they could buy into. It sounded good.

So now at least we had a name, a squad who knew who they were playing for, a set a fans who knew who they were supporting and the colours to wear. We had a board of directors, admittedly without a chairman, but all seemed to be there to support what we were doing on the playing side. But of course this was the Warriors. Suddenly on 1 August, a month before we were due to kick off the Celtic League season against the Borders, chief executive Gareth Thomas announced his resignation. He had taken enough, and had suffered enough. It finally dawned on Thomas that his relationship with Samuel was unworkable.

There were two reasons why Gareth resigned. He couldn't believe many of the things Leighton told him, and Gareth also knew that the financial situation would become untenable as well. He had produced financial forecasts which showed that we were heading for big debts. The squad costs were horrendous. As their share of the WRU funding each month, the Warriors would receive £137,500, but the wage bill alone was £200,000.

Also the WRU money arrived in the club's bank early in the month, but the salaries went out a month in arrears, so there was always a scramble to cash the cheques in case the money ran out and the cash situation was always tight.

Leighton wanted total control of the Warriors, and like a runaway train nothing was going to stop him until he hit the buffers somewhere. Where Gareth slipped up was in thinking that he could work with Leighton. The two of them had got on well enough when it was Pontypridd and Bridgend. Now this was a joint venture, things were different. Samuel had to be in control and could not stand people disagreeing or opposing him. Gareth resigned and went back to trying to sort out the financial mess that was Pontypridd. Samuel now returned as chief executive. He had virtually a free reign as there was no one left to stand up to him.

Pontypridd supporters welcomed the return of Samuel. The chairman of the supporters' club, Phil Lycett, is on record as saying, "Leighton realises the need to get Ponty fans on board. We were honoured he met with us." With Leighton as chief executive, he continued, "I think we will see more action, more publicity and the region being sold more."

I don't blame Phil Lycett for those comments at the time, but he would want to eat his words in a few months time. It just showed how Samuel was and how he told people what he thought they wanted to hear. Within a very few weeks he went back on just about every promise he made to the Ponty fans.

The problems and the comings and goings off the field didn't really affect us. We ploughed on regardless. We had our first squad sessions at the University of Wales Institute, Cardiff, where we had lots of meetings with the players to set protocols in place, and then got to work on the conditioning. We eventually got our base and our training facility, the agricultural college at Pencoed, just outside Bridgend. It had everything we wanted: two pitches, gym, kit room, medical room, weights room, restaurant, meeting room. It was a great centre for us and it was down to Leighton Samuel who got the facility for us. What it cost in financial terms and what it did to the budget I have no idea, but it was just what we needed.

The squad of players came together really well. We were without our World Cup stars, so the rest of the boys got down to forming a close-knit group. Despite the fact that we were amalgamating two teams, there were never any cliques, never any them-and-us feelings, never any battle lines. Everyone got on with the job of creating this new concept of a region, and from those early days team spirit was good. Even later when the World Cup lads returned, they just seemed to melt into what was there already and everything carried on.

We planned three pre-season matches, and before that as seems to have become the tradition now, we went on a week's fitness training at a military camp. These are ideal for pre-season camps as they are well away from the public eye – not that we had anything to hide – but secure, and there are few distractions. We chose the RAF Halton camp near Aylesbury in Buckinghamshire. This was ideal as they had a couple of gyms, a big fitness room with machines galore, pitches and a swimming pool. The only problem was the weather! The first week of August 2003 was boiling. Often the fitness side of the camps is left to the military guys who are used to breaking the backs of the new recruits, and they can put even the fittest athlete through hell. We decided against this. Instead Allan and myself would do the coaching, with Nick Johnson working on the fitness and conditioning. We met with the players to try and put into place what we expected from them during the week: our philosophies, a code of conduct, and how we wanted to play.

It wasn't all graft. On the Wednesday afternoon we planned a golf tournament which we all took part in. I think I probably took the prize for walking further than most and visiting more areas of long grass and bushes than the rest of the party. Golf is not one of my strong points, but needless to say there were one or two who showed their competitive instinct. But we all took part and it was all part of the team building.

Thursday was a milestone day. It was the day we sat down to select our first Warriors squad. Another reason for choosing RAF Halton was that we could easily get from there to our first match at London Welsh on our way home. London Welsh were at this time in the second tier of English rugby and would prove to be a good test for us. We couldn't play at their traditional ground Old Deer Park as that was still in use for cricket, but we did get to play them on the Metropolitan Police pitches at Imber Court.

It was ironic that after all the problems we had encountered setting up the region, all the delays in the name, the launch, etc., that we should be the first regional team to take to the field. Everyone realised the significance of the occasion and that this was the start of something new and something special. Around a hundred supporters came up to watch the game and to see Ponty and Bridgend fans standing together cheering the same team was strange. I had a special feeling, as well. Being there with my good mate Allan brought a lump to my throat. We split the match into four twenty-minute sessions with lots of stops for water as the weather was boiling. The score was 20–5 to us at the end of the hour, but that was insignificant compared with the occasion and the effort put in by our group which included so many youngsters.

We continued our build-up against two other English clubs, this time stepping up to the Premiership. We wanted to share them between our two playing venues, Sardis Road and the Brewery Field. Bath, from just across the Severn Bridge, came to Sardis on Sunday 17th. It was ironic that one of the players we hadn't managed to sign, Duncan Bell, had opted for a move to England where he had international qualification. He thought he would stand a better chance of international recognition if he played in England, so he had signed for Bath. Here he was back at Sardis Road, destroying our front row. As a result I sent on Gerald Cox with the strict instructions to sort out Duncan. This he tried to do at the first scrum with a mighty punch which didn't sort out Mr Bell, but did get Gerald ten minutes in the sin bin. It also got him the bollocking of a lifetime from Allan Lewis to whom he explained that he was only following out the instructions he was sent on with from Lynn. I smiled and shrugged my shoulders. Bath, who were only a couple of players short of a full-strength side, were just too strong for us at this stage of our development and beat us 29–22. Over 2,500 turned up to watch the game which was encouraging, and there were even a few chants of "Warriors, Warriors".

On the following Friday the Brewery Field hosted the visit of Sale. It was encouraging not only on the field, where we won 33–22, but off it as well. The kick-off had to be delayed to allow the entire crowd to get in. They saw Neil Jenkins kick seven goals out of seven attempts, and we saw that even without our international players we were capable of competing with one of the top dozen teams in England.

I was pleased with the pre-season. There was always the problem of bringing everyone together and the team bonding, but what I saw in the friendly matches showed me that we had achieved what we set out to do. The players had all been very positive and we were ready to take the Warriors into battle.

3

They Can't Take That Away from Me

So WE WERE ready to go. We knew what we were called, the team on and off the field was set up, the pre-season had gone well and we were up and running. Well, not quite. There was the problem of the Rugby World Cup. It was the year the Webb Ellis Trophy was brought back to the northern hemisphere for the first time, courtesy of Jonny Wilkinson's last minute drop goal. There is a supporters' code in Wales that you support two teams: Wales and whoever are playing England. I go along with that to some degree. If England are playing in the Six Nations then, yes, I am up for Scotland, Ireland, even France or Italy. It's our heritage, our tradition. England has been expected to win so much that it is probably supporting the underdog. I think a lot of the Celtic nations are the same, all against England. On the occasion of the Rugby World Cup, though, I was supporting England in the final. It was the northern hemisphere against the southern hemisphere; a team from up here against Australia. Also I am glad they won because it did the game up here a big favour. Interest in the game increased, gates went up and for the players it was a big stimulation to be playing against World Cup winners.

So how did this affect us as Warriors? Well Wales wouldn't be returning from that World Cup in Australia until early November. We had nine players in that Wales squad, which showed even before a ball had been kicked in anger the strength of the squad we had assembled. The nine with Warriors after their names on the World Cup team sheets were: Kevin Morgan, Gareth Thomas, Sonny Parker, Ceri Sweeney, Gareth Cooper, Gethin Jenkins, Mefin Davies, Rob Sidoli, and Brent Cockbain, and not to forget Richard Parks who was named in the original 42, but didn't make the cut. We had to negotiate the start of the Celtic League season without nine of our best players, although we did have Sililo Martens who was yet to meet up with Tonga. True, other regions including the Irish and Scots were in the same predicament, but for all of us in Wales it was the start of something new and we would have liked to have begun with everybody in place and everything settled.

Our first game couldn't have been much further away from home, up at the Borders, a long old trek. In a way though that was just what we needed. The journey and being away from home cemented everyone. It pulled everyone tighter because we were travelling together. We had of course been working on pre-season and all of us had got on well, but this was the real thing and it made us feel as if we were a team. Everybody had bought into the regional concept; the players were looking forward to the season starting. As for me, after everything that had gone on, and was still going on with the growing problems between Leighton Samuel and Pontypridd with regard to Pontypridd's financial position, I was glad to be getting a team of players onto the field to play a game of rugby. Once we had done that and focused the players on rugby matters, I knew we could take things onto the next step whatever that might be. But I had to get that first competitive game under the belt. Borders would be difficult opposition. Pontypridd and Cardiff had found games there difficult, but even though we didn't have the World Cup players at our disposal, I felt we had a good enough squad to survive those first few weeks.

Cardiff airport at five-thirty in the morning for a seven o'clock flight is not the place you would choose to be at such an ungodly hour. But if we wanted to fly and do the job professionally, so be it, and the guys looked good and were looking forward to the first game. We had another late problem as well, as Jonny Bryant's wife decided to go into labour the day we were due to leave for Scotland. As a result we were short of an inside centre, but David Bishop stepped up to the mark and with Jenks' experience and help he got us through the game. We felt we had built well and that the squad we had was good enough to compete.

Scotland coach Ian McGeechan had released Gregor Townsend from the World Cup warm-up game against Ireland the following day, but to our delight Borders coach Tony Gilbert had decided to start Scotland's most capped player on the bench. On paper they had a good side. As well as Townsend they had Doddie Weir and Gary Armstrong, all three British Lions. Also in their squad were Nikki Walker, George Graham, Chris Cusiter and their captain Kevin Utterson, all Scottish internationals.

The build-up at the hotel on match day was nervous. The infighting was put behind us and, on the morning of the game, when we saw the quality of the opposition we felt that it was a bloody good game to win. The team meeting which was always held in the hotel before we left was one of: 'us against all the odds and great expectations. Let's get this game on.' There was just that feeling in the water that things would go well.

Little, though, did we expect that first competitive match to go as well as it did. Jenks got us going with a couple of penalties, then the Warriors' first-ever try was scored by Aisea Havili. We touched down five times. Shaun James, who had an outstanding match, scored two of them, with Gareth Wyatt and Nick Kelly getting the others. Neil Jenkins converted three of them, and kicked six penalties for a personal total of 24 points. We were 31–0 up by half time, our pack dominated and the Borders were, as one newspaper put it, reduced to 'a disorganised shambles'. They did bring on Townsend for the second half, and Borders scored a couple of late tries, but 49–12 in our first-ever game we had inflicted the biggest ever Celtic League defeat on the Scotsmen.

We didn't return home until the Saturday morning, so there was a chance to enjoy the victory and there was a great feeling of relief, and optimism for the season ahead. We had won our first game with a squad of young players and the old war horse Jenks had pulled the strings. We had done well and we all enjoyed a few beers together. I must say on this topic that I have never been a coach who stops his players enjoying themselves after the game, as long as they weren't carrying injuries, and these players had earned it.

I spoke to Neil Jenkins on the Saturday morning as we waited for our flight home and he was very relaxed. He said that he felt that way because he didn't have the demands of the international game to worry about. Now he just wanted to enjoy his rugby. It had been a clinical performance by him and the whole team. It was a good win away from home and a good start. The thing that pleased me most of all was that the players took onto the field the game plan we had been working on all pre-season. Despite the ease of the win we knew there was more to come and it gave us real confidence, not only for the future, but for the immediate games ahead when the strength of the squad would be tested without our World Cup stars. The other piece of news we received when we got home was that Jonny Bryant had become the father of a bouncing baby girl named Tia.

Having won so convincingly away at Borders, my big concern now was to show our fans that it hadn't been a flash in the pan. It couldn't have been set up better. The next game was at Sardis Road where all the squad wanted to play. Even the former Bridgend guys in the set up knew the atmosphere at Sardis Road so it wasn't just the former Pontypridd players who wanted to be there. The environment was special, though I would say that of course, with my Pontypridd hat on. The point, though, was proved that Saturday afternoon against none other than Leinster. Mind you, like us they were missing their international stars, with no less than ten of them away in Spain for pre-World Cup training with

Eddie O'Sullivan, and a load on the treatment table. One man who wasn't, though, was second row Leo Cullen who had been left out of the Irish World Cup squad. Leinster coach Gary Ella had made him captain for the day, but we didn't know whether he would sulk or try to show Eddie that he had made a big mistake. As the Irish region had kicked off their season the previous week with a local derby defeat by Munster we also wondered if they were about to take revenge on us.

In this new regional set-up we had to pay far more attention to detail than we had got away with in the past. Attention to detail had to be paramount. For example we made sure that our team run was held at Sardis Road, which might seem a little obvious as we were playing there, but it also gave the former Bridgend players in the squad a chance to experience the 'luxury' of the home dressing room which they would not have experienced before. All of them had played at Sardis Road before, but on those occasions they had turned right into the away changing room where, to be honest, you couldn't swing a jock strap. Now they were to sample the great expanses we had enjoyed for years. Well, at least you can move around without bumping into anyone else. It may seem strange but you could see how difficult the Bridgend lads found it now being the home players. The game plan was to start strongly and get the supporters behind us. Also to keep their backs quiet as Leinster were always a good running side.

We made a couple of changes. Kevin Morgan came in at full back for his first game since suffering a serious knee injury. He had been injured in the Six Nations game against Scotland at Murrayfield six months before, but we never had any doubts that he would fully recover after conversations with the specialists treating him. Steve Hansen had surprisingly included him in his World Cup squad, so was thankful that we were prepared to give him some game time, to prove his fitness, and to gain some match fitness. Don't worry, Steve, we would have done anything to help! New dad Jonny Bryant made his Warriors debut at centre, but only lasted half an hour as he picked up a shoulder injury.

Sililo Martens had joined up with the Tongan World Cup squad so Pontypridd favourite Paul John played at scrum half, but having been asked to pay for his own insurance during the World Cup, Aisea Havili refused to go, and so we were more than delighted to have him on the wing. We also made a couple of changes in the back row where Nick Kelly and Richard Parks came into the starting fifteen. I say fifteen, make that sixteen. There is no doubt that for this first home game in regional rugby, the fans had taken up the challenge. The kick-off had to be delayed for ten minutes, something football fans had often experienced, but almost unheard of in rugby. The problem apparently was that our fans, 4,500 of them, had found problems parking around Sardis Road. The latecomers missed three Brian O'Meara penalties as we made an awful start, and referee Iain Ramage was on the whistle like a canary. Nine minutes gone, nine points down. Jenks missed a sitter which the crowd couldn't believe, but did land one when Jonny Bryant announced his arrival in regional rugby with a thundering tackle on the Leinster flanker Des Dillon.

The scores were level into the second half, all penalties, when Gareth Wyatt began a one-man crusade to not only beat Leinster, but to show Steve Hansen what he was missing by ignoring his claims for an international call-up. It always amazed me how Gareth was not given the recognition he deserved by the Welsh selectors when everyone else in Wales recognised his talents. Wyatt dropped a goal to level the scores, before Brendan Burke went over for a try in the corner, and I thought we had been beaten when O'Meara stuck the conversion over from the touchline. Thankfully the boys on the pitch had other ideas. Mefin Davies, who I had sent on at hooker to give him some game time in preparation for the World Cup (I think Hansen thanked me), went over for a try, Jenks converted that and kicked a penalty which gave us the lead for the first time. When O'Meara landed another penalty with time ticking away and the scores locked at 22–22, it looked like honours even, until Gareth Wyatt produced the try of the season. Neil Jenkins started the move with Kevin Morgan racing up from full back, passed to Wyatt who twice chipped the ball over would-be tacklers, stretched every sinew in his muscles and used every ounce of his energy to win the race for the touchdown. Sardis Road, the House of Pain, erupted into a cauldron of jubilation. We went mad on the bench, hugging and exchanging high fives. The crowd were bouncing, hugging and embracing each other. It meant something. The try itself was absolutely fantastic, but add to that the fact that it was two minutes into injury time in our first home game and that we were about to beat Leinster, and the script could not have been better written. There was a sense of relief and jubilation that we had won our first home game at my spiritual home ground Sardis Road. Not only had we won, but we had been by far the better team on the day. We had persuaded a lot of people that regional rugby had arrived and we had given it a good chance of being accepted in the Valleys.

The fans, as I suggested earlier, played their part by supporting us, but more importantly they became Warriors. There were chants of "Ole; Ole, Ole, Ole; Warriors, Warriors". It took some of the other regions several years before their fans started chanting the name of their region rather than the name of their former teams. Ours were doing it during the first home game. The travelling Ravens and the Ponty faithful had given the Warriors the thumbs-up in emphatic fashion. The match had been a real bruiser, but the squad had put into practice an unbelievable amount of our work at this comparatively early stage.

In the bar after the game the feeling and the atmosphere was fantastic. There was certainly a sense of relief from the Pontypridd officials that the night had gone so well, but both sets of supporters had come together and were very excited about the season ahead. The home players had always been well treated and as for me, well, I had never had to buy many beers, but on this night Allan Lewis was given the same hospitality.

After such a good night the Monday morning was surreal to say the least. We had just gone top of the Celtic League but all the talk from the officials of the club was how poor the Pontypridd organization of the game had been handled. The criticism had come from Leighton Samuel who didn't want any of the games in Sardis Road, and he would go to any lengths to find fault in the Ponty organization. The problem for us was that the criticism had got through to the squad, and several of the former Pontypridd players had relayed the stories to the management. They were asking whether we were ever going to play at Sardis Road again. It was down to the rugby management to keep the lid on it, and all we could tell them was that we'd just keep playing the rugby.

Next up was the newly introduced Celtic Cup competition, and the chance for us to get a taste of what Leighton Samuel would have liked us to experience every week at the Brewery Field. This was a new cup competition and we felt that it gave us an opportunity to see some of the younger players in the squad. In all we made nine changes in the squad of 22. Kevin Morgan, having come through his first game since his injury the previous week against Leinster, had been taken out to Wales' warm weather camp in Lanzarote. Former Wales captain Phil Bennett was one of those who believed that with his lack of match fitness Kevin would have been better staying with us and getting as much game time as possible. One criticism of his performance against Leinster had been his kicking out of hand, but his rustiness there was only to be expected after being out for so long. What he had shown was that his confidence had returned and that he would be a real attacking threat in the World Cup. I think that Steve Hansen might have been nervous about Kevin playing too many matches so close to the start of the World Cup, something I can understand with his injury record.

We had ten players away at the World Cup, and with Jonny

Bryant and Nick Kelly both succumbing to injuries during the Leinster match, we were struggling for numbers. Mind you, Glasgow coach Hugh Campbell had selection problems as well. His squad had been hit by a flu bug, but in addition he had four players injured, and so made no less than seven changes from the side which lost quite heavily in Ulster the previous week. We were top of the table, admittedly after just two games, but with the way we had played we didn't feel we should have any trouble getting into the hat for the second round.

There had already been rumours that off the field things were about to take a turn for the worse. Pontypridd rugby club were about to go into administration with debts of about half a million pounds. Buy As You View had been a great supporter of Pontypridd rugby for several years, but their financial commitment to the club was very different to the benefactors who supported the likes of Newport, Llanelli and Cardiff. Buy As You View had their name on the shirts and if one of the players needed a car, it arrived with the company logo on it. They helped the club and got their return from being associated with a successful local rugby team. Their financial commitment was more in kind than in hard cash. If Cardiff Newport or Llanelli needed money then Peter Thomas, Tony Brown or Huw Evans would reach into their pockets and pull out the cheque book. That didn't happen with Buy As You View. They paid for guys like Neil Boobyer, Dale MacIntosh and Chris Jones to go out to the schools in the Rhondda, Merthyr and Cynon Taf areas as development officers. The Pontypridd players were expected to go with them to coach the kids and spread the word. The company had also become the shirt sponsor of the Celtic Warriors, but naturally as the importance of the club game waned, so did their spending on Pontypridd.

Pontypridd's debt of around £700,000 was mostly owed to the tax man, and he was not inclined to hang around for his money. The option for the club was to go into administration, which they did, but that meant that their share of the Warriors became available for anyone to purchase. Leighton Samuel had offered to clear the debt in exchange for Pontypridd's half of the region. The Welsh Rugby Union refused to allow this, as they said the Warriors were an amalgamation of the two clubs, and they wouldn't agree to one man, Leighton, having total control. This was a poor argument as Cardiff and Llanelli were both owned by one person; Cardiff by Peter Thomas and Llanelli by Huw Evans. Also Tony Brown was calling all the shots at the Dragons. In hindsight this was probably their first move to wind up the Warriors. In the end Leighton did buy the Pontypridd share from the administrator, for £100,000 according to administrators Begbies Traynor, but then on 14 November 2003 he gifted it to the WRU, which made them joint owners of the region. A generous gesture? Not a bit of it. Leighton was paranoid about someone else coming in as a benefactor and taking over control from him, hence his eagerness to buy the other half. This was yet another hurdle to put in front of us which kept disrupting the way the squad and the whole group of staff were settling into the new set-up. It would roll on and affect us over the next few months.

Having said that it should not and probably did not affect our performance against Glasgow. Neil Jenkins landed a couple of early penalties, but their defence was good and we couldn't break them down. Calvin Howarth levelled things up and just before half time they almost scored the first try, but thankfully the referee Alan Lewis said he was unsighted. This was before the referees were sponsored by Specsavers opticians! The relief was short-lived though as Glasgow scored two tries just after the break and we were beaten 19–9. Our bubble had burst, big time. One national newspaper even went with the headline, 'Warriors Humiliated'. There was a feeling of disbelief and disappointment. We had won against Leinster in front of a big crowd and that was a great occasion. Now we had lost to a team we should have beaten. A lot of questions were answered about the 22 players selected for that game, and I finally made my mind up that Ryan Jones was not a second row. Don't get me wrong, Ryan is a good player, as has been proved by his success on the international field and as captain of Wales. In my opinion he was far better suited to the back row than the second. He was dynamic, a big ball carrier and his distribution skills were good. At the time there was only one other player of that type in Welsh rugby, Scott Quinnell. In this game we were out-muscled and that was one thing that would never happen again.

By the time we came round to the next two matches, our first meetings with other Welsh regions, Leighton Samuel had achieved his aim to have full control of the Warriors. Yes, he had gifted half the region to the Welsh Rugby Union but having had his attempt to take over the running of the region on his own blocked, we were now run by Samuel and the WRU on a fifty-fifty basis. It was meant to allay the fans' fear that Samuel would own the region outright. Having said that, Leighton wanted total control of the Warriors, there is no doubt about that, and now with Pontypridd appearing to be out of the regional rugby picture, he more or less had his way. He must have been aware that Moffett would not help either Pontypridd or the Warriors financially, even though the Welsh Rugby Union had bailed Llanelli out of financial trouble. After all, Moffett always wanted four regions and here were the first signs that one could go to the wall at any time. Leighton Samuel announced that the Warriors would continue to play at Bridgend and Pontypridd for the rest of the season, but the decision about the future beyond that would be made at the end of the campaign. He said that he had been accused of wanting to take regional rugby away from Pontypridd. In *The Guardian* on 27 September he was quoted as saying, "Nothing could be further from the truth." He also gave assurances that Pontypridd would continue to receive the bar takings and hospitality money from games at Sardis. "It would be hard to take games away from Sardis Road," continued Samuel. "But my ultimate aim is to build a ground between the two towns to reduce our overheads." He also made it clear that it was not the end of rugby in the Valleys. It appeared from these statements that the future was a little clearer as far as rugby in Pontypridd was concerned. But this was Leighton Samuel talking.

Our meeting with the Scarlets brought together the top two in the Celtic League, and a crowd of around 5,000 hinted at green shoots of growth in the regional game in Wales. Scott Quinnell was injured, but as one of that famous rugby family moves over, another is ready to take his place and so we faced 'Little Gavin', the latest Quinnell off the famous family production line. It was different playing another of the Welsh regions. For a start the crowd was much bigger and obviously that lifted the atmosphere. Wherever you went in Wales the crowd was the 16th man. They were as keen for their team to win as the players were. The difference with the regional matches was that the desire for bragging rights became even more intense. These were the games to win. From a coaching point of view it became more difficult. Yes, you knew the opposition players' strengths and weaknesses, and what the coaches might have up their sleeves, and you could be pretty sure how the opposition would play. But then they knew the same about you.

We took an early lead through Gareth Wyatt's try which Neil Jenkins converted and he kicked five penalties which took him over the 50-point mark for the season. But it was our discipline which let us down. Cory Harris was sent to the sin bin just before half time and with the extra man Scarlets scored a try through Barry Davies and, with Gareth Bowen matching Jenks kick for kick, we ended up on the losing side 27–22.

There was some good news the following week as Steve Hansen named seven of our players in the team to play Canada in Wales' opening Rugby World Cup match: Kevin Morgan, Gareth Thomas, Sonny Parker, Ceri Sweeney, Gareth Cooper, Gethin Jenkins and Brent Cockbain were the guys to carry the Warriors name onto the international pitch for the first time. To say I was proud to see their names on the team sheet is an understatement even if it did leave me with a headache with team selection looming for the game against the Ospreys.

I went down the road of most coaches who have a similar problem of players being away with international teams, by coming out with the positive line that it gives others a chance to make a claim. I felt then and still feel now that it was right for us to have kept playing through the World Cup as we were trying to create interest in regional rugby. There would have been nothing worse than having one or two games then taking a break during the tournament in Australia. Not that the rush of interest was overwhelming, but we would have lost whatever momentum we had.

Although Steve Hansen had decided against selecting two of our players, Nathan Budgett and Gareth Wyatt, they did receive a measure of notoriety on the eve of Wales kicking off their World Cup campaign. Someone decided to run a poll of 800 women to choose the sexiest player in Wales. They even suggested quite seriously that it might help to boost the gates if we signed a player or two for their appeal to the ladies rather than just their rugby ability. The marketing department might have gone for it, but unfortunately for the fairer sex our budgets didn't quite have that flexibility. Gareth Wyatt came in at number eight, Colin Charvis was third and Scott Gibbs was runner-up. But Wales's sexiest rugby player for 2003, standing at 6ft 5in and weighing in at a lean, mean 17st, and bald, was none other than Nathan Budgett. You can bet he took some stick, not only from us and the players, but also from the supporters and just about everyone involved with the Warriors. Again, though, it all helped to bring the squad together with a bit of light relief. Thank you, ladies.

The top two sexiest players in Wales were due to meet two days later when we played the Ospreys at the Brewery Field. Scott Gibbs was due to captain the Neath–Swansea partnership, who were fourth in the table. Who exactly would be coming up against Gibbs for us was a problem. Despite my enthusiasm for playing during the World Cup, it did leave us short, especially in the centre. Dafydd James, David Bishop and Jonny Bryant were all injured, and in the end I went with

Shaun James and Matthew Nutthall, who was either a wing or a full back. We intended to keep the ball away from their backs as we knew our midfield was our weakness, but we felt our forwards were stronger than theirs and if we could keep the ball for long periods they would concede penalties, with Neil there to kick the points.

The problem was that we came up against one player who had a point to prove to Steve Hansen. Gavin Henson, despite being the new pin-up boy of Welsh rugby, had been left out of the Wales World Cup squad. He was apparently distraught, and decided to take his frustration out on us. He played at full back and set up both tries for wing Gareth Morris, converted them both and banged over six penalties as our discipline let us down again. Neil Jenkins, who could teach the upstart a thing or two, replied with five penalties for us and converted Richard Bryan's late try, but we were beaten by ten points. Lyn Jones was keen to play down Henson's recent performances but, much as it hurts me to say it, the upstart upstaged the maestro. He provided the moments of class in the game and his supporters were probably right, he should have been out in Australia.

Mike Powell set something of an unwanted record in this game for the fastest sending off of a replacement. I sent him on with instructions to get stuck into them. Well, fair play to Mike, he carried out my instructions to the letter which is always good for a coach to see. The problem was he went just a little over the top for the liking of referee and lasted just thirty seconds before seeing the red card.

I was a little upset after the game as no one from the Ospreys came into the Bridgend clubhouse for food and a drink. They went straight back to do pool recovery. OK, we were now in the professional age and enough has been said and written about how players didn't grasp the professional ideas, but no one informed us of their intentions which I found showed a lack of etiquette and manners. Also, was this the beginning of the end of what had traditionally been part of rugby union, the socialising in the bar after the game? I'm sure the management and officials of the Ospreys didn't all have to do pool recovery. We may have been professional but could still maintain values and responsibilities.

A crowd of 2,500 had turned up at the Brewery Field, although it must be remembered that at the same time Swansea were playing Newport in the Premiership at St Helen's in front of 1,200. Just to put that into perspective, though, the night before Cardiff had attracted 3,500 for the visit of Leinster, and the day after Newport Gwent Dragons had a crowd of around 3,200 at Rodney Parade to watch them beat Glasgow. It was a chance for us as coaches to compare notes on the way regional rugby was going. A chance missed, though. Gareth Jenkins, through no fault of his own, could never relate to any problems we had at the Warriors because his region was basically just Llanelli under a new name. He didn't have any of the problems we had in amalgamating two squads and playing at two venues. That said, we did talk about the integration of the clubs within the region and how we at the Warriors could use his experience in this area, as Llanelli had been doing this successfully for many years. As for Lyn Jones, who had similar problems with Swansea and Neath, well, Lyn was always great company, there was no one better to have a pint with, but serious rugby chat? Forget it. I always found Lyn very dismissive and difficult to talk to about serious rugby matters. Some of his interviews and comments were just off the wall and that was probably the reason why he was never seriously considered for the Wales coaching job. He had all the qualifications, but just couldn't be serious for long enough.

In-form Ulster provided our next opposition. They were second in the table with three league wins out of four, whereas we had lost our last two. Ulster won 26–20. Was I worried? Yes and no. I felt we had to try different people in different positions and try to put a squad together. If we were going to go forward we had to see who was capable of playing in the squad, and during that period it was all part of the build-up to the Heineken Cup so we had to get it right. We knew players would be coming back from the World Cup so it was just a case of moving things forward.

So going into the next game against Mike Ruddock's Dragons we needed a win. The game was at Sardis Road and we needed to get back on the winning road. We had been hampered by injuries, especially to senior players who we were relying on whilst the guys were away in Australia. Dragons captain Andy Marinos appealed for a free flowing match, hinting that in previous Welsh derby games there had been a lot of niggle and not much decent rugby. His words were wasted. The game was awful and what made matters worse was that it was played in front of just 1,477 supporters. As dear old Andy Howell said in his *Western Mail* report, if Leighton Samuel had been thinking of building an all-seater stadium at Sardis, he could have managed with a big shed. The game was live on television, the marketing had been poor, and it was cold. But with all that we had said about the passionate support from the Valleys, that shouldn't have been an excuse. After three defeats on the trot we needed a win, any win anywhere and anyhow. We managed to get the win and so stopped the rot, but apart from that there was little to get excited about. There was a cheerful note for the commercial department, however, as it transpired that our shirts were the second-most sought after in the sports shops.

The luck of the Irish did for us in our next game, as we went to the reigning Celtic League champions Munster. Now if the game against the Dragons had been dull, this was far from it in more ways than one. The referee was from Scotland but his name was Ireland, and he had a 'mare'. Things went against us even before the kick-off with Jonny Bryant pulling a calf muscle in the warm-up. We had to put 19-year-old Lee Thomas in at centre and he did a brilliant job. I wouldn't blame the groundsman for the injury to Jonny, but he didn't help matters. On arrival, as always, I checked the field then approached the groundsman to ask which side of the field we could use to warm up. He replied, "Out on the back field behind the stand." I then pointed out that Munster had laid their warm-up equipment out on one side of the main field, to which he replied, "I have relations and very good friends playing for Munster, they can do what you like, but you are still warming up on the back field, and by the way do you want a cup of tea?" After I threatened to raise all hell he relented and we warmed up on the main field, but you have to love the Irish!

We scored two tries for the first time since that famous win against Leinster, Aisea Havili and Phil Booth scored them, and needless to say Neil Jenkins stuck over three penalties and a conversion. We were on for a win until Mr Ireland, who made some bemusing decisions throughout the game, killed us a minute before the end. He spotted one of the forwards coming in from the wrong side of the ruck, fair enough a penalty, but then played an enormous amount of advantage which seemed to go on for ever and a day. Jenks was so frustrated that he wellied the ball and, as luck would have it, it caught Mr Ireland smack on the head, knocking the bugger clean out. When the referee came round Neil apologised and the referee accepted his apology. Maybe he was still concussed! I understand that the incident became a 'What Happened Next?' question on TV's *A Question of Sport*. When the spat had died down, Jeremy Staunton kicked the penalty and they had won by a single point. We were devastated as we had outplayed Munster, and with a very young team, but Jenks had shown again what a class player he was. He always seemed to grab the headlines when the chips were down. That performance was no exception.

We now had two games against Scottish opposition before the most important part of the season came along in the form of the Heineken Cup. There was mixed news on the injury front. Maama Molitika was fit but Jonny Bryant's warm-up calf injury in Munster would keep him out for at least a month. There was an immediate replacement for Bryant, as our former Wales and British Lions centre Dafydd James had come through a premiership match for Bridgend following his shoulder injury. We had an agreement with Bridgend and

Pontypridd, our two Premiership clubs, that we could use their games to ease injured players back to full fitness. It benefited both parties as they got the use of a regional player and we got our man some game time at a slightly less intense level. If Dafydd had been fit there is little doubt that he would have been out in Australia as well. He had a great physique and was a real presence at centre or on the wing. He had been injured playing for Bridgend against Swansea back in the April and had to have an operation on the shoulder. As a result he was yet to make his debut for the Warriors.

We were on a revenge mission here as Glasgow had beaten us in the Celtic Cup back in September, and we knew we had to improve our ball retention and cut out the turnovers which had been the worst of any side I had been involved in. They out-muscled us that night and we couldn't let it happen again. Hugh Campbell, the Glasgow coach, had made changes in his backs as they attempted to halt a run of one win in their last six league games which had left them one place off the bottom of the table. Thankfully we extended that losing run, winning 29–23 and it was our turn to behave ourselves whilst the opposition gave away a string of penalties which Neil Jenkins converted. It also provided us with the first win at the Brewery Field for a regional side. Not such good news for us in the next game though against Edinburgh as we lost 30–19, but a host of events had happened off the field in Wales and across in Australia between those two matches.

Wales had finished their World Cup campaign with a couple of performances which set the tournament alight. After expected victories in the group matches against Canada, Sililo Martens' Tonga and Italy, they then played New Zealand. This was a defining moment in the international career of Gareth Thomas. He was named on the bench as Steve Hansen, knowing they had already qualified for the quarter-finals, rested several of his front runners. Alfie's rest didn't last too long as he was needed as a replacement when Garan Evans went off four minutes into the game and he came on at full back. What happened next is now history, and the performance, despite the 53–37 defeat, was an inspiration to the Welsh rugby faithful. So too was the defeat by eventual winners England, when Wales continued their running attacking style which brought them a total of four tries against New Zealand and three against England.

On their return from Australia one or two of the players told me the secret of their success in these two matches. They said it had been a case of 'Sod Steve Hansen, we are going out to play our own game in our own style'. Others have put it down to the players who felt that they weren't going to play any part in Hansen's plans for the quarter-finals having a point to prove. The decision came after New Zealand had scored an early try, and Garan Evans had been injured. The players had got into a huddle and decided to go for it, all guns blazing with nothing to lose. The game just exploded. Everything Hansen and his coaches had been drilling into the players clicked and the results gave Wales a fantastic performance. Even though the 28–17 defeat by England denied Wales a semi-final place, Steve Hansen was right in stating that it opened up a bright new dawn after years of doom and gloom. He went on to say that now was the time for supporters and sponsors to get behind the five Welsh regions and that we all had to move together.

With Wales on their way home we would soon be at full strength, and hopefully then the fans would see just how good the Warriors could be. But not, it appeared, at Sardis Road. At the end of September Samuel had promised that regional rugby would be played at Sardis until at least the end of the season. By the middle of November, we had had one of Leighton's famous U-turns. A message appeared on the Warriors website saying, "For financial reasons the regional side has decided to play all future games at Bridgend's Brewery Field." In hindsight it showed how naive I had been regarding Leighton. I had trusted him. He had promised and delivered so much for us to establish the region. In some cases he had gone too far, but at the time he could not have done more for us. Now he was showing his true colours. I had been completely wrong about him. He proved, in my view, that he was a person who could not be trusted. As far as I could see, he had misled me about Sardis Road. For me it showed the true character of the man. I was gutted by the news and could have strung Samuel by the bollocks from the nearest cross bar! I have always been a person who makes up his own mind about people rather than relying on others' opinions. I got this one wrong in a big way, and it was small compensation that I wasn't the only one. It was a difficult position to be in and Allan and myself tried to run the Warriors with as little contact with Samuel as possible. It became a need-to-know situation, I told him what he needed to know and only asked for anything if it became necessary.

Even the former Bridgend players knew how much of an advantage it was to us playing at Sardis Road. There was a good crowd at the Brewery Field, but at Sardis it was different. Whether it was the hills, the stands, or maybe the wins Ponty had experienced there, there was something about Sardis Road which gave us an advantage and this was going to be taken away. The players had been quite happy with the fifty-fifty split that had been decided at the start of the season. They weren't happy, the fans weren't happy and I certainly wasn't happy.

It was another step, the final step, towards taking rugby away from the Valleys. The Dragons had said they would play all their matches at Rodney Parade, so the Gwent Valleys had already been denied top-class rugby. Now the same was happening to the Rhondda Cynon Taf and Merthyr Valleys. It was the final nail in the coffin of top rugby in Pontypridd, and probably the biggest mistake Samuel made. If he had stayed even until the end of the season, sweet-talked the Ponty supporters, put his arm around them and got them on-side, he could have made the Warriors a better supported team than they were. That, of course, wasn't Leighton's way. With him it was either his way or no way. Leighton had built a huge hospitality area at the Brewery Field that stretched the whole length of one side of the pitch. It cost him a reported £750,000. At Sardis we had made do with a temporary structure at one end. It served its purpose but never made any money. It cost the club £72,000 to hire the facility, and the twelve boxes were sold out at £6,000 each for the season. It broke even but in the modern climate a facility like that breaking even was not the idea. It had to make money; it didn't. Also there was a feeling amongst other teams in Wales, and even further afield, that we had a massive support at Sardis Road for the big games and could pull in big gates. But for the smaller matches against the less fashionable teams we would be down to less than 3,000 supporters. Our grandstand held 1,700 people, whereas Cardiff, Newport, Llanelli, Swansea would get far more than we did, so their weekly income was far bigger than ours. The Celtic League didn't help either, as very few fans, if any, travelled down from Edinburgh or Glasgow, and the same could be said about the Irish sides. So we could be playing one of them with no away support coming through the turnstiles. Our fans were fantastic, but our catchment area and the sheer number of fans available to us was limited.

There was no way, though, that Leighton was going to allow his monument to stand idle. You cannot argue with the fact that it looked great, and you cannot argue with the fact that he put the money upfront to build a very useful facility. But it was going to be heart-wrenching for those of us with Pontypridd connections to leave our beloved Sardis Road. Supporters' club secretary Alun Jones called the move a "breach of faith", adding that, "We brought season tickets at the start of this season on the understanding that a proportionate number of Warriors home games would be played out of Sardis Road." The only consideration to the Pontypridd supporters was the provision of buses to take them to the Brewery Field. Moffett, still out in Australia, seemed more concerned with the plight of the Dragons, who had gone into administration, than with us. It was another chance to have a dig at those who opted for five regions instead of four. As he hadn't got his way he was not going to miss an opportunity to bring the matter up again. He had a perfect opportunity to get down to four. Why didn't he take it? The answer is simple. There are 43 clubs in WRU district A, the Gwent area, which is more than any other district in the WRU. Now Moffett may have had little knowledge or little consideration for rugby in Wales but he could add up, and he could see that to get rid of regional rugby in the most populated area of the country was suicide. He was daft but not that daft.

He also said that it was a shame that Pontypridd had turned down Samuel's offer to buy the lease and turn Sardis Road into an all-seater stadium.

So there was a pretty subdued mood going to the Brewery Field for the game against Edinburgh. For us as a management group it was the most difficult problem for us to deal with. We had become very close as a group and it was no surprise that it was not just the former Pontypridd players who became affected by the decision. The players were quite happy to play at the Brewery Field as long as a fair proportion of the games were played at Sardis Road. Other problems started to emerge as well. The players would be handed a salary cheque only to be told not to cash it for a couple of days. Most of the players did wait, but some, probably to test the system as much as anything, did cash them straight away, and sure enough they bounced. Sometimes on payday it was like the Wacky Races as the players raced off in their cars to cash the cheques. Usually it was the last three or so who were unlucky and theirs bounced. Somehow Leighton always managed to persuade them that it had all been down to a banking error and the money really was there.

It was obvious to them that things weren't right off the field. But it was a credit to the players that the off-the-field problems seemed to pull them closer together as a group. They were a great bunch. Some of the players probably felt that if we could overcome the early teething problems then everything would turn out fine. Even the venue for the games would be sorted if Leighton, as promised, built the new stadium. This was certainly the belief of many of the players. Yes, we had problems. Yes, we had a loose cannon at the head. But if we could just get through this first season then maybe next year things would be more settled.

This was the first match with our World Cup players available and we played eight of them. Gareth Thomas, despite his success at full back, captained the side from outside centre. Kevin Morgan, who had played for Wales against Canada, found that luck deserted him again. He had suffered a calf injury in a collision with Sonny Parker which had ended his tournament. All he wanted to do now was get back and play rugby, with the hope of making an impression on Steve Hansen for selection in the Six Nations. We also had Gethin Jenkins, Robert Sidoli and Tonga's Sililo Martens, with Mefin Davies, Brent Cockbain and Ceri Sweeney on the bench. So the only two missing now were Gareth Cooper and Sonny Parker. We hadn't used Dafydd James against Glasgow so he, like the World Cup returnees, was making his Warriors debut. That to me looked like a pretty strong outfit. Edinburgh had their international players returning as well but coach Frank Hadden had his selection critics. The big debate in Scotland was where to play Chris Paterson – at number ten or at wing. Hadden selected the player, voted Scotland's best at the World Cup, at fly-half and he killed us. We looked disjointed as you might expect with all the new faces in the side, but it was a poor performance and had Brendan Laney not missed with five attempts at goal the score might have been nearer 50. As it was, 30–19 to them was bad enough.

With a crowd of around 2,000, way under the estimated 6,000 we needed to break even, Leighton Samuel again had a go at the supporters, and hinted that unless things improved, the top earning players would have to look for a new team next season. So far just under 13,000 supporters had paid to watch our home games, about 2,500 per match. Samuel estimated we were losing about £50,000 per month, a figure he was prepared to subsidise in the short term. We needed more supporters; maybe the Heineken Cup would attract them.

At this stage of the tournament's history, you had a good chance of going further if you had an Italian side in your group. Thankfully in our group we had the Italian champions Calvisano, and we started with them at the Brewery Field. I made a plea to the supporters to get behind the team. We needed them and I promised an entertaining style which they would enjoy watching. People were looking for something special from the Welsh regions following the World Cup as if we had suddenly caught whatever Steve Hansen had injected into the players out in Australia.

I promised an entertaining game, and so it proved to be. We led 21–3 after half an hour but trailed by a point at half time thanks to three tries by the Italians. It was entertaining for the fans, but a nightmare for yours truly. Brent Cockbain spent ten minutes in the bin during the second half, but thanks to Ceri Sweeney, whose 19 points earned him the man of the match award, we won 34–25. It was certainly a better performance than the previous week. The boys stepped up to the mark, and we won with a try bonus point as well, but I was disappointed. We looked like a combined team, when we thought by now we were putting our best team out. Maybe I was expecting too much too soon. The World Cup players were only now beginning to become accustomed to the Warriors' game plan and it was difficult for these guys not to drift back into the Wales mode in which they had spent the last few months. But we had won.

There was better news off the field with the crowd given as 2,900. They had after all either rallied to my appeal, or had been attracted by the status of the Heineken Cup. It proved to be a decent weekend for three of the Welsh regions. Apart from our win, the Scarlets beat Northampton, Dragons beat Ulster, and even Cardiff Blues put in a good performance at Sale getting a losing bonus point. Unfortunately the Ospreys lost at Leeds.

Steve Hansen threw his pennyworth into the mix as well by highlighting the results, the fact that there was now more competition for places, and that the system was now bringing out the best in people. He could also see that some good young players were starting to come through the regions as a result of all the World Cup players missing the start of the season. These would "give Wales a good base of players to work from" said the Wales coach.

As always after the game I stayed around for a pint and then drove home to Maerdy, meeting up with my wife, Jeromin, and some friends. I have always made a point of getting home and meeting up with the crowd who have always been loyal and supportive and seem to say the right things at the right time. Whether this was to bring me back down to earth or give me support if things hadn't gone well I don't know, but they have been important to me whether I have been coaching Wales, Pontypridd, Cardiff or the Warriors. Needless to say, having got our first Heineken points tucked away safely, the beer tasted better than if we'd lost.

With five points in the bag we topped group six, but we would have to step up another gear for the next game, away at the previous season's beaten finalists Perpignan. To play in front of a crowd in the region of 12,000 and behind an 8ft fence would be one thing, but there would be an atmosphere of hate. We weren't just the opposition, we were the enemy, make no mistake about that. Perpignan's ground is known as the Bull Ring for good reason. To make matters worse Perpignan had been beaten in the opening game, 28–7 at Wasps. Wasps had really fronted up to them, denied them possession and kept a great deal of pressure on them. They had been demolished by the English side and my fear was that there was likely to be a backlash. I had watched the game, and towards the end had seen the real Perpignan retaining the ball and demonstrating their ball carrying skills. In Australian Manny Edmonds, recently recruited due to an injury to Nicolas Laharrague, they had a fly-half who was a great controller of the game. We knew they would be physical and we would have to match them in that department.

We had a crisis in the front row. Chris Horsman, Phil Booth, Andrew Joy, and Martin Jones were all missing, and to add to our problems hooker Mefin Davies fractured an eye socket in training. Thankfully we had signed Christian Loader as cover. I and many of the former Pontypridd players had been involved in matches in France before, especially a particularly tough encounter in Brive, so we knew what to expect. The instructions were simple: meet fire with fire. It is the only way they give you any respect. If we took one backward step we would be done for. The group seemed confident enough, though. They had a tremendous respect for each other and they knew the squad was full of good players.

We lost 26–19. With the record of the French clubs at home in the Heineken that might not be a surprise, but again I was disappointed. We had done enough to put ourselves into a winning position and should have won that game. We lost it in the first half by making some poor decisions and were 14–3 down at the interval. Our scrum was under pressure and our line-out wasn't as good as it could have been. Their first try came from a rolling maul, something they used well, and the second showed the strength of their flanker, Lionel Mallier, who was brilliant throughout the match.

Two incidents in the first half, though, showed how the French often played the game in front of their own fans. Second row Christophe Porcu landed punches on Christian Loader and then Gethin Jenkins. The sly bastard skulked away from both incidents, which unfortunately were not spotted by the referee, Gregg Davies. How many times throughout my coaching career has a Scottish referee had an influence on the result of games? Thankfully video evidence seen after the game allowed us to cite Porcu and he ended up missing the remainder of Perpignan's Heineken matches.

We played much better in the second half and the frustrating thing was we put ourselves into a winning position. Kevin

Morgan scored a try which Ceri Sweeney converted, then Jenks came on and struck over a couple of penalties and we were hammering away at them, only to concede a late try which killed us. We had secured a bonus point, but the feeling was that the game was one that got away. It was rough, tough and dirty, but you wouldn't expect anything else out in France.

A fortnight later we made a Christmas visit to Cardiff. There is always an edge to a game at Cardiff, but this game proved particularly significant because I sensed that with it we finally came together as a team. There was a great team spirit beforehand, with everyone wanting to go down there and win, and you could sense something special was going to happen. Revenge was sweet as we won 26–10. Unfortunately I wasn't there to enjoy it.

We had arrived in Perpignan on the weekend of a seafood fair – right up my street. After the game there had been a spectacular show of shell food and I had made a bit of a pig of myself. I paid for it by contracting food poisoning. All my joints became swollen and I ended up unable to move. While Allan looked after things at the Arms Park, I was stuck at home watching the game on the television.

"We all laugh and joke about it, but Lynn has been quite seriously ill actually," revealed Lewis. "He's still suffering and it's been two weeks now since he was taken ill. I know that he wanted to be with us and he did try and ring me a couple of times during the game to suggest a few things. With the way the game was going it was very difficult to answer questions and shout at the same time! He is getting better now thankfully and we hope we'll have him back on board pretty soon." I wonder how much of that was said tongue in cheek!

One newspaper gave almost as many column inches to my illness as they did to the match report. "Ailing Warriors coach Lynn Howells could hardly have received a better tonic from his troops than this commanding Arms Park victory," it said. But it was a great day for Gareth Thomas who set us up for victory with a hat-trick of tries.

If we had come together for the Cardiff game then we certainly came together in the New Year when the Heineken Cup resumed and we faced Wasps. It would prove to be the Warriors' most memorable win in their short history. Everything we had planned to do going into the Heineken Cup came together in that game against the team many people thought could lift the cup. We outplayed the certain players that we had planned to outplay. We knew we had to outplay Lawrence Dallaglio and Rob Howley and sure enough Sililo Martens bottled up Howley and Maama Molitika sorted out Dallaglio. It was as clinical as that. It was a game plan that we put together and it worked for us and it was nice to read Howley's admission the following week that we "had done a job on them". The weather was wet, windy and muddy, and Wasps were sunk in it. Aisea Havili scored our only try, and Ceri Sweeney kicked three penalties to give us a 14–9 win and Wasps had been beaten for the first time in two months. Looking back, some of the senior players have admitted that this game was the one where everybody came together. It was the Warriors unification point. There was no Pontypridd or Bridgend faction. This was one team and we had something special. To go up there and beat Wasps, who were probably one of the best teams in Europe on their own patch, proved that. If we could only get things right off the field then this was going to be a big team. There was now a genuine feeling we could progress in the competition having performed so well in the three games so far.

There was one moment straight after the game, while I was giving some words of wisdom to the press, which will remain with me forever. Here we were at one of the top clubs in England in the so-called professional era, and while the rest of his team mates were out on the field 'warming down', Wasps' Samoan hooker Trevor Leota was standing at the bar, all 20 stone of him, with a pint in one hand and a cigarette in the other. Maybe this was the way forward after all.

Injuries and unavailability caught up with us for the return game against Warren Gatland's men. We didn't have a second row. Though Brent Cobain had suffered a hamstring injury, I kept saying he would probably play. I also let it be known that Rob Sidoli, who was suffering with a groin injury, might make the squad as well. But without those two we had to put Nick Kelly alongside Deiniol Jones in the second row. As Deiniol was a front of the line jumper, and we had to use him in the middle, we had little or no line-out presence at all. Ryan Jones wasn't eligible for the knockout stages. Chris Horsman had recovered from a knee injury, but I decided to leave the front row as it had been, and started Chris on the bench. Gatland made no less than six changes to the Wasps side, with only one of those down to injury.

At last we drew a crowd. The stand had been sold out for several days and the rest of the ground was full as well, as 10,000 pushed and shoved their way into the Brewery Field. The kick-off was delayed by ten minutes but needless to say there were no complaints from Samuel this time as there had been following the delay at Sardis Road before the Leinster match. There was an announcement by Derrick King before the game kicked off that a proposed merger between us and Cardiff had been put on ice. That got probably the biggest cheer of the night.

"There is one special announcement we want to make here tonight," said King. "And that is, as far as the Celtic Warriors are concerned, the merger with the Cardiff Blues is off. Celtic Warriors as a region will continue to stand alone." The *South Wales Echo* had been running a campaign against the merger, enlisting support from Warriors and Blues fans. Sometime later Leighton Samuel announced that he had received death threats from people who knew that talks about an amalgamation with the Cardiff Blues were taking place. I promise that even though there were times when I could have swung for him, it wasn't me!

Of all the problems we had this was probably the most difficult to deal with. The players were constantly concerned that Samuel would go, but those off-the-field matters may just have brought the guys closer. Rumours that the Warriors would merge with the Blues were different. Both regions thought they had done the hard work in getting their squads together successfully, and getting the season off to a pretty good start. We had worked this hard and come this far and now there was a chance of it all being thrown up into the air again. A merger would certainly have meant the culling of another load of players, as there was no way that the remaining region could have carried two squads. If anything the rumours of a merger with the Blues brought the squad even closer together.

The game wasn't a classic but there were a few dust-ups to liven the crowd. Nick Kelly landed half a dozen really good punches on Dallaglio. How the touch judge missed it I'll never know. Dallaglio got a yellow card for body-checking Gareth Wyatt but returned after his spell in the bin and nurtured them home in the last fifteen minutes. It was enough for a bonus point but not the win we were after. Nick Kelly had come into the side and put his body on the line and performed very well out of position, but we missed the extra bulk of Cockbain and Sidoli. A major factor in our set piece had been the absence of key personnel. Having looked at the video, I was frustrated because we could have won the game. What you can't do in Europe is give away as many penalties and lose as much set piece ball as we did. Even so with a home game against Perpignan and then having to travel to the weakest side Calvisano, I didn't think we were out of it by any means, but we had to win them both and pick up a bonus point from somewhere. You have to win your home games in this tournament and then if possible sneak a win on the road. We had done that with the win at Wasps, but with them having beaten us at the Brewery Field we were no longer in control of the group.

So the Frenchmen came to us also needing to win as they faced Wasps away in their final match. Rob Sidoli was fit, so we brought him into the second row, and Chris Horsman was brought into the starting line-up with Gethin Jenkins moving across to his favoured loose-head side. Nearer the day

Ceri Sweeney went down with a septic knee so Neil Jenkins started at fly-half and what a night it proved for him. Porcu had of course been suspended after his antics in the game out there, but they were full of talented forwards, and had Manny Edmonds controlling things behind the scrum.

Aisea Haveli should have scored a try from Gareth Cooper's chip, but dropped the ball over the line, and that was about the only excitement in a pretty dire first half in which Edmonds dropped a goal and kicked three penalties, whilst Jenks landed two penalties. The Ginger Monster's third just after half time was significant as it took him to 500 Heineken Cup points, only the fourth player to reach that target, joining Stephen Jones, Diego Dominguez and Ronan O'Gara. Referee Guilio de Santis was appalling but did get among the French ball-killing and sent a couple of them to the sin bin. In the last few minutes, with Frederic Cermeno still in the sin bin, we drove from a line-out, they collapsed the maul once too often for the ref's liking and he danced over to the posts to award us a penalty try. Jenks didn't miss from in front of the posts so we scraped home by a point 16–15, but the French had a bonus point. It is hard enough to play the French teams, but when they have sixteen men on the field it becomes even more difficult. During the last few manic minutes with sin bins, penalty tries, and replacements coming on and going off, the referee didn't notice that they had sixteen on the park. He was soon made aware of it from our bench in no uncertain terms!

What amazed me about that game was that our set piece was awful and yet we beat the previous season's Heineken finalists. We went about ten minutes during one stage where we didn't touch the ball! Our line-out didn't function and one player who was particularly depressed about that was Rob Sidoli. It was Rob's first game back for a month after his groin injury but he was really upset with his performance. We had to work hard on him the following week to put our arm around him and persuade him it was only a one-off and not to blame himself. We were helped in that matter by Steve Hansen who included

Sid and seven other Warriors in his Wales squad for the Six Nations. Rob was joined by Sonny Parker, Gareth Thomas, Gareth Cooper, Gethin Jenkins, Ceri Sweeney, Richard Parks and Kevin Morgan. I thought that Deiniol Jones should have been there as well. I can't even today recall a game when he didn't perform well for us. The work he got through in a match was incredible, and he was an expert line-out tactician. Having so many Warriors named by Wales was great encouragement for the boys in the squad and the rest of us going into what could be the most important game so far, with the prize being qualification for the knockout stages. Us, Wasps or Perpignan could still win the group with one round of matches remaining. It was complicated. We had to win out in Calvisano and get a bonus point, and also hope that Perpignan beat Wasps, but didn't score four tries in doing so, which would have given them a bonus point.

Everyone thought we had an easy task. People were talking about how many tries we would score as if the Italian side were a pushover. Things had changed and Italian teams, although not as strong as the other nations, had come a long way since they first entered the European tournaments and the Six Nations. We had to worry about winning, first of all, then think of tries and bonus points.

As one newspaper so aptly put it, we won in Italy and lost in France. Yes, we beat Calvisano 28–26 (I said it wouldn't be a walkover), and, yes, we got the bonus point thanks to tries from Gareth Wyatt, Gareth Thomas, Deiniol Jones and Gareth Cooper. But Wasps smashed Perpignan 34–6 to top the group. The record books now show that it was to be Wasps' year as they went on to win the Heineken beating Toulouse 27–20 in the final at Twickenham. At least we had beaten the winners and on their own ground, but more importantly for us our European campaign had been a good one. We had won four and lost two, and there are plenty of sides today who would love that sort of record at the end of a European season. The one we felt we should have had was the one out in Perpignan.

That was the one which disappointed us. The Wasps game at home we can look back on and say that we just didn't have the personnel but, yes, a very good first European season.

Having tasted Europe, we now had to make sure that we qualified again. Between the start of February and the end of the season we had some notable scalps. We thumped Leinster 37–16 out there, on a roll of four wins in four games. We then lost to the Ospreys, and Ulster at home – the only time we failed to score all season. What was noteworthy about this game was that a record came to an end. Neil Jenkins had kicked 44 consecutive attempts at goal – 30 penalties and 14 conversions – a record which stretched back to October. I don't think it was a record which Jenks relished. I think all the talk about it in the papers got him down, and he did say to me on a couple of occasions that providing we were well ahead in a match he would miss a kick just to end the sequence and end all the talk. Some of those kicks had been routine, but in some cases we had relied on Jenks to get us out of a hole. It just showed what a fantastic kicker he was. The only success that night against Ulster was the performance of the youngster Ryan Jones. Hansen thought he was a second row, but for reasons I have already mentioned I saw him as a number eight, and that night he was brilliant.

A defeat by the Dragons made it three in succession, but that defeat was upsetting for other reasons as well. Maama Molitika was sent off in the second half for punching. I had no argument with the decision, but as he left the field a small number in the crowd at Rodney Parade shouted racial comments at the Tongan. Derrick King heard them and confirmed that a small section of the crowd were making racial comments. There is no place for that in rugby and we could have taken the matter further by reporting the incident to the WRU. When Dragons director Martin Hazell said they would launch an investigation and deal with the 'scum' in the appropriate manner, we were happy to leave the matter in their hands.

Our form returned after our internationals came back

from the Six Nations, and we put together successive wins, starting with a great Sunday game against Munster. Regional rugby came back as a one-off to Sardis Road after a gap of over five months, and the crowd was treated to a real thriller with us winning 29–25. Looking back at the league records the crowd is quoted as 4,157. I've also seen somewhere that it was as many as 5,000, but also there was a spot on the television coverage when the crowd was announced, and Jonathan Davies burst out laughing at the figure given and hinted the figures might have been doctored a bit. He was probably spot-on. The crowd was a big one. The players had been looking forward to returning to Sardis all week and the atmosphere and support justified their anticipation. I know several of them went public on wanting more games there next season. Ceri Sweeney, in particular, after his 19-point haul was keen to suggest that everyone wanted a fair fifty-fifty split in matches. I echoed those thoughts and added that the crowd had shown how intimidating a place Sardis Road can be.

There was a theory put forward as to why we suddenly had this one game back in Pontypridd. Leighton Samuel wanted out. Again. So what better way to do it than to go along with what so many people wanted, a game at Sardis Road, and then find something wrong. He was looking for hostility from the Ponty fans, and sure enough he got that alright. He also claimed that Pontypridd had refused to allow the sale of Warriors goods from the souvenir shop and the Warriors were forced to sell the goods from the back of a van. Perhaps his plan was to see what trouble was stirred up by this game, and then look for a way out.

It was about this time that the players were starting to worry about their futures. We were all sick and tired of not knowing whether Samuel would stay or go. So Allan and I arranged a meeting between Samuel and some of the senior players at Decor Frame's offices. Rich Bryan, Alfie, Jonny Bryant, Rob Sidoli, Deiniol Jones were there, and apparently it got pretty heated. Samuel was asked the question straight: are you in or out? He assured the boys he was in. They were happy. New contracts were signed by some of them, new kit for next season was chosen, everything seemed to be in place for a rosy future.

Wins over Glasgow, Edinburgh and Cardiff Blues ensured that we qualified for the Heineken Cup the following season and that from the outset had been our main aim.

There was one disappointment about the Blues game, though. It was the final competitive game in Wales for Neil Jenkins. He had been such an important part of Pontypridd over his career, and also for the Warriors, and the only reason we had been able to hold onto his services was down to the sponsorship of Buy As You View. Rumours were rife on many occasions that Jenks was a target for the rugby league clubs up north, and the only reason we could keep him in Wales was thanks to the generosity of Buy As You View partners Gerald Coleman and Bernard Jones. The morning of the Cardiff game had seen the funeral of Gerald Coleman. Gerald had been a big supporter of Ponty, the Warriors and Valleys rugby. I was surprised and not a little disappointed that the Warriors board had not seen fit to have a minute's silence before the game as a mark of respect. I realise that Gerald had been a Ponty man, but without his support Jenks would not have been around to become the world's most prolific international points' scorer, and I don't think it would have been out of place to have acknowledged the contribution of such a generous supporter of Welsh rugby, even at the Brewery Field.

The success of that first season is something they cannot take away from me or from the rest of the Warriors. The further the season progressed, the more people started to buy into it. There were certain games where we played very well and people could see it all starting to happen, and I think that for me showed what we were trying to do. So we set off for the final game at Connacht in good spirits. Little did we realise that this was now the end of the beginning and the beginning of the end.

4

The Darkest Day

THE MATCH AGAINST Connacht would be a game of finals. It would be the final competitive game for one of our great servants and a great servant of Welsh rugby, Neil Jenkins. It would be the final Warriors game for Gareth Thomas. Paul John, who had been such a big part of Pontypridd and at the Warriors, would be retiring from regional rugby, and it would be the final game for me as Warriors coach. There would also be another final for all of us, but as we sat at the airport waiting for our flight to Cork we didn't see that one coming.

I had set up the team and on the pitch things were going pretty well. It was now time to address the wider aspects of regional rugby. Remembering back to the interview I had done for the job as coach, I had told the panel that being the head man in a region would mean more than just coaching the team. It would be the development of a pyramid within the region, "to create a pathway for coaches, players and administrators".

At the top of the pyramid obviously was the Warriors team, but we needed a structure below us which would give everyone a chance to make that top level in their own particular field. They needed us, and we needed them. If we had a player who needed game time, returning after injury for instance, we needed teams playing in the Premiership to give him that time. They also needed us to provide them with those players when they were in need. To make sure the players were treated as we would want them to be, on and off the field, we had to have a system whereby the Premiership clubs knew what we were doing and how we did it. Likewise the Premiership clubs could use the teams below them in the same way, and so the pyramid would move down to the bottom clubs in the region.

The next level below the Warriors consisted of the four Premiership clubs in our region at that time, Pontypridd, Bridgend, Maesteg, and Llanharan. Below them came the Division One teams such as Beddau, Treorchy, Tondu, etc. Next came Division Two, right down to Division Five and the likes of Gwernyfed and Porthcawl.

I felt that if we sent a representative of the region to these clubs it had to be the guy at the top. If they were prepared to buy into us then I had to give them the courtesy of meeting them in person. I made plans. I produced maps, I made lists of coaches and club representatives, I even did geographical breakdowns of the regions, schools, factories, places of interest and much more. Not only did we have to win over the clubs, but we had to win over the potential supporters as well. Our region had the largest catchment area of supporters and also the largest number of clubs.

This I believed was essential for regional rugby to be a success. It's interesting to see even today how many years later that little work like this has so far been done in Wales. The exception being at the Scarlets where Gareth Jenkins has gone back there and continued the work, but to be fair Llanelli have always had a fabulous link with their junior clubs taking players and players going back at the end of their careers.

In spending time doing this it was clear I would not have as much time to run the Warriors team. That is not to say that I was intending to give up the coaching. Richard Webster would come in and help out with the forwards, while Allan would take the training sessions. I would still have the responsibility for selection. I thought about this in February 2004 and spoke to Webby and Allan and we all agreed on the new plans. So for me as well, the game at Connacht wasn't so much the end of an era, but the start of a new one developing other things within the region.

There was nothing to play for at the Sportsground in Galway that Friday night. We would be fourth and had already qualified for the Heineken, and Connacht had little or nothing to play for apart from a bit of pride maybe. They would finish the season in ninth place. It was destined to be an exciting night for two of the Welsh regions as the Scarlets and the Dragons were both, along with Ulster, in with a chance of clinching the Celtic League title. The Dragons had the more difficult job having to play Leinster away at Landsdowne Road in Mike Ruddock's last game in charge before he became the new Wales coach, while the winners of the game at Stradey Park between the Scarlets and Ulster would take the title. They could fight it out. It didn't bother us. We had achieved what we had set out to do in that first season, which was to make sure we continued our involvement in the Heineken Cup. As it turned out the Dragons lost, but with the Scarlets winning 23–16 they took the title. So in the first season of regional rugby, for Wales to have three of the five sides in the top four places seemed to suggest that regional rugby might be the answer after all.

Before our game Connacht made a presentation to Jenks; a glass rugby ball. It was a wonderful gesture by the Irish as Neil had never done anything particularly outstanding for Connacht, but it was just the respect they had for him. They were almost honoured that his last competitive game should come against them and they felt they should do something on behalf of rugby to mark the occasion.

Neil and Gareth had been given a rousing send-off at the Brewery Field with our victory over Cardiff Blues the week before. Alfie started, and Jenks came on after an hour but, rarely for that season, he didn't contribute a point in our 20–3 victory. So now the celebrations could begin.

A few days before we were due to go to Ireland I had a deputation from some of the senior players who thought it might be a good idea if everyone went on the final trip of the season. That was a call for Leighton Samuel and, fair play to him, when the idea was put to him he came up trumps. He paid for all the squad, the coaches and the medical staff, to go out to the Connacht game, another example of how generous the guy could be. This gave us the opportunity to celebrate what we had achieved during the season. A couple of players were leaving, Nick Kelly was being released, Alfie was off to Toulouse, and it was a chance to sink a few pints of Guinness. Well why not? There was also another major event to celebrate as Mefin Davies was due to get married, so what better excuse than to have his stag do with the boys after the final game? So the playing squad flew out on the Thursday, with the rest of the party coming out on the Friday morning. It was a good weekend.

After the match a kangaroo court was convened, a regular feature of rugby trips and tours, with Maama Molitika as the enforcer. Whatever the court decided as punishment, he made sure it was carried out. He took his role very seriously, so much so that the daft sod started the celebrations as early as eight o'clock on the Saturday morning, and as the day wore on and the Guinness went down so Maama got into the role and started fighting with everyone. The court decided that Matthew Rees, who everyone called 'Smiler', so idolised Neil Jenkins that he should be taped to him. Nick Kelly was returning to his old trade as an electrician, so he was given a Bob the Builder belt which he had to wear all weekend. Our conditioning coach Mark Bennett always thought he was a bit of an Adonis, so was given a leopard-skin thong to wear. It was a good weekend, job done, plenty of enjoyment and a good end of season. We had qualified for Europe, and even though one or two players were leaving everyone knew in that group we had a good squad. People were looking forward to the next season believing that all the teething problems of regional rugby were behind them and we had something to build on.

Even though a lot of the players had signed new contracts it now appears that some of them had started to make plans in case the Warriors ran into difficulties. There was a feeling that with Leighton Samuel running the show then we could either fold or win the Heineken Cup! Things had been building up for months since before Christmas, and some of the players had started to find out, through their agents, if other clubs would be interested in their services. It might sound as if they were prepared to leave a sinking ship, but they had careers to consider, families to support and mortgages to pay. I don't blame them. Eventually though, with assurances from Leighton Samuel that he was honouring his commitment to the Warriors, they had refused moves to other teams and signed new contracts with us. Jonny Bryant was one who could have gone to the Blues or the Dragons, but after assurances from Samuel he signed a new contract. Jonny Bryant wasn't the only one either. Samuel must have known at this time that he wanted out.

According to the statement of company history, which eventual liquidators Begbies Traynor presented to creditors, the Welsh Rugby Union contacted the Celtic Warriors company on 9 April as part of its 'overall review of the finances of the regional operations'. There were concerns about the finances of the Dragons and the Warriors but to show no discrimination against any region the same letter was sent to all five. Remember, there was still a desire to get down to four regions. The Scarlets, Ospreys and Blues were financially alright, the worry was the Dragons and the Warriors. There was never a danger of the Dragons going out of business. Tony Brown, their benefactor, had deep pockets. But good old Leighton Samuel took the bait, hook, line and sinker.

According to the statement, the letter, 'prompted a response from Mr Samuel on that day which culminated in a request to the WRU that it formulate an exit plan for him. This was again raised at a meeting between Mr Samuel and Mr W. J. Morris (the WRU solicitor), as representative of the WRU, on 4th May 2004. Further discussions took place during the following days which culminated in an agreement dated 11th May 2004 for the WRU to acquire Bridgend RFC's share in the company. This agreement was completed according to the document on May 19th.'

That agreement came about between Samuel and the WRU two days before we flew out to Connacht for the final game of the season, with no inkling that this would be the last time we would be together as a squad for a game of rugby. There wasn't a hint of what was about to happen, although looking back maybe we should have expected trouble as everything was too quiet. Leighton hadn't threatened to pull out, there were no rumours of amalgamations with other regions, everything was quiet. It was the calm before the storm. The only time that Samuel wasn't bleating to the press or websites, he was negotiating with the Welsh Rugby Union to get rid of his Warriors share.

Richard Webster had returned home on the Saturday evening and got word from somewhere that news was already breaking that the Warriors were going to fold. He phoned me on the Saturday night, but to be honest I could easily have thought that this was just another 'Samuel Going' rumour. I left it for the time being and joined the rest of the guys for party time.

We arrived back in Cardiff on the Sunday morning, and by the Sunday afternoon the grapevine was in full swing. One of the players was phoned by a press man to tell him that the news was out that Leighton had sold out to the Welsh Rugby Union and the Warriors were going to fold. I had called Leighton as I needed to know what was happening, not only for the players, but the coaches and backroom staff as well. Just as important to me was the reason for his decision, which he told me was because he couldn't work any longer with the WRU as he didn't have any control. He admitted there were money problems, but was adamant that the Union had told him the Warriors would continue. I think, though, as soon as I put the phone down I knew the Warriors were finished.

One of my senior players, Jonny Bryant, rang me to find out what was going on and I could assure him that yes Leighton had sold out, but the WRU had promised him that the region would continue to play rugby. Nothing would change apart from the fact that we would be run by the WRU, which in the long run might not be a bad thing as there would be more stability. On Monday morning we had a phone call summoning us to a meeting at Wales' training centre at the Vale of Glamorgan Hotel. By now a lot of the players had found out what was going on and that the WRU had no intention of the region being closed down. Therefore we went to this meeting expecting simply to be told that Samuel had sold his share to the governing body, but the Warriors would continue as normal.

Samuel, in true Samuel tradition, looked for a scapegoat. He was away on business, but the newspapers caught up with him and he didn't disappoint them with his outspoken comments. He rounded on the supporters. It was their fault for not coming to support the region in big enough numbers. "The fans may be devastated but they should have come through the turnstiles," he said. Well, he was right to a certain extent. According to the statement of company history the crowds averaged 3,000. But who moved the Warriors away from the potential fan base? Samuel. The crowds at the Brewery Field only went above 2,000 for games with the other Welsh regions as compared with over 4,000 for games at Sardis Road, and those were against regions which didn't bring much, if any, travelling support. We can only compare crowds for the Celtic League games as none of the Heineken matches were played at Sardis.

Samuel blamed arguments about the name, arguments about where we played. He said he had received death threats when he was talking to Peter Thomas about an amalgamation with Cardiff Blues. He blamed the financial problems at Pontypridd and the fact that they had gone into administration, claiming that the club had not been honest with him about their finances. Then there was the failure of the WRU to work with the Warriors board after Samuel had given them the fifty per cent he brought from Pontypridd's administrators. "That," said Samuel, "brought the whole situation to a head."

Although the deal had been agreed with Samuel, it couldn't

go through until it had been approved by the full WRU committee. It wasn't possible to set up that meeting until 4 o'clock on the Monday afternoon we were called to The Vale. Whoever called that meeting was a little premature as it only gave the WRU committee an hour to pass the resolution to take over the Warriors, and to get the result to WRU solicitor John Morris and general manager Steve Lewis. It was later obvious, from the way the meeting started at five o'clock, that they didn't know the result. They waffled, they hedged, they stalled, until Moffett rang them to say go ahead, make the announcement.

We were all in a room: coaches, players, and backroom staff together, and Steve Lewis read out a statement telling us that Leighton Samuel had sold his share of the Warriors to the WRU who, as from five minutes ago, were now in total control. But, Lewis said, they didn't know what they were going to do with it. There was no confirmation that the region was going to continue. Jonny Bryant and Richard Bryan did most of the talking because there were a lot of young players in that room, and they may not have had the confidence to speak up in front of Lewis and the solicitor. The solicitor took a lot of the questions, and deflected the attention away from Lewis. Apparently Lewis knew more than he was allowed to reveal at that stage. He knew that the Warriors would not be continuing, but couldn't reveal that because the most important consideration throughout the whole winding up of the Warriors was to keep the players in Wales. If anyone had been told at that stage that there would be no Warriors next season, they could have signed within hours for clubs in England or elsewhere.

The players asked repeatedly what the WRU intended doing with the Warriors. I can say now quite honestly I feared for the safety of both Lewis and the solicitor. Here were some pretty feisty characters whose futures were in the balance not getting answers to a question they had every right to be asking. People were on their feet. Some of the senior players were ready to take out their frustration on the pair of them. Lewis didn't help his cause with the smug smile he carried which didn't go down well with the lads. I think the biggest factor was the shock, not only of the news which people had known about for the best part of twenty-four hours, but the disappointment that neither Lewis nor the solicitor were confirming that the Warriors would continue to exist. We all thought that this was just a meeting to inform us of a change of ownership. It proved to be something very different.

Lewis did say that there would be a meeting the following day, the Tuesday, when the players would be given further news about what was going to happen to them.

It was amazing, just like herding cattle into a room for the slaughter. That's it, you are finished, you are gone. I couldn't believe what was being done, or the way it was being done. Lewis left the meeting and we just stood outside talking about what we had heard. It was a mess. A group would get together and talk about things, then another group would get together, people were just milling around, going around in circles not knowing what to do, where to go, who to talk to next. Everyone was shell-shocked.

The WRU had not been able to stump up the estimated £1.2 million needed to buy Samuel's shareholding in the Warriors. So they persuaded the other four regions to put up a quarter each with the temptation that they would get the pick of the players they wanted, and of course the seven million pounds annual share-out from the Union would be divided four ways instead of five. The actual figure asked for by the WRU was £1,250,000 with each region contributing £312,500. Therefore from an outlay of just over £300,000 the surviving regions would get back £1.75 million every year. No contest. I have been told by at least two people who would know the facts that Tony Brown at the Dragons offered to pay the whole lot himself, but was quickly told by Peter Thomas that he wouldn't have to because Thomas would pay half. No need, the other two benefactors jumped in and offered their share. Such was the dislike, no, hatred, they held for Leighton Samuel, that they got their cheques into the pot so quickly the ink was hardly dry. Samuel wasn't one of their sort. He didn't have as much money as they had. He wasn't a rugby man. Dare I say he wasn't of the same stature as them, and yet ever since the start of negotiations about regional rugby he had made sure he got his point across.

So with that fifty per cent, and the fifty per cent gifted to them by Samuel earlier in the year, the Union would control the whole of the Warriors. They could do exactly what they wanted. Reports from those who were involved at a higher level than me say that the only reason Leighton Samuel sold his fifty per cent share to the WRU was because they assured him that the Warriors would continue to function. Well initially, apparently, that was the plan, but when the deal was eventually done and the financial people got a look at the books they discovered that the Warriors were far deeper in debt that they had been told or had imagined. At this time the WRU were in debt themselves to the tune of £70 million so there was no way they could have afforded to have taken over the Warriors and kept them going.

The important point here, though, is that Samuel was without doubt told, when he handed over his share, that the region would continue to function, a claim he kept repeating to everyone, a claim he has always continued to hold. All I can say on that is that Samuel was a businessman. If you do business with people, do you do it on a nod and a wink, a promise and a handshake? I doubt it. In the world of business things get written down, contracts are signed and sealed, and knowing the lack of trust between Samuel and the WRU was he just foolish to accept their word? On the part of the Union, though, should they not have gone through the books before they did the deal and seen exactly what the state of the finances were? Samuel got his money from the Union. He got £875,000 out of the £1,250,000, but there were rumours around for a long time that businessmen were willing to get involved in the region, and he could have sold his share to them for far more than he got from the WRU. That would have assured us of a future.

As a result it was always difficult for all of us to know exactly where to aim our anger. Was it at Samuel or at the WRU? Regardless the WRU got plenty. Moffett kept well out of the way, which shows what kind of individual he was, and Steve Lewis and the solicitor copped most of it.

There was definitely no way of going back, the Warriors were finished. It was just a matter now of what to do with the players. The big fear was that our Welsh stars would move across the border to England, or take lucrative offers out in France. Gareth Thomas was already heading for Toulouse, and Stephen Jones was leaving the Scarlets for France, but these were for different reasons. The other four regions were apparently pleaded with to take up as many of the Warriors players as possible to keep them in Wales.

So the players assembled again on the Tuesday morning at the Vale and met with Steve Lewis, the solicitor and Richard Harrhy who was there as representative of the Welsh Professional Rugby Players' Association. The other four coaches had been asked to make a wish list of the Warriors players they would like, and I am told a scenario was agreed whereby whoever got first pick in one round of players got last pick in the next. It must have been rather like kids in the schoolyard picking their players for a playground game. The Scarlets only took Matthew Rees, Arwel Thomas and Aisea Havili as they had already more or less finalised their squad for the new season. Chief executive Stuart Gallagher and coach Gareth Jenkins then left and let the other three get on with the horse trading.

The other regions knew exactly what our players' contracts had been worth, and they agreed not to out-bid each other for a player's signature, so they were at a disadvantage from the start. Players would be offered less than they had been on at the Warriors because the other regions knew they either accepted what was on offer, or looked elsewhere. One thing was for certain, no one got a pay rise from their move to the Blues, Dragons, Scarlets or Ospreys.

So on the Tuesday morning when they were called back to the Vale the players were put into a room to await their fate. John Morris, the WRU solicitor, came into the room and told everyone, "I know some of you are concerned about your contracts", at which point he was shouted down by some of the players, who told him that was not what it was about. "You are out of order. We've built something up here and you have just got rid of it overnight." There was a lot of anger. Morris told them that those who were wanted would be picked up by other regions and would have the opportunity to take the offer, but they could also refuse it if they wished. So there was no doubting now that the region was going to be put into liquidation despite what Lewis had told everyone around twelve hours earlier. It was obvious to everyone that he didn't know what was happening the night before. Players were also told that if they weren't taken on by other regions their contracts would still be honoured.

After that Richard Harrhy came in and told the players how the process would be conducted. If they wanted to, they had the right to refuse to go to the region which had selected them, but as far as the Warriors were concerned that was out of anyone's hands apart from the Welsh Rugby Union, so legally that was gone. One by one they were called into another room where Steve Lewis and John Morris were sat with Richard Harrhy. But there seemed little Harrhy could do to alter the way events were heading. One by one they were told which region or in some cases regions wanted them, or the knife was stuck in and they were told no one wanted them. For most of these guys this was the second time in 18 months or less that they had been faced with this kind of scenario. Allan and I had been in a similar position when choosing the Warriors squad, of telling players they were wanted or not. That was bad enough, this was worse.

It was brutal and it was savage. Here was a player like Aisea

Havili who could hardly speak a word of English having to agree or not agree to what they had decided was his future. Mefin Davies, who was one of the current Wales hookers with 17 caps to his name, wasn't wanted by anyone! For those players who didn't get a place with the other regions things were going to be difficult. Mefin ended up playing for Neath in the Premiership and with no disrespect to the Welsh All Blacks, that wouldn't do his ambitions with Wales any good at all. Eventually he was picked up by Gloucester. The players were up against it because new contracts are normally signed in the early part of the calendar year. Now the clubs knew that the Warriors players were in a desperate position and they had little or no bargaining power. At no time was any money mentioned to any of them, the Warriors went into liquidation and their contracts were just chopped, finished.

Some of the players who came out of that room were relatively happy, though relieved might be a better word. Others were devastated. Tongan Maama Molitika for instance, one of the toughest men you could wish to meet, wasn't wanted by anyone, and he was in tears. Some of the guys who were sorted with new clubs mingled around waiting to see if they could help those less fortunate. Some have told me they couldn't stay. Standing up to the likes of Steve Lewis or the solicitor was something they could handle, but what do you say to someone who has just lost his livelihood? It wasn't just the players, either, it was the other people who were affected, the families with a house to pay for, bills to pay. Who had taken the wider picture into account? Certainly not Moffett and the WRU.

The BBC had got wind of what was happening and they were filming outside. Richard Bryan went out and spoke to them and asked them to stop filming which, after a bit of protest, they agreed to do. The trouble was they put the camera on the floor and carried on filming, so things got a bit heated with Rich saying to them that maybe they should go and knock on David Moffett's door as the real story was there.

There was no sign of Moffett. It was once again Steve Lewis

who had to do most of the talking, and despite what I had thought about Lewis before, I actually felt sorry for him and the solicitor as they were the ones doing the shit work. The players, some of whom didn't know who Lewis was, hated him from the off because he was the spokesman. He was the one who told them that the team they had wanted to play for, the team they had enjoyed playing for, and the team they had busted a gut for, was finished. Gareth Cooper and Rob Sidoli had played through pain. Despite needing operations they had played on until we had qualified for Europe, only because they thought it would be worth it for what was to come the following season. Now some of these players were being told they were worthless and no one wanted them. It was bitter. Seeing some of their team mates coming out of that door with nowhere to go was totally disgusting.

Alfie could have walked away from it all, as his future had been settled for some time. He had negotiated a transfer to Toulouse and needn't have been anywhere near the Vale or the carnage which was taking place. But, fair play to him, Alfie was there for the lads. He might have been a reluctant recruit at the inception of regional rugby, but he stuck by his team mates through their darkest hour. When a senior Welsh player from another region who was training at the Vale came out with the cheap comment, "don't worry, boys, I have a few contacts in France if you need somewhere to go", Alfie ripped into him, saying that these lads were in a shitty situation and comments like that were out of order. Alfie proved to be a top captain who stood on the bridge with his players when the ship was sinking.

The players did get paid. Of the £1,250,000 received by the WRU from the four regions, £875,000 went to Samuel, some went to pay off creditors such as the local clinic, the coach company, etc., and a cheque for £141,000 was handed to Richard Harrhy to pay the players their month in arrears. Those players who were picked up by the other regions then went onto their payroll, but for those not offered other regions that was the end of their payments. Their Warriors contracts were just ripped up, they got no more. It would be nice to say that the players were paid because they had been the most important part of the region, or that they had done a brilliant job, but no way. The players were paid for the same reason they were not told on the Monday night that the region wouldn't be kept going: to keep them as happy as possible and keep them in Wales.

And what about us? Well, Moffett actually said to me, "Don't worry, Lynn, we will look after you," to which I replied, "Don't worry about me, I don't want you looking after anything to do with me, I'll look after myself." That is another thing which annoyed me about him. He never said that to anyone else in my management team. He didn't do anything for me or the rest of the backroom staff. I am still owed money; Allan is still owed money; we are all still owed money to this day. It wasn't as important to the WRU that the backroom staff stayed in Wales, so we didn't get treated the same as the players. I had just signed a new two-year deal, but our contracts were just finished and we were told that was it, we had to go.

Go I did, as there was nothing left to argue about. I think I went back to the Maerdy Social Club and had a couple of pints. The first thought that went through my mind was what the hell am I going to do now I am out of work? I had just signed a new contract so everything had appeared to be in place. Now I had nothing: no job, no prospects of a pay-off, nothing. And at that time of the year all the other teams had everything in place for the next season. Now I had to go home and tell my wife that I didn't have a job. Thankfully Jeromin is one of the most positive people you could ever wish to meet. Her reaction was, "Well, stuff them. I'm working. You will get something fairly soon, so we won't starve." If it hadn't been for her during that period of time when realistically I was probably at the lowest point I have ever been, I don't know what I would have done. She was the one who pulled me through that. My other friends were good as well and they were very supportive. You can go out with them, but for people who have never been in that situation they may not realise that once you close your front door, your home can become a very lonely place as well as a sanctuary. There was a feeling of shock, of despair. There was nowhere to go. Rugby was my life and it had been taken away from me, and there didn't seem any way back into it. I just wasn't motivated to do anything. I just sat around and I am sure it was upsetting for the family to see me in that state. I went on like that for a couple of weeks until Jeromin just got at me and said, "Pull yourself together."

The players had their union, but for us coaches there was no support. I suppose we could have taken legal action for wrongful dismissal, broken contracts or whatever, but the players had tried that and got nowhere so there was no chance for me on that score. I even considered going back to Telecom. It was the first time in my life that I had felt so totally dejected and hopeless. There are things which happen in your life which you can say are your fault and you can't blame anyone else. There are things you can control, directions which you can alter, but there was nothing I could do about this, and that probably made me as angry as the way the whole matter had been dealt with. I know the evidence may be against it, but I am convinced that the coaches knew that the Warriors were going to the wall before that final weekend of games. After all, the benefactors were negotiating with the WRU to buy out Samuel. Do you mean to tell me that they didn't mention anything to their coaches? They must have done, and discussed with them the players they would like. They knew from the start that the WRU wanted to keep as many players as possible in Wales.

A day or two after the meetings I went back to the office in Pencoed to pick up what belonged to me. I walked in, picked up the stuff, and just wanted to get out. I didn't want to be there. I left what was theirs but made sure I took all the paperwork. The plans I had made for the region the following season, the structure of the region, that all came with me. It was a selfish move in a way. I had done all the legwork going around the region and if that was now finished then anyone coming along to try and incorporate our patch into something else, well they could start from scratch. They weren't having the benefit of my graft after what had happened. I am not a vindictive person, but at that point I could cheerfully have swung for Moffett. As for Steve Lewis, well, it would have been shooting the messenger. I may have thought he lacked credibility to be on the interview panel for the regional coaching jobs, but this was different. I felt sorry for him; he was hung out to dry by Moffett. He was stuck in front of people because the person who should have been at the meetings and making all the statements and answering all the questions from the players and the staff, didn't have the balls to be there.

John Morris, the solicitor, was in the same position. I have spoken to John since those events and he has told me, "It was the worst day of my life of dealing with other human beings. I can't blame them for hating me."

Towards the end of the week everyone was called to a meeting with Leighton Samuel at Decor Frame. He was asked why he hadn't got anything in writing. The answer, if there was one, seems to have been lost in the chaos. From that point of view it was difficult to direct our anger. The WRU copped most of it, but did we believe Samuel? Was he stupid not to get negotiations in writing, or had he been stitched up as much as we had? Samuel was keen to profess his innocence but there was always that lingering doubt.

The meeting was quite angry; Samuel claimed he had been stitched up and had tried to rectify what had happened. He told the meeting, in his usual style, that he intended to take the WRU to court over their promise to keep the Warriors going; that he planned to take back all the contracts and resurrect the region. He wanted to know who was leaving and a few hands went up. By now, of course, it was all too late. A lot of the players had accepted offers from the other regions, or had made their own arrangements to go elsewhere. When he asked one or two of them why they were going, the answer he got was that they couldn't carry on not knowing if their contracts were safe or whether it was all over.

There was no way the WRU was going to allow Samuel anywhere near the contracts. They were dead and buried. Also the future for a lot of the players looked a lot more secure than it had while they played for the Warriors. It was a case of nice try, Leighton, but it's too late. I got the feeling from a lot of the players that had there been a significant chance that the team could be saved, they would have delayed signing for other regions, as they had enjoyed their season and wanted the Warriors to continue. The meeting broke up with Leighton claiming he would return the money the WRU had paid him, and if necessary fight them in the courts. Needless to say, nothing came of Leighton's claims.

Everyone who was interested met for the final time at a meeting in June called by the liquidators, Begbies Traynor. All the backroom staff and coaches went to this. As we were all owed money, we were all creditors. This was the first time Moffett had lifted his head above the parapet. Needless to say some of the players and staff didn't give up on the chance to let him know their feelings. Richard Bryan was one of the most eloquent of the players, telling Moffett in no uncertain terms that he should have been present at the very first meeting, and that we had been lied to by his representatives. I can see Rich now looking at the floor and shaking his head as Moffett replied to him. Moffett got really aggressive and shouted at Rich not to look at the floor when he was talking to him. He obviously decided that he had to attack before he was attacked.

Suddenly the door opened and in walked Ryan Jones. He was late because I think he had just been called up to the Wales squad on the tour. Well, the meeting had just about gone as far as it was going to go, but Ryan laid into Moffett, telling him what he thought about what he had done and the way he had gone about it. Moffett sat there with his jaw almost on the floor, and he wasn't the only one. Here was a young lad who had the balls to stand up to the WRU chief executive, and I think Moffett and a lot of the rest of us thought here is a young guy with character and some bottle. Little did we realise that here was a future captain of Wales.

History tells us that there was no bid by Samuel to resurrect the Warriors. That would have taken months to follow its legal course, far too long for players to hang around to see what the outcome would be. The players who were wanted signed for other regions. Some, like Chris Horsman, signed up for teams in England, and others managed to make a living from the Premiership. Alfie went to France, although that move wasn't as straight forward as it once appeared, as the WRU now claimed that Leighton Samuel had negotiated with Toulouse that they would pay the Warriors the remainder of Gareth's contract. As the new owners, they would have to pay the WRU. The French thought they could get away without paying anything as the Warriors now didn't exist.

The Warriors went into oblivion and the Blues got their place in the Heineken Cup. The game in the heartland of Welsh rugby was dead; killed by a governing body whose Memorandum of Association states its duty: 'to promote, foster, encourage, control and improve rugby football in Wales'. The bastards. They had got what they wanted, four regions. You can be very certain nowadays that if one of the four remaining regions got into difficulty the WRU would bail them out.

It wasn't quite the end of the matter as in October 2006 Leighton Samuel and the WRU were due to meet in court. Samuel had started legal proceedings over the way the WRU had acquired and wound up the Celtic Warriors. His lawyers had served papers, with Samuel claiming the WRU promised the contracts of the Warriors' players and staff would be honoured by the Union and the Warriors would play in both the Celtic League and Heineken Cup under the ownership of the WRU in 2004/5, and future seasons. Here again the WRU had been very crafty. The £1.25m. they had asked the other four regions to contribute was well over the amount needed to buy out Samuel and close the Warriors. They took into account that in the future they might well be involved in a legal battle with Samuel or someone over the demise of the region, so they built up a defence fund. The amount left over, after the bills had been paid and Samuel had received his payment, was £125,006.25p which was paid to the WRU.

The WRU pulled out of the court battle with Samuel and settled out of court, much to the disappointment of many people, including Moffett. The court case would have blown apart, once and for all, whether the WRU had said that the Warriors would continue or not. The WRU did the sums. It would have cost a quarter of a million pounds in legal fees for both the WRU and Samuel, with the loser picking up a half-million pound legal bill. Add to that any compensation payable to Samuel if they lost, and it wasn't worth the day in court. They settled out of court with Samuel receiving a sum far less than the legal fees would have cost the WRU. They knew Samuel didn't have a case. I suspect Samuel knew he didn't have a case. He didn't have any commitment in writing from the WRU to keep the Warriors going, but the point must also be made that the WRU should have taken more diligence in assessing the true state of the region's losses before making that commitment. But this wasn't like any normal business buyout or takeover. Samuel's first concern was getting out and getting as much money as he could. The WRU's priority was getting their hands on the other 50 per cent of the Warriors, while the other four regions wanted to get rid of Samuel and get a bigger share of the WRU budget. From the start Leighton probably lacked the vision to be the head man. He got exposed for not knowing what to do with the Warriors; he was weak in his decisions. The WRU sensed that, and that's how they managed to get control of the Warriors. They exploited him because they could see he was weak.

Moffett, however, didn't have the bottle to be there. He didn't care. For me that was probably the way he dealt with everything to do with the regions, the way everything has gone on from the word go. There can only be one reason why he wanted that region to go. It was nothing to do with playing ability. Remember we had beaten the eventual Heineken Cup winners. We had come fourth in the Celtic League table, we were hardly a struggling side. The only reason he wanted that region to go was financial.

To this day some of the players blame Samuel, and snarl at the mention of his name. Others, and I am one of them, still blame Moffett and the WRU. This was certainly the lowest point of my rugby life. It was not just that my job was at an end. At the Warriors we all knew the potential that had been there. With the squad we had, and the set-up we had, it could have been a great region.

As for Leighton Samuel, well, he wasn't done with Pontypridd. Within a month of the Warriors going under, he is reported to have put a five-figure sum into the town's soccer team. He said it was to help a long-term friend of his and wasn't an attempt to get back at the rugby club.

Later that summer, while I was on holiday in Scotland, I had a call from Dai Young offering me a job with the Cardiff Blues, going around the Valleys to try and get them to buy into, and support, the Blues region. At the same time I had a call from Italy offering me a job with Leonesse. I had no problem with Dai or with the Blues, but I didn't want anything to do with Welsh rugby after the way they had treated the players. The person who had done that, and could do that type of thing again, was still in charge of the Welsh Rugby Union. For me Welsh rugby had lost all credibility and I just wanted to get away from it.

5

Little Moscow

On my mother's side, there have been three or four generations of the Jones family living in Maerdy. Like so many of the towns and villages in the Rhondda, coal was the reason for its existence and many in our family made their livelihoods from the pits. For me it has always been home, and always will be, although if you visit the village now it might be hard to understand my attraction to the place. Maerdy is no different to anywhere else. For me it has a spirit. It's not just a home; it is a place you go back to. You know the people, you feel comfortable in the place, and you feel comfortable in their company.

Maerdy is the last village in the Rhondda Fach. At Porth, just above Pontypridd, the Rhondda Valley splits. To the east it is the Rhondda Fach, the small valley, going up towards Maerdy. To the west goes the Rhondda Fawr, the big valley, leading to Treorchy, famous for its choir, and Treherbert.

The houses in Maerdy are a mixture of terraces, built in neat rows along the west side of the valley, and a couple of council estates built in the early Sixties. Everything is built in a straight line. I can't think of any curves in any of the roads. It's neat and tidy in that respect.

In my early years, like so many of the villages in the coal mining areas of Wales, the place was dominated by the pits, Maerdy had two, and spoil tips: grey, filthy, man-made mountains on which nothing grew. Not in my back yard? They were in everyone's back yard. How there were not more disasters like the one in Aberfan, when a coal tip engulfed the primary school and part of the village killing 144 people, 116 of them children, is a miracle. When I was doing an apprenticeship I was with two men who had family in Aberfan. On the day of the disaster they rushed home as soon as the news came through of what had happened that never-to-be-forgotten October morning. Thankfully now in many of the areas the eyesores and the danger have been removed, and the tips landscaped. I'm not saying you would never know a pit had been in Maerdy, but the areas have been covered with grass and trees, and sheep graze where the waste from the collieries was once discarded. In those days the environment was the last thing to be considered. As kids we often played on the tips and on more than one occasion my mother had to call the police because I had a habit of wandering off with the dog for hours on end. She said they would find me either on the tip or by the river.

Even now, though the place doesn't look like much, within five minutes of walking out of my front door I can be alone with my thoughts or tramping with friends to the top of the mountain. I can survey the view over the valley I love, recall the scene which would have spread before me forty or fifty years ago and relive the memories.

Another route might take me to the reservoir, and the peaceful sound of water lapping on the bank. Gone is the noise and the smog drifting from the valley below, where every house and every chimney once belched the fumes from burning coal. A black, polluted cocktail used to flow through the village, collecting the legacy of a hundred pits before joining the River Taff and emptying its contents into the Bristol Channel at Cardiff. But now the river runs crystal clear compared with the black polluted cocktail which wound its way through the village before.

Another thing that people who don't know the place probably don't appreciate is that within an hour you can be on the beach, or in the unspoilt beauty of the Black Mountains. Maerdy, at the very top of the Rhondda Valley, can be the gateway from one extreme to another. The unfortunate thing is that there is no work left here. People who have the means and the opportunity leave Maerdy. If I was a youngster now I don't know that I would stay. If I was twenty-five I would probably feel different about the place. I think it is the same for most of the mining villages; the bottom has fallen out of them. In my day the pits were open and there was always something going on. People shopped in the village. The stores in Ceridwen Street, long since gone, were bustling. People did not have to go out of the village for anything. The biggest place in Maerdy was the Workmen's Institute. That has gone, and for me that was where everything was happening.

The dulcet tones of Lynn Howells were first heard in the Rhondda Valley, on 29 May 1950. My grandfather was the caretaker of the Workmen's Institute, and I was born in the house next door. We were a big family. Not many people left the family or left the village in those days, although those that did go either went to get employment, or to escape the pits. A couple of my aunties and uncles left to go to England and got work there. I remember, though, they always came back for Christmas. It was a happy place. I was always able to run around, and because my grandfather was the caretaker, I more or less had the run of the establishment.

It was a huge three-storey building with halls, a billiards' room, ladies room, and on the top floor a hall which held a thousand people. The most frightening place I had ever been in was the library. It was always full of people and you had to be quiet. The atmosphere was tainted by the clammy grey fug of tobacco smoke. It was full of miners who had just come out of the pit, and you couldn't move. If you walked into the room their heads would shoot up and they would glare at you. It was frightening. There was no other way to describe it.

I had a good childhood, but the one thing I missed was my father. It sticks in my mind that I rarely saw my father because of his work. He worked down the pit, but suffered from the effects of pneumoconiosis from an early age. He therefore had to leave his more lucrative employment underground to get a job on the surface, and as a result had to work longer hours to make up the money. But from what I can remember I was a happy child.

One story I recall from my early years was when the Queen toured Britain after her coronation. When she came through Maerdy the bunting was out and schoolchildren lined the streets. In among the Union Jacks being waved by the crowds she might have spotted the red flag with the hammer and sickle on it which my grandfather had hung from the house window. It makes me chuckle now although my grandmother was not very happy about it. He was a staunch communist, as most people were in Maerdy in those days. The main paper in the Institute library was the communist newspaper *The Daily Worker*. Maerdy was, and sometimes still is, known as 'Little Moscow'.

My grandfather was a short, stocky man who never allowed a drop of alcohol to pass his lips. When they turned the Institute into a club and served alcohol, he never set foot inside the place again. Despite his temperate beliefs he was a rum bugger. In those days you could 'run the terrace'. All the attics in the terraced houses were linked, so when the bailiffs came in, and they were frequent visitors, people moved their furniture up into the attics and it travelled along before coming down in someone else's house. When the bailiffs had gone it was moved back again. In the great depression of the Thirties, my grandfather was in a group arrested for breaking into a shop. It was not for their own advantage, they distributed the food they stole to those families who were without. Unlike in more recent recessions, in those days there were no haves and have-nots. Nobody had anything and so everybody was exactly the same. Grampa's principles were good. They were true communist. He never forced his principles onto anyone, it was up to you and what you felt as to whether you agreed or not. His name is bolted onto the Kremlin wall in Moscow. Apparently during one of the mining strikes the Russians sent people over to Maerdy and they were so impressed with what they saw at the strike centre that they had the names of the six ringleaders embossed onto a plaque which still hangs on the wall in the Russian capital.

He smoked a pipe, and one of my tasks as a child on a Sunday morning was to roll his Condor pipe tobacco. He was always talking to me and became a great influence on my life, especially later when I started work and became involved in the unions. But I was never as Bolshie as Grampa.

The whole family seemed to be living on the edge of the law. My uncle would go up onto the mountain and kill a sheep so we always had food. It was no more or less than anyone else was doing at that time, even in the early Fifties. During some of the miners' strikes men would go up onto the mountain and dig out the coal for their homes, it was part of life.

My mother was always at home. She was simply, and I don't mean it in a derogatory way, a housewife, although she did have to go and clean the local doctor's house to make up the money. She was always there. For me she was the stable influence, and that was probably the same for most of the families in the Valleys. She was a typical mining valley woman. Short, plump, always to be seen in a 'pinny'. We didn't have a lot. We didn't have any more or any less than most of the other families around us. I think that people from outside the Valleys and outside the mining communities might have wondered how we survived. My sister and I might not have had a great deal of what a lot of people had, but we never went short, we never went without. People in our street probably had a television before we had one, but we never went short of food or clothes. It was a struggle for my parents and after grandfather retired from the Workmen's Institute they had to support my grandparents as well. But while we didn't have much, it was a happy environment. It was just managed, there was never a fuss made about it. As kids we probably didn't notice any problems, we were more likely to be out in the streets playing. We never knew anything about whatever went on as it was never discussed in front of us out in the open. Family holidays were only possible as one of our relations lived in the seaside resort of Weston-super-Mare. Another lived in Warminster. That enabled us to have holidays, one by the sea, another in the countryside. There was no other way we could have afforded holidays.

When grandfather retired we moved into a brand new council house in Tanybryn. The pits were going strong, lots of people were coming into Maerdy and the council estate had to be built to house them. Again, it was basic. There was nothing fancy about the way you lived and, thinking back, life was probably still difficult for my mother and father.

After my father retired we moved again to Wilson Place. By now his chest was really bad and it was a move out of necessity. It moved us nearer to the shops, nearer to the amenities, and nearer to the Workman's Institute. Life itself was a struggle for my father. Tanybryn, where we had lived previously, is on a bit of a hill, and by the time we moved there he had left the coalface to work the crane on the slurry beds. Even so, his time underground had left him with a legacy, a struggle to draw every breath. He would come from the pit to the bottom of the road on the bus and then take on what was, for him, the tortuous climb towards home. By the time he reached the front door he would have had to have stopped three times to catch his breath before moving on. I could hear him coming.

By now of course I had started school, first of all at Maerdy Infants. Since I passed through the doors other generations of Howells have followed, the latest being my grandson, Kian.

The only thing that sticks in my mind about the infants' school was the teacher Miss Burgess. She was a tall middle-aged lady, very quiet, but a massive disciplinarian. A total part of the community, she lived among us, taught us, was very kind, and was just a lovely person. The sad thing is that because of the dwindling numbers in the village now, the infants' school and the junior school have been combined on one site.

Junior school, for me, was a lot different. People who know

me may find this strange to comprehend, but I was bullied. It has always been my nature to be fairly tolerant, and it takes a lot to rouse me. So I was reluctant to get involved in any trouble, even if it meant standing up for myself. I was a tall, skinny kid, and my family background and our financial situation I suppose was the root of the problem. I was probably the last boy to go into long trousers. My mother couldn't afford to keep buying me long trousers as I wore out the knees so quickly. So I was always in shorts while other boys of my age looked more grown up. Being a tall, skinny boy it stood out more, and other boys would pick on that. It was mostly verbal bullying, and they probably wanted to see the small kid hit the big one. I probably did not help the situation at that age by not sticking up for myself. I wasn't comfortable with fighting, to be perfectly honest. It wasn't in my nature and I became an easy target. It wasn't a continuous thing, it was not frequent. People today see bullying as something that happens day after day after day. It wasn't just me, it was other people as well. There could be weeks without anything happening, and then it would be my turn again.

I didn't tell anyone what was happening because at that time there were a few things you didn't do. If you got a clip round the ear from your teacher or a policeman you didn't go home and tell anyone, because they would give you another clip. Also you didn't tell them at home you were getting bullied because I would imagine they would simply tell you to get in there and sort it out and, as I have said, that was not in my nature. In those days there was no Childline at the end of a telephone. It was up to you to survive the treatment as best you could. I was upset at being bullied, but I made sure I kept away from certain places where this group of people hung out and stayed away from them as much as I could so that it didn't happen. Thankfully, even though we lived in a small community, the bullying didn't carry on outside school. I would not have been playing outside school with the group of kids who were doing the bullying.

When you reached a certain age in the junior school, you had the chance to play in the school football team. People might find it amazing that despite living in the Welsh Valleys we always played football at school and in the streets. Never rugby, always football. Rugby was never the main sport, not where we were anyway. The one teacher from my junior school who sticks in my mind was Mr Will John Griffiths. He was one of the teachers you didn't mess with. He was tall, stocky, a dominating figure.

I played in goal thanks to Mr Griffiths' unique selection policy which makes me laugh to this day. "Right boys," he would say. "Stand up against that wall, stretch your hand up as high as you can. Howells, you are the tallest, you're the goalkeeper." Needless to say the method had its faults. I was pretty bad. I went on to play for Maerdy Juniors outside school, never as a goalkeeper I hasten to add, not after they found out how bad I was. But to be honest I was not a very good footballer.

Neither was I a very good pupil. The eleven plus was still in operation in those days. Needless to say, I didn't pass and ended up going to North Road School, Ferndale, just down the valley. This was a big, four-storey brick building which was knocked down a few years ago. If I explain that just before I went to North Road School a couple of boys from there were sent to borstal, you can tell what sort of place it was. North Road toughened me up, it was that sort of environment.

Thankfully the bullying didn't continue. The move up to secondary school probably acted as a natural break, but also I think I began to stand up for myself more than I had done. At the North Road School you either stood up for yourself or you had problems. All in all, they were good times at North Road.

There was no way that I could be classed as academic, and it didn't interest me. I must have been a late developer – a very late developer come to think of it – because, from being a boy who failed his eleven plus and couldn't get into the grammar school I gained my masters degree when I was fifty! I must have had something, but I certainly didn't use it at that age.

I got through school. I think that is the best way of putting it. I certainly didn't see school as the most important thing in life and the key to a bright future. You wouldn't find me with my head in a book. I would be out playing football all the time. Having said that, while I was at North Road, I was always in the top half of the class, so you could say that despite my reluctance to do academic work, I was doing very well. Sport was becoming my favourite subject. I was a good runner and my mother reminds me that I ran the 110 metres hurdles for Glamorgan while at the school. I liked the practical subjects, woodwork, metalwork, art, and surprisingly maths. I hated English, but really school held little interest for me and my parents never pushed me into anything. Looking back, I believe that if I had wanted to, I could probably have done a lot better than I did. I always thought there was something better to do than the schoolwork. When I left school at sixteen I had a school leaver's certificate, but it was nothing like GCEs.

In many mining households it was expected that a son would follow his father down the pit. One of the options was an apprenticeship with the Coal Board, but there was no way my father would allow me to go underground. I was told I was not going down the pit. It was never an option for me. I would probably have gone down, as all my friends were going down, it was near to home, it was well paid, and the miners' apprenticeship was recognised as being a good one. I think I did want to go down the pit, but my father could see what it had done to him, and he did not want that happening to me. I am not saying that I was heartbroken. Having been down a pit just to see what it was like, it was not something I would have liked to have done. It was claustrophobic, dark, wet, and frightening. There was no way out apart from the cage if anything went wrong. And yet if I had been forced by circumstances to go down, I would have done. I cannot understand to this day how fathers were happy for their sons to follow in their footsteps down the mine. They must have been able to see what it was doing to their health and that of their workmates, their neighbours, and other people around the village. And yet without the generations of miners and the pits, there would have been little for the people of the Rhondda Valley and Maerdy. Don't get me wrong, I admire every last miner for doing the job they did, but thankfully it was something I avoided.

My intention after I left school was to join the police force. I even started a shorthand course at a local college, but within less than a year a friend of my father arranged for me to get onto an apprenticeship at the electrical engineering firm South Wales Switchgear. This involved me travelling to Blackwood. A bus to Pontypridd, and another to Blackwood took the best part of an hour and a half, so I had to leave home at six in the morning.

As a sixteen-year-old kid this was certainly the longest distance I had ever travelled on my own, and my horizons began to broaden. Once I started to go away from our valley environment, albeit into another valley, I think friendships developed and I had a different outlook. Suddenly life began to expand; I started to go places to see things. I went to see bands. Something I must explain here is that unlike these days when bands or groups play at big venues in the big cities, like the Motorpoint Arena in Cardiff, back in the Sixties and Seventies these places didn't exist. There were no big venues, and bands came to you. I went to see Cream, The Animals, The Small Faces, and they would come to places like Pontypridd or Merthyr and play in a cinema or a hall. I must be one of the few people to have walked out of a Beatles concert before the end. They were an up-and-coming group, just another group on the circuit, and they were playing in Cardiff. So I got onto the train, which rattled down the valley to the big city. It was the most disappointing concert I ever went to. With all the girls screaming over the band's playing it was an absolute waste of time. It might seem a big thing now for me to be able to say I once saw the Beatles, but that was all I did. I never heard a note. These days my musical tastes are diverse, anything from AC/DC to opera.

I wasn't the only one with a musical interest in our family. But while my only participation was listening, my sister Wendy was far more involved. Our house in Wilson Place was often graced by the sound of her singing voice. She was part of a group called Sweet Rain. They sang on Hughie Green's *Opportunity Knocks* only to be beaten by Iris Williams who went on to have a distinguished career and became an iconic Welsh singer. Wendy, along with four others in the group, continued singing around the clubs in Wales, until marriage and family commitments became the priority.

The apprenticeship at South Wales Switchgear was one of many available to youngsters at that time. Now, of course, they are like gold dust, but in those days moving from school to an apprenticeship was no big deal. There weren't the pressures of going to a university, not that anyone did from North Road, but you still had to do the written coursework at college. After a year in the practical training environment, you finally got to go down to the main Switchgear factory at Treforest, just south of Pontypridd. This was a lot closer to home and a lot easier to get to than Blackwood.

South Wales Switchgear made transformers and had contracts with just about all the electricity boards in the country, and also exported a great deal. The interesting aspect of the training was that you went through the whole process. You did a few months in one place before moving on to another part of the job. I think though, looking back on it, I fell back into the old bad habits, or perhaps I never grew out of them. I was pretty lazy. The apprenticeship was an easy environment for me, as long as I passed the exams at college it kept everybody happy. The work environment was easy because I was an apprentice. Again, it was an easy option. What proved harder was coming home at night and meeting up again with my friends, many of whom were on the mining apprenticeship and earning a lot more money than I was.

That was hard because, at that age, you wanted the money that they were spending on drink and on generally enjoying themselves.

Religion played a big part in my early life. I went to Sion Chapel on Maerdy Road, and joined the Rachabites. It was their belief that you didn't drink, you didn't smoke and you didn't swear. Needless to say I have broken just about all their rules many times over. I remember going to one of their meetings and the minister delivered his sermon with a glass of whisky in his hand. He dropped a worm into the glass and of course it died. That is what will happen to you if you drink this stuff, was his message. Whatever your religion, you feared the minister in those days. I read in chapel and was committed to it, but my days of attending probably ended when I came home one day with my Sunday best covered in mud. I hadn't been to chapel at all, but had been playing football with the boys. My mother decided then that if I was telling her I was going to chapel and wasn't, then it was time to finish.

By this time I had switched from playing soccer to playing rugby, and this led to a very important event. After one game for Treherbert we had the usual few pints before setting off for a night out in Pontypridd. Here, while adding a few more quid to the profits of Brains' brewery, I noticed a group of girls. One in particular had great legs. It was the time of mini-skirts and hot pants, so there were plenty of legs to be seen. I staggered over and started talking to her, but we didn't make any arrangements to meet again. On the way home that night, and this was before the breathalyser or drink-driving campaigns, we ran the car into the kerb and buckled a wheel, so we had to sleep in the car all night. A few weeks later a group of us went out to a nightclub in Tonyrefail. By coincidence the legs were there again. I must have impressed her as we started talking and this time we did arrange to meet. Jeromin lived with her mother in Rhiwbina in Cardiff. Her father had died and I never met him, so it was her mother I had to ask before Jeromin Stonham could become Mrs Howells. We were married at Pontypridd registry office in 1973, and a year later our son Lee was born. In 1977 the family was completed with the arrival of our daughter Claire.

After finishing my apprenticeship I spent a year at South Wales Switchgear before moving to Post Office Telephones. As a trained electrician I visited the exchanges doing the electrical work rather than work on the telephone lines. Although the job paid less than Switchgear, there was better security, and by this time job security was beginning to be an issue. There was a period in the early Seventies when you could walk from one end of Treforest Industrial Estate to the other and be offered ten jobs. Not now.

I was working for British Telecom when the 1984 miners' strike, the biggest event during my time in Maerdy, began. People could see it coming, but the main topic of conversation was that the miners' leader, Arthur Scargill, was going to call the men out in the summer. That had never been done before. It had always been done in the winter when the demand for coal was at its greatest. It would have made little difference. Prime Minister Margaret Thatcher had made sure every power station had stockpiled coal. It would not have made any difference when the strike started. I think listening to the miners back then, the biggest concern was that it would be the end of the coal industry, and everybody knew it. Even so they still went on strike. Such was the militant attitude which still existed in the valley that the men honestly believed that they would beat Maggie. They thought that they would be in control because whenever the miners had gone out on strike in the past the government of the day had capitulated. The people I knew thought the strike would be a short one. It would not be very long before they were back in work. How wrong they were. No one in the village hid from the strike. There was animosity between the miners and the managers because they were continuing to go into work, but that had always been the case during strikes. As the strike continued, though, attitudes towards them became bitterer.

More than a quarter of the families in Maerdy were not affected directly by the strike, because like me they had jobs outside mining. Being the last pit in the Rhondda, people came to Maerdy from all over the valley to work there. Obviously, though, there was an effect on the village. People didn't go out as much, the pubs and clubs weren't as full as usual. The workmen's hall was used as a distribution point for the aid which was sent from supporters all over the UK and even from foreign countries. So people were to be seen going to and fro collecting what they could. As always happened during strikes, people went up onto the slag heaps to try and collect coal to keep their fires burning. It was a dangerous occupation and three youngsters were killed in Yorkshire doing that very thing.

Those in work tried to help those who were on strike – that was the big thing in Maerdy. Each time someone went shopping they bought a little bit extra and gave it to the families who were on strike. I think that happened throughout the communities.

There were no big meetings or demonstrations in Maerdy, there wasn't any picketing. There didn't need to be. The strike was rock solid. No one even thought about going back to work. The Maerdy boys went off to other areas picketing, and came back with stories of how they were being dealt with by the police and the violence. They went to a lot of the Yorkshire pits, and to Nottingham which was particularly violent because they had gone back to work. I learned while coaching Doncaster RFC that to this day people there refer to those in Nottingham as 'the scabs'. When they go off to play them at rugby, they say, "We're off to play the scabs," never Nottingham.

I took an interest in it all because my friends were involved. None of my family was employed in the pit by then, so it didn't affect us as a family. It affected the community. Because it was not a short strike it became a gradual wearing down process, and you tended not to notice so much. You got used to it. By the end of the strike, even after all they had been through, the boys didn't want to go back. They knew they had to go back, but they certainly didn't want to.

I had supported them one hundred per cent. Virtually all of the people in Maerdy supported them at the time. I thought they were doing the right thing. I still think they were called out at the wrong time, but she, Maggie, was clever enough to manipulate that. They were looking after their jobs. I think if they hadn't gone on strike she would have closed the pit anyway, so it was right that they were fighting for their jobs. The miners' strike of 1984 certainly made me take more of an interest in politics. It influenced but didn't change my way of thinking. That was down to my upbringing, and my grandfather the communist who would be willing to have a fight about anything. I have always been a member of a union, and I believe in a worker's right to strike. All a worker can withhold is his ability to work, and he should have the freedom to be represented by a union.

The closure of the pits did not just break the NUM, it broke mining communities, and Maerdy has never been the same in that people move away from there now. There are no people coming into the valley because there is no work. The infants' school is amalgamating with the junior school because of a lack of numbers. They only need one school. It shows how the valley is shrinking. We used to have an expression when I was at school that a squirrel could go from Maerdy to Cardiff in the trees without touching the ground. I can see the valley becoming more like that; it won't be a built-up area like it is now.

When the strike finished, Maerdy was the last pit to go back. It became one of the defining moments of Welsh history. I marched with them. I felt I had to do that for my father. The mine had been a big part of our family, but at a cost. My father had died in the early Seventies with no quality of life. It is always difficult losing a parent, but looking back it was probably the best thing that could have happened. He had got to the stage where he couldn't walk upstairs, but he would never have his bed brought down into the front room. It was probably part of the miners' instinct. If their bed came downstairs that was seen as the end for them. He was a proud man and he did not want that to happen. He was on oxygen and was more or less sat in a corner, gasping for breath. At the time it was devastating. He had no life.

My uncle Bill, who was apparently on the verge of a Welsh rugby cap, was badly injured when a lift cage fell on him and after that he couldn't work never mind play rugby. His son, my cousin, who was working away, came back and we marched with the miners together. It wasn't just miners, their wives and children; there were a lot of people like me marching with them. The sad thing was that they were marching behind the band on that cold morning, knowing they were going back to a pit which was going to be closed anyway, and the site is now gradually going back to what it was before the pit was opened.

I am proud of my roots and proud of my upbringing. It was so typical of valley life. Jeromin and my first house had a living room, a lean-to kitchen attached to the back which had a gas geyser to provide hot water, an outside toilet and we bathed in a tin bath in front of the fire. But it was our house and our first home.

In the mining villages this was not unusual. Yes, one or two people had a little bit more, but generally speaking that was the way people lived in those days. The big difference now is that there are people who have a lot, and people who don't have a lot, and there is a big gulf between them. That is where conflict comes from – envy. In those days most people had exactly the same so there was no envy no jealousy.

You got used to not having things; if you asked for something and you couldn't have it, usually for financial reasons, then you just accepted it. The mining community gives you that sense of value. If you can't afford something then you don't have it, and when you do get something it means more. If households did get something new then it came on the old higher purchase, and when you had paid off the H.P. then you might get something else. I don't of course think for one minute that Maerdy was the only place on earth where people lived this way. There are plenty of other communities in Wales and in the UK who lived life exactly as we did.

Looking back I have been very lucky with my jobs and especially with the rugby. There is no doubt that when Jeromin and I first got married we had very little, but thanks to professional rugby we have been able to improve our way of life. If things were to change it would be relatively easy to go back to the old days for us. The people I feel sorry for are those who have always had wealth and then lose it.

I live in a fabulous house now, although people who might come and see it from 'Middle England' as it is called might not agree. It is two terraced miners' cottages knocked into one, and at the time we were spending the money to create it I felt guilty, and still feel a little like that now. We were lucky as it is something we were able to afford because of the money I earned from the rugby. But that makes the point; because we have had to wait, and because we struggled in the beginning, we probably appreciate what we have far more than if my father had been very rich and just bought us a mansion.

Just as there always have been poor people, there have always been people who will help them out. If you went into the pub and someone was in there who you knew had hit hard times you might buy them a pint, and not expect one back. It sounds condescending, but I don't want people to get the idea that it was condescending, it was just what we did, without a second thought. There was never a case of thinking that someone who helped out was flaunting their good fortune. It was just how people are in the mining communities.

When coaching in Doncaster I got very little chance to get back to Maerdy, in fact I got back more often when I coached in Italy. Now it is all over we are back there, and I am quite happy to be back, but it wouldn't have bothered me if we hadn't gone back, and I would not have said that a few years ago. What draws us back is our family and friends. My son and daughter both live in Maerdy and the grandchildren keep us here.

6

Playing Days

IT IS A pretty well accepted fact within sport that the best players don't necessarily go on to be the top coaches, while the top coaches have seldom been heard of as players. A look at England's World Cup-winning football team of 1966 is a point which well illustrates that theory. Nobby Stiles, Bobby Charlton, Bobby Moore, Alan Ball were just some of the stars of that day at Wembley who had a go at football management and coaching without much success. The only exception was Jack Charlton who did well with several clubs and the Republic of Ireland. In rugby it is a little different. Take Clive Woodward, who won 20-odd caps for England in the days when caps were harder to come by, and made two appearances for the British Lions. He went on to win the Rugby World Cup as England's coach. Andy Robinson has coached England and Scotland and not done a bad job, Shaun Edwards won just about everything there was to win in rugby league and is a well-respected coach, so rugby has bucked the trend a little.

I did eventually wear the Prince of Wales feathers, but it was on my tracksuit rather than a red jersey with a number on the back. It was certainly the highlight of my rugby career. I was able to go further with my coaching than I did playing, there is no doubt about that. But to do whatever you do for your country has to be a fantastic achievement, and I am certainly proud of what I eventually achieved. But there was a long way to go before that honour.

I came into rugby relatively late. I was 18 before it dawned on me once and for all that my football days were at an end. Not for me the likes of Cardiff City, Swansea, Newport County, who were still in the league at that time, or even non-league Merthyr. Howells the goal had retired. So my father took me along to his old rugby club Tylorstown. They had a curry and pint night so it would be an ideal opportunity for him to introduce me to a couple of people and we would be up and running. Dad had always wanted me to play rugby and I think he was tickled pink that I was going to play for his old club as well. The thought made him quicken his step as we made our way to Penrhys Park.

It appeared that with Dad's connections the introduction to Ralph Davies the youth coach would be a formality. Not so. "Had I played any rugby?" asked Ralph. When the answer from this 18-year-old was no he didn't think there was a place for me at Tylorstown. Dad wasn't happy. I wasn't either, but that was because I was halfway through my curry when he grabbed me by the collar, lifted me out of my seat, and dragged me out of Tylorstown muttering all sorts of comments under his breath. So there I was, a converted rugby player with the first obstacle in my career standing in my way. It wouldn't be the last.

I must have mentioned my exciting curry night at Tylorstown rugby club when I got back to college at Llwynypia the following Monday. A guy called Johnny Pool who was on my course suggested I joined him up at Treherbert. "If they don't want you there just come up with me and we'll see what you can do," he said. Sure enough, I was given a chance and Johnny's advice was, "All you have to do when you start to play is follow me wherever I go and you'll be alright." It worked very well. Considering I hadn't played any rugby I ended up as one of the top try scorers for the year we played together, just following Johnny around and picking up the pieces. Treherbert was a good club for me and I made a good fist of that first season in 1968. I progressed through the successful youth system and made the Boys' Club for Wales side along with several other Treherbert players. It was down to some good players in the team and some good people around the club. It must have been the first time I came into contact with any type of coaching. We had a fitness instructor called Gwyn Davies and he for some unknown reason put his arm around me and helped me.

I remember one Christmas, and this wouldn't happen now, we had a double header against Treorchy. It was a real needle match. We played them on Christmas Day and then had the return on Boxing Day. On Christmas Eve we all went over to Treorchy and wound up some of their players with a few drinks. That was when it would start, as the two clubs didn't get on. It continued in the first game and any retribution was taken out in the second. The year I played down at Treorchy I got a raking on my ear from a stud. Being the hard man I thought I was, I carried on playing until one of our players said, "Lynn, I think you had better get someone to have a look at your ear, it's bleeding a lot." So I went to the sponge bucket (the old fashioned equivalent of today's physio), put the sponge to my ear and pushed towards the top of my head. Apparently my ear was like a sole flapping off a shoe, and so hard was I that the next thing I remember was being in an ambulance off to hospital. I'd passed out.

There were some talented players in that Treherbert side and some of them went on to realise ambitions they harboured as youngsters. Alyn Paul, who was related to Roy Paul who lifted the FA Cup as captain of Manchester City in 1956, went to Cardiff playing stand-off. He was understudy to the great Barry John when he went off on international games. Johnny Pool went on to play for Neath and had a final Welsh trial, only to miss out on a cap because of the consistency of Steve Fenwick. Alan Nicholas, a full back, went to Glamorgan Wanderers who in those days were up among the top sides in Wales, and hooker Gary Davies went down and captained Cardiff.

Rugby in those days was very different to today. Players didn't travel much and a lot of the players in one district would stay around and play for their district sides, which was an honour. It was probably the equivalent of the English counties who had a very strong competition going in the Sixties and Seventies. A lot of our players went on to play for the mid-district team which was one of the strongest, if not the strongest in Wales at the time. I had ambitions, but you must remember at this time Wales were almost invincible at rugby. The international team was full of legends, and although players like Johnny Pool went off to the bigger clubs to try and progress, they could only get so far. International matches consisted of the Five Nations, and a few games against touring sides, so players would get five or six caps a season. These days there's the Six Nations, the autumn internationals, plus summer tours, and also it was only in 1969 that a player could be replaced in the case of an injury. So the fifteen which started were often the fifteen which ended a game. These days, 20-odd players can be capped in one international.

When my time came to move on I could have gone to Neath, but I was enjoying playing where I was, with friends and in a good team. When my move did come it was to Pontypridd. Their big second row, Bob Penberthy, lived in Tylorstown just down the road from us in Maerdy, and they obviously had heard about me, so he knocked on the door and asked me to come and have a go, which I did. I had a trial and was lucky enough to get offered a place. Pontypridd rugby club wasn't the club it was to become later. We played at Ynysangharad Park and went to the Athletic Club in town for a beer with the opposition afterwards. Pontypridd was not in the top flight of Welsh rugby. The likes of Newport, Cardiff, Swansea and Llanelli played against the touring sides and also against the big names in English rugby. We played the lesser known names, and if you wanted to stand a chance of getting a cap you went from Ponty to these big guns.

Our chance against the big Welsh clubs would come on a midweek evening when they might play us under lights as part of the Welsh Merit Table or in a cup game. It would be at about that time that Ponty began to buck the system and beat one or two of those sides. People weren't happy. The WRU certainly didn't want Pontypridd to break into that cartel of big names. As usual, all that did was to make Ponty stronger. It began to make the club what it is. People began to realise that the club was producing good players. True, Tommy David had to go to Llanelli before he got a cap, but Bob Penberthy stayed and I am certain that staying at Pontypridd for an incredible 876 games cost him the chance of playing for Wales. There were a lot of players there who if they had moved on would have stood a far better chance of playing for their country.

It was while I was at Pontypridd that I played in probably the most memorable game of my career, and it was against Pontypridd! The club arranged to play against a Barry John XV to raise money for a new clubhouse. I was lucky enough to play with current internationals such as Graham Hodgson, Ian Hall, John Bevan, Gareth Edwards and Denzel Williams. There are certain things you can remember about games. Denzel was the Wales and Ebbw Vale prop, and I remember looking at him and thinking I had never seen a guy with a bigger head on his shoulders. He had a massive head. It was also memorable because it was possibly the first game of rugby where a replacement was used. The referee was the famous international ref, Gwynne Walters, and he turned to someone near to me and said to them that the introduction of the replacement was a first in a recognised match in which he had officiated.

I only played at Ponty for one season because someone upset me, although before I mention his name let me add that as I have progressed in rugby I have realised that what he was doing in those days would now be readily accepted and he was probably simply way ahead of his time. The player is a Pontypridd legend and it's none other than Tommy David. Tommy carried the ball miles in a game, but what upset me was that he did little in the way of grafting to get the bloody thing. He also had plenty to say after the game about those who failed to get the ball when it wasn't in our possession. I had no problem with Tommy getting the credit for scoring or laying on tries for others, but I didn't like him blaming others because he didn't get the ball at certain times, or saying that we weren't tackling enough when he wasn't doing it either. That didn't sit well with me, so I went back up to Treherbert. I had played eleven games, but as I look back now perhaps I do regret not staying and fighting for a regular place in the team. However the realisation then also was that I wasn't good enough for that level. I think I fell between two stools. I was very comfortable at the Treherbert level, but wasn't quite good enough for the level Ponty played at. I know now that I should have stayed and fought for a place and I am disappointed at the way it ended. It was my decision, it was nothing to do with selection, but I don't think in all honesty I would have achieved a regular spot in the Pontypridd team.

I returned to Treherbert, captained them in their 99th year, and the following season, the centenary year, we played a Max Boyce XV as part of the celebrations. Max was at the height of his fame at this time, touring the UK and other parts of the world with his show, which consisted of fantastic humour about Wales and the Welsh rugby culture. He filled venues wherever he went, and was lucky in a way that his arrival on the entertainment scene coincided with the great Welsh team of the Sixties and Seventies. Max played in the game at Treherbert, and I can remember him singing some of his stuff during the game!

Little had changed in the season I had been at Ponty. I saw exactly the same faces when I returned, as players in those days, unless they had great hopes of an international cap, stayed with their local club. You didn't get the crazy situation you have now where someone is tempted to move for stupid money to help a side win Division Four East, or Division Three West. As for me, I was happy playing at this level. I was comfortable playing at that standard and, having had the season at Pontypridd, I could see that this was my mark. I was good at that level, but

I wasn't good enough to go any higher. I had no aspirations to go and play in the big time. Rugby was to be enjoyed, and I enjoyed Treherbert.

It was during my time here that I suffered a knee injury, and in those days when you had to have a cartilage out it was a long job. Unlike today, when the surgeon goes into the knee with a probe, does the job, and you are back playing within a couple of days, in the early Seventies it was a matter of weeks. It was ten days in hospital with your knee bandaged up, then the gradual movement back into the knee, then running, then back to fitness. There were no rehab programmes, no physios to monitor your recovery, especially at Treherbert's level.

In the meantime I had been asked by the local club at Whitchurch if I fancied going along and helping out with their coaching. Obviously it had got around about on the bush telegraph that I had played a full season at mighty Pontypridd, and the opportunity for them was too good to miss! Well, that would be nice to think anyway. The truth was that my brother-in-law, Roy, was playing at Whitchurch, and he asked me to go along and lend a hand while I was recovering. The important thing, though, was that Whitchurch put me through my first coaching exams, and while I was with them I gained my level one coaching badge. I got the taste for coaching and enjoyed it, and for that I will always be grateful to Whitchurch.

I went back to play for Tylorstown, forgiving them for not having welcomed me with open arms when I was 18. Where we were living then meant I passed Penrhys Park to get to Treherbert, so not really worrying about standards or ambitions to become a future international, I opted for the short journey to play, and more importantly the shorter journey home after a game and a few beers. Dad, no doubt, looked down and had a chuckle, but the past was forgotten.

Eventually my playing days came to an end when I suffered a back problem. I was getting to the stage when I was probably ready to give up anyway as it was taking me longer to recover from the Saturday exertions every week. Tylorstown asked me to become their coach, and as this is the closest you can be to actually playing, I realised that it would keep me in touch with the game and keep me in that rugby environment. You still get involved in the build-up, obviously you can't do anything about individuals on the pitch, but you have the same adrenalin rushes during a match, the same elation when you win and the same downers when you don't, and I didn't want to lose that as I was still only in my early thirties. So for me it was a natural progression when I finished playing. Although I had my level one badge, that didn't matter as in those days you just went from playing to coaching if you were interested. Unlike today when you have to have qualifications to take up coaching posts even at lower level, in those days it wasn't a requirement.

Looking back at my early sorties into coaching, I must admit I was something of a control freak. I had been lucky enough to captain sides, and I like to be in charge. As a coach you have total control of the team, of the way they are going to play, and the game plan is down to the coach. I enjoy that as you can see players improving and you can see whether the game plan you were implementing is the right game plan. I think the biggest thing is the influence the coach has over the players and you only need a couple of the things you have been planning all week to come off, and you begin to think that it's not a bad job. I can honestly admit now that I have learnt lessons from those early experiences; I suppose it was a kind of insecurity. You thought you had to be in control, otherwise the players you were coaching would think you either didn't know what you were doing, or you didn't have the knowledge to be in the post. Now my coaching is very different. As I have moved up the ladder, as it were, and coached more experienced players, I have learned that they have a contribution to make, so I let them speak and put over their points of view. You tend to let people have little parts of it and empower them. Starting out, you want it done your way. Whereas now I can take advice from players I certainly didn't do that at the beginning.

The other difference between coaching and playing was the

involvement after one game and before the next. Even more so today you have to prepare your side for the next challenge. These days, of course, that involves pouring over stats and videos, whereas in those days at Tylorstown video analysis was about as far in the future as the internet and the mobile phone. But I still did some preparation, I made notes during the game, and gave some thought to our next opponents, but that was me. It seemed a natural thing to do and it showed the players, most of whom I had played with, and many who were my age, that I was taking the job seriously. I was so successful at the end of that first season that I was sacked! It remains the only job I have ever been sacked from, but they decided I wasn't the coach for them despite our mid-table position. I think they thought I was too close to the players. So from my first appointment at Tylorstown I went over to Penygraig, another small valley club which was looking for a coach. This wouldn't last more than a season and a half as I received the biggest fright and the biggest shock of my life.

It was 1989 and Jeromin and I had been married fifteen years. I was still working for Telecom at the time while Jeromin, who had stayed at home while the children were growing up, had decided they were old enough for her to go back out to work. She wanted to do something she had always wanted to do, so took up nursing. Everything seemed to be going pretty well. One day we noticed that I had a kind of pimple on the back of my leg and it looked like the head of the pimple had come off, as a result it wouldn't stop bleeding. So I went to the doctor who sent me to a specialist who gave me the news that it was cancer. Even today when, thankfully, there is a good recovery rate from certain cancers, the 'C' word puts fear into the minds of people who are connected to someone who is diagnosed with such a frightening disease. In those days, just knowing you had been diagnosed with cancer, no matter what type, was one hell of a shock. It certainly changed my outlook on life. Things which hadn't been so important before suddenly became a priority. I accepted it, but I know that the people around me found it very difficult to accept. I remained positive, while others thought of the worst that could happen. It's the word, it's nothing else but the word. There are many different types of cancer. Some kill you, some don't, but when you are told you have cancer your immediate thought is not what type, and can it be cured, it's that it's going to kill you. When the specialist told me, I was frightened; terrified. I managed to come to terms with it fairly quickly. You focus on things. But it's the people around you who have the problems coming to terms with it emotionally. I know it affected Jeromin badly and how she managed to keep going and do her nursing training I will never know. It just shows how strong she is and what a special woman she is. The children were relatively young. Lee was 14 and Claire 12.

It was even more difficult, I think, because I had to go into the East Glamorgan Hospital in Church Village and was put onto the very ward where she was doing her training. She had to be taken off that ward because they weren't allowed to nurse family or relations, so that would have disrupted her work as well. It was a bad time for Jer.

Mr Foster was the specialist, and I was lucky because he had big associations with Pontypridd rugby club, so at least after the operation there was a friendly face staring at me when I came round and he could give me the news that they had cut out the cancer and it hadn't spread.

When the cancer scare was over I went back to work after a break of about two and a half months and I also wanted to get back into coaching again. But Penygraig had needed to find a new coach when I had become ill, so at the invitation of Mike Dwyer, who had been the scrum half at Pontypridd when I had played there, I went to coach at Porth. They weren't in the league system operated by the WRU; they were what was called a junior union club, below the league system.

It was during this time at Porth that I started moving through the district sides. I coached the Rhondda and East Glamorgan side which went on to win the Howells Cup (no relation). That was a cup which all the junior clubs from all the regions took part in. I coached the district team which played New Zealand, and then moved up to the mid-district set-up, so I suppose I was starting to build something of a reputation as a coach through the junior clubs and the district. I was also making my way through the WRU coaching system but I found out, even as early as the level one course, that if you were a teacher you had a big advantage. Your rugby knowledge is taken very much for granted, simply because you are on the course and interested in becoming a coach. I found a huge part of the courses involved organization and communication. Well, teachers are doing that all day and every day, and they had all the organizational skills, so it was a big disadvantage for someone coming from a non-teaching background like British Telecom.

My big break came in 1991 when Dennis John asked me to join him as the forwards coach at Pontypridd. I had known Dennis both as a team mate, and as an opposing coach with the junior teams for many years. Dennis had been coach at Llantwit Fardre when we played them at Tylorstown. Also, we often talked to each other about rugby and coaching, so we knew each other well. The big change at Pontypridd since the season I had played there was that they were now regarded as a top tier club along with with the Newports and Cardiffs. Two brothers, Clive and Chris Jones, had been the coaches before Dennis and I arrived, and they had built Ponty's reputation as a tough side, and a team not to be messed with. I suppose it's fair to say that the foundations of the Ponty tradition had been built up by Clive and Chris. The club had moved to their own ground in 1974, Pwllgwaun, which I doubt many people in world rugby will have heard of. It might be better known from Ayr to Auckland and from Tucuman to Tredegar as Sardis Road, and this was the time when it got the nickname by which people in Wales and beyond came to know the place: The House of Pain.

Pontypridd in those days were a bullying side. They didn't

stand any nonsense from the opposition and if there was trouble in a match, the Ponty boys could sort it out. The club had had a series of coaches who, let's just say, had played the game on the edge of the laws and expected their teams to do the same. As one of my former players put it, "Ponty were a physical team with the odd thug in the side." They had a lot of hard boys from the Valleys with a valleys mentality. For four consecutive seasons the club had received letters from the WRU warning them about their players' behaviour on the field. There was one particular cup game against Llanelli when things got very out of hand and the media got stuck into Pontypridd and their methods of winning matches. Whatever the rights and wrongs, as a result of the battle in that game Llanelli called off fixtures against Pontypridd, and they wouldn't play each other again until the formation of the Heineken League two years later. Leicester also called off fixtures against Ponty after a game at Welford Road saw one player sent off for stamping and others could have shared the early bath as well. In one game against Ebbw Vale even the touch judge had been sent off by the referee. (It was still the time when the clubs provided the touch judges.) These difficult times for the club culminated during the 1989–90 season with the resignation of coach Clive Jones. According to Alun Granfield's excellent record of Pontypridd rugby club *In Black And White*, this was over 'a difficult relationship with the Pontypridd committee and the controversies over the team's disciplinary record.' Clive's brother Chris took over as coach, but after him another controversial appointment was made when former Wales captain Mike Watkins took over the coaching duties. There were several people who were concerned about his disciplinary record as a player, and again he did not enjoy a happy relationship with the club, lasting just one season before being replaced by Les Brown for the 1991–92 season. The league programme started with five defeats out of six, and Les was out.

So that was the club which Dennis and I inherited. There

was no way we wanted to take away that hard edge, because it was a big part of Ponty, but we wanted a style which people would want to watch and enjoy playing. Players had to realise that you had a far better chance of winning if you had fifteen players on the pitch, but rugby was different in those days. If you played in the forwards you expected to get a good leathering. There were no television cameras looking at every angle, there were no touch judges to help the referee. A lot went unseen. Make no mistake, the previous coaches and players had done an awful lot to put Pontypridd rugby on the map and to give the club something to build on, and we didn't want to throw that away.

I was also dealing with a different class of player, certainly different to any I'd ever come across. Then there was the opposition. I went from Porth v Bedlinog, to Pontypridd v Cardiff, a massive jump. We were coaching a side to play against the best teams in Wales, containing the best players in Wales. We had some quality. Nigel Bezani was there, Paul Knight was a current international and Dale McIntosh and Mark Rowley both went on to play for Wales. There was an 18-year-old ginger headed fly half who had just come out of youth rugby by the name of Neil Jenkins, who would go on to make something of a name for himself. The quality of player was a big step-up, so potentially, I suppose, there could have been a problem for me. If you tell a player at Porth this is the way to do it, or this is the way something is done, he would probably gobble up your words and ideas with great enthusiasm. At this level they could very easily have questioned my knowledge, my skills, and my coaching credentials. I didn't have a great playing career to fall back on, so I had to ensure that my organization was good and this was what I worked on as much as anything else.

A great deal of my introduction to this quality of coaching was down to Dennis. Dennis was an awful lot of what I wasn't. Even though he had been coaching at lowly Llantwit Fardre, he had also been involved in the Wales national set-up at various levels. He had coached some of the best players in Wales, and was known to them, and his reputation was enough to initially carry both of us forward at Sardis Road. He handled it so well that my experience was never a problem. I have so much to thank him for, and learned so much from him at this time. His knowledge of the game was immense, his organization was first class.

Of course we were still in the amateur age when I joined the coaching team at Pontypridd, so training was on a Tuesday and Thursday evening. When the first Tuesday night came I couldn't wait to get home from work and get down there. It was like the first day at a new school. There was an excitement at being involved in a club as good as Ponty, and yet a certain amount of nervousness to be working at a much higher level. I was lucky in that I knew a lot of the players anyway and that helped so much. Nigel Bezani had been at Tylorstown with me, and I had come across a lot of the other players as well. Whatever anyone said, I was a former Pontypridd player returning. The fact that I had only played there for one season wouldn't have been held against me. You always question whether you are good enough to be doing this. You have to do that because if you don't then there is only one way you are going to go. You have to keep proving to the players that you are good enough to be doing it.

I found the intensity of the sessions something I had not encountered before. There we were on a Tuesday and Thursday night, doing just what we had been doing at Porth, but because of the standard of the players and the quality of the work, the intensity was worlds apart. It was difficult for me to come to terms with, and also the level of knowledge required was so much more. If you didn't have that knowledge then the players soon found out and you were dead meat. You might just as well walk away from it. I was helped greatly by Dennis, and it was a bit of good cop, bad cop with us. Dennis was always on at the players, driving them, moaning at them, cursing them, but he could get away with that because of his record. He coached

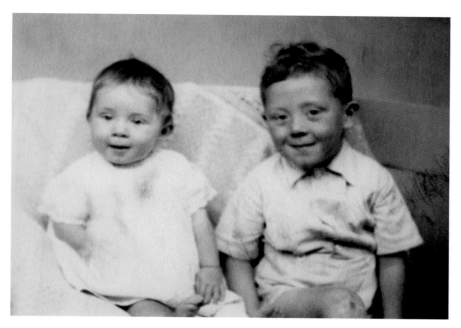

Me with my sister Wendy at an early age.

My mother and father enjoy retirement.

The most important day of my life. Jeromin and me on our wedding day in Pontypridd.

Mum, dad and me at my sister Wendy's wedding.

My son Lee with my granddaughter Kia.

My daughter Claire.

My granddaughter
Caitlin with my two
grandsons, Dale
and Kian.

Lynn Howells MSc – I never would have thought it possible!
Photo: Dave Daggers

My first club Treherbert after being told that I wasn't required by Tylorstown. Front row left, you could rest fruit on those sideboards!

Gone up in the world and my first association with Pontypridd. Second right, back row, I still had the sideboards. Bob Pemberthy, who took me to Ponty is the giant in the back row. Tommy David, who went on to play for the Lions has the ball in his hands, as usual.

It hadn't worked out at Ponty, but at last there was a welcome at Tylorstown. I was captain for the 75th anniversary celebration game. The referee is Wales' top referee at the time, Ken Rowlands.

Coaching at Pontypridd. Dennis John is on the left. Richie Collins is third right, back row. The Chief, Dale McIntosh, is next to him. Paul John is second from the left in the front row, Steele Lewis is next, then the ginger monster Neil Jenkins. Phil John is sat behind the mascot, alongside captain Nigel Bezani who's dog – who's name I can't remember – is stood in front of me.

Pontypridd's first major trophy. Nigel Bezani lifts the Swalec Cup with two other senior players Steele Lewis and Phil John who has already swopped a Neath shirt. In the Wales blazer is Glanmor Griffiths, then the secretary of the WRU. If it hadn't been for him being stubborn and ignoring the doubters, there would be no Millennium Stadium.
Photo: Huw Evans Agency

The Swalec Cup was followed the next season by the League Championship. A young Neil Jenkins lifts the trophy watched by the typical massed Sardis Road crowd.
Photo: Huw Evans Agency

Cardiff, a team bursting with internationals. Dai Young was my captain, alongside John Humphries, Rob Howley, Neil Jenkins, Mike Rayer, and Kevin Ellis who played rugby league for Great Britain as well. Rhys Williams was just a kid coming through. In the middle row Gareth Thomas is peeping through behind Peter Rodgers. Pieter Muller is on the right, and in the back row a young Martyn Williams and Craig Quinnell amongst others.

In the Arms Park dugout with my good friend Geraint John. We would later take the Wales team on tour to Japan together.

Photo: Huw Evans Agency

HOWELLS QUITS CARDIFF JOB

..and he's pulled out of Wales set-up

LYNN HOWELLS has quit as coach of league champions Cardiff after two years in the job – and he is standing down from the Wales management team.

Howells, who joined Cardiff from Pontypridd two years ago, made his shock announcement to the players at the Arms Park yesterday.

And it comes after telling Wales coach Graham Henry that he was withdrawing his application for the post of national forwards coach.

Retain

Howells will be seeing out the season with Cardiff, who still have a chance of becoming the first club to retain the Welsh-Scottish League title.

But the Arms Park clash with Caerphilly on Thursday week will be his last in charge.

Howells said last night: "I have a few offers to consider.

COACHING ROLE: Dai Young

two outside Wales. Before I enter into negotiations, it was only fair to let Cardiff and Graham Henry know, so that they can plan for the future."

An English Premiership club and an Italian outfit are said to be interested in Howells.

He had grown weary over his negotiations for a new contract with Cardiff which had dragged on for five months.

Cardiff skipper Dai Young could end up taking on a coaching role next season.

TURN TO PAGE 47

PARTING OF WAYS: Lynn Howells with Wales coach Graham Henry

At least the end at Cardiff made the headlines.

The original five regional coaches plus someone I had little time for, Steve Lewis, on the left. Next to him, Lyn Jones (Ospreys), me, Mike Ruddock (Dragons), Gareth Jenkins (Scarlets) and Dai Young (Blues).
Photo: Huw Evans Agency

The Warriors – probably the most talented side, other than the national team, I have ever coached. Captain was Gareth Thomas, with the unmistakable hairstyle just behind, and to the right of me is Richard Parks, who raised thousands of pounds for Marie Curie climbing the highest peak in every continent. Of the coaching staff Alan Lewis is on the left, in front of him is the kit man Simon Harris. At the other end is Tim Atter, physio, and inside him Nick Johnson, the conditioning coach. All of us would be on the scrapheap within twelve months.

All smiles now, but after just one season the Warriors would be disbanded.
Photo: Huw Evans Agency

I had plenty to think about at Edinburgh and not just on the pitch.
Photo: Huw Evans Agency

My singing partner. Alan Lewis and me celebrate becoming the first British team to win a Test series in Argentina.

The coaching team celebrate after beating South Africa first and, so far, only time. Me, Graham Henry, Steve Black and David Pickering.
Photo: David Williams

Holding court before the press in Japan. Me, Sam Simon – another Ponty man who was the WRU manager on the tour, and team captain Andy Moore.
Photo: Huw Evans Agency

Sitting alongside Stephen Jones. He made his Wales debut on the fateful tour to South Africa, but would go on to make over a hundred appearances for Wales. What is written in Japanese I don't know. Maybe it's better I never knew.
Photo: Huw Evans Agency

A young Gavin Henson on his Wales debut in Japan. If only he had concentrated on the rugby.
Photo: Huw Evans Agency

Watching with long-time team manager Trevor James. He was my team manager on the tour to Japan in 2001 and was involved with the WRU from 1989 until 2002.
Photo: Huw Evans Agency

Working with Leigh Jones. It was Leigh and I who walked in on discussions between Graham Henry and the WRU officials in a Sydney restaurant.
Photo: Huw Evans Agency

Alongside the maestro. Graham Henry became a lifelong friend.
Photo: Huw Evans Agency

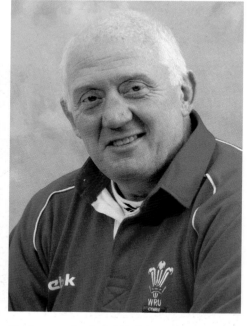

Having coached all the club sides I have been involved with, and now in Romania, still my proudest moment was putting on a Wales kit as part of the coaching team and head coach in Japan.
Photo: Huw Evans Agency

Another proud moment was coaching the Barbarians against the South of Scotland in November 2011. We lost but the next man to coach the Barbarians, one Graham Henry, lost to England by more!
Photo: Barbarians FC Archive

A tiring business this touring. Leigh Jones and I relax on the tour to Japan.

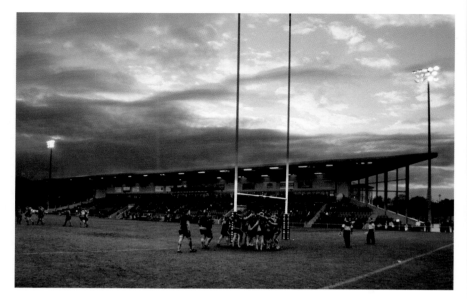

With the advent of professional rugby it also brought in benefactors who ploughed vast sums of money into clubs around the country. Tony De Mulder gave the club fantastic facilities at Castle Park, Doncaster.
Photo: courtesy of R J Cadman Construction

Management team for the Romania national team: Neil Kelly (defence coach), me (director of rugby), Olivier Rieg (conditioning coach), Marias Tincu (forwards coach), Harry Dumitras (head coach), Eugen Apjok (backs coach), Horatio Bargaunaus (team manager, not in photo).

with his head and his heart. I seemed to be the one who they came to, to have a moan back at. I would not have done anything to undermine Dennis but it helped that they saw me as the good cop. We worked hard and talked a lot, planned a lot and I think I earned the respect of the players. Also Pontypridd is a friendly place. The people around the club off the field are friendly and would do anything to help you settle in.

We wanted to set about changing things on the field. Both Dennis and I knew what Pontypridd had been about and how they operated. They bullied teams and built the team around that mentality. Neither of us wanted things to be that way but we knew we couldn't change that overnight. We had to bring in players to play the style we wanted, and move the bully boys out. Eventually we got to where we wanted to be, but we couldn't do that with a lot of the players we had inherited. We weren't daft enough to think we could win every game by running the ball from behind our own posts, throwing it about even on the wettest and windiest days, but we wanted to play with a certain style and eventually we got there. By the time we won the cup in 1995–96, and the league a season later, I think we had the players and we had coached them to play to the conditions on the day. We could play any style. We never lost that capability to play the physical game if we had to. If teams wanted to throw in some dirty tactics we could hold our own, but we could also play in a style that people wanted to watch and that was the big thing about Pontypridd. We had players like Paul John at scrum half, Neil Jenkins outside him, arguably the best halfback pairing in the country at the time. There was Phil John at hooker, Steele Lewis, and Mark Rowley. Later the likes of Martyn Williams and Jason Lewis came through to play alongside one of the legends of Pontypridd rugby, Dale McIntosh. Dale was a New Zealander who had a remarkable resemblance to a character called the 'Chief' in a film called *One Flew over the Cuckoo's Nest*. So Dale got the name by which he is now known at Pontypridd, and just about everywhere else he has travelled with rugby. Other young players would follow, like Kevin Morgan, Jonny Bryant, Sonny Parker, and Gareth Wyatt on the wing. Players who could entertain. We had the best of both worlds.

As we were progressing along this road, rugby union went through the biggest change in its history. The summer of 1995 catapulted Vernon Pugh, a well-respected Welshman, and a former Pontypridd player, into a permanent place in the history of rugby. He was the man who guided rugby through the difficult period towards professionalism, and made the announcement in South Africa on the eve of the World Cup final that the game would go professional. That announcement affected rugby more than any other decision had ever affected the game. It wasn't like a law change, or a tinkering with try values or the worth of a penalty, this affected rugby players, clubs and coaches and also our families. My thoughts when I heard the news were very selfish. What is going to happen to me? There will be some people reading this book who have never known anything but professional rugby union, so let me explain. In the amateur days you did a job of work then you trained and played rugby in your own time. At most clubs you actually paid an annual membership fee to be a member of a club so that you could play for them. They would provide a shirt in the club colours for some teams; in lower teams players brought their own shirt. You paid a match fee which went towards the running of the club. No one was ever paid to step onto a pitch and take part in a match. No one was paid to coach, to be a physio. Even being a club administrator was an unpaid office. Anyone who was found to have received money was banned from the game. It provoked all sorts of disputes. Players who left rugby union to go and play rugby league were not allowed into a rugby union clubhouse. Former internationals were barred from receiving international tickets. They were treated like lepers. Even if you wrote a book after you retired, or went to work in the media and got paid, you were no longer allowed into contact with rugby union.

There were rumours that players in the southern hemisphere

were receiving money for playing, and I know that in England there were very strong rumours that players in the big Welsh clubs were given a brown envelope containing a few quid at the end of a game. Unfortunately one never came in my direction, and I don't think any did at Pontypridd. The club didn't have enough money to pay players. I have no doubt that there was a reward system at some clubs even if it was in kind rather than in coins of the realm. I believe that one club had an arrangement with local stores that if a player needed something for his house then it was delivered.

That nonsense all came to an end in 1995 when the decision was made that union would go professional. It didn't affect every club. Even today some have never been touched by money and still operate exactly as they did before the summer of 1995. How it has benefited the game or not could be the subject of another book. All I can say is how it has affected me. I don't know what it was like at the money clubs, but certainly it didn't come as a sudden new dawn at Sardis Road. We still trained on a Tuesday and Thursday. In the early days no one gave up their jobs. Yes, payments started to be made, and came above board, but that was about the only change. It may have had an immediate effect at some clubs but not at Pontypridd. I'm not sure at that stage people knew what professionalism meant other than getting paid.

People had to decide whether to give up their jobs and go full-time rugby, or play the game as it had been played for a hundred years in the Valleys, alongside work. As late as 1998, three years after Vernon's announcement, Pontypridd still hadn't gone totally professional. The club had started to find sources of income other than gate receipts. Marketing was a word which was creeping into the game and one or two players had left their jobs and become this new breed of full-time rugby players. These guys would train and play matches, but they would run around in cars emblazoned with 'Just Rentals' – which later became 'Buy As You View' – because they had come on board as the club's sponsors. In return the players would promote the company in the Valleys, becoming the public face of the organization. They in effect topped up the wages of those early professionals and without them Pontypridd would never have been able to hang on to the likes of Neil Jenkins and Dale McIntosh.

As for me, I was still worked for BT for another three years and then two things happened which would change my life. BT decided it was looking for redundancies, and for the 23 years service I had put in, I discovered I would get a decent pay-off. Secondly, Wales were going on tour to Zimbabwe and South Africa. Kevin Bowring had resigned as Wales coach after the defeat by France in 1998, and Dennis had been asked to take the tour. He wanted me as one of the coaching team. So two strings were pulling me towards a full-time coaching career. By now Pontypridd had got its finances on an even keel and money was there for the players and staff to be full time. I had to consider the family in all this, as everyone else in my position had to. I had to consider that I would be entering a results driven environment. If the team wasn't successful, the coach and his staff would get the chop. That didn't matter so much when you had a full-time job to fall back on. But now this was your job. It all went through my mind.

The kids had grown up by now and were working, so there was no problem there. Jeromin was working as a nurse, so we had an income, but it was still a big decision. Again it was another example of how she has supported me during our life together. She was behind me one hundred per cent and in fact she was pretty influential in me going for it. I was certainly going to be on less money as a coach than I had been at BT, but the big temptation was the Wales tour.

Going professional changed my coaching methods as well as my life. A new part of the job was analysis. Previously we had been forced to do this in the evenings outside work time, but now at least we had time to do it properly. Players could come in, or we could get them in, at any time, and all day if necessary as they were under contract. But this had to be managed properly as well. Although we had them available for eight hours a day, you can't train a player and expect him to run around or do a weights session for eight hours at a time. That was a big learning curve for us, managing players to get the best out of players. Because we had them every day we had to prepare training programmes. That for me was probably one of the biggest challenges that professionalism threw up, managing the players' time. Plans had to be put in place, plans for periods of the season. Plans for the Heineken Cup, which would be very different to the plans for the Celtic League. Training plans, travel plans, hotels, food, recovery, plans, plans, plans. At least everyone found it easier in the professional arena when it came to matches which involved travelling. In the amateur days players had to ask their employers for time off to go to Ireland or Scotland or France. Now the club was the employer and we had the players all the time.

All these things evolved gradually, but once the set-up became more professional then there were no half measures. Physios, medical staff, rugby staff, back-up staff, all these had to be in place. If the players were in you had to have the physio there. All these aspects needed arranging by the coaches, and they became as much managers as they were coaches. In the old days you just came along on a Tuesday and Thursday and coached the side. This was a different set-up altogether.

As the professional side of the game came together, so there were other challenges on the field. When Dennis and I first went to Pontypridd we were just playing the Welsh sides and a couple of English teams. It was the first year of the new Heineken Leagues in Wales which replaced the old merit tables. They had been the only competition we had had, and your position depended on your results against other teams in the table. The problem was that not every team played every other team so the positions were worked out as a percentage of games won to games lost. Now at least with the new leagues every team in the division played every other team so a proper table resulted.

Another big challenge came for the start of the 1995–96 season with the decision to create a European tournament, which has now become the biggest tournament in the northern hemisphere. This gave us a chance to play new teams from outside Wales and Scotland. At first it was a bit of a mess. There was no sponsor, and the English and Scottish teams didn't take part, it was just the Welsh, Irish and French. We were in a group with Leinster and Milan, and you only played one game against the other two sides, there was no home and away fixture like there is now. We beat Milan at Sardis Road in front of a crowd of 4,500, and wrote ourselves into the history books as the first Welsh team to play in the European Cup. We then lost out in Leinster, so came second in the group, not good enough to move onto the knockout stages. With no sponsor the clubs had to fund their own travel arrangements, but teams were excited about playing in this new competition because they could see it might be the start of a European league.

The Heineken Cup, as it became, helped the game enormously. As a coach it gave you new challenges against the other nations who would play a different type of game to the one we played in Wales. For the players it gave them a chance to play against internationals from the other four nations. It was hoped that this would raise the game at international level, and raise the players' awareness of what was required in this new age. Our Pontypridd squad had been together for some time and had tasted success, but now the bar had been raised and this new competition showed what was expected. It changed the mentality of the squad and the players realised that they had to change physically. They would now be coming up against athletes.

An example came early on when we played Bath. In those days the players could swap shirts with the opposition and Neil Eynon, one of our props, swapped shirts with his opposite number, Victor Ubogu. Now Victor was a specimen, muscles on muscles, a lean, mean scrummaging machine who had benefited from Bath's professional approach. Our Neil's shirt fitted him like a tent, whereas Victor's shirt showed Neil's every bulge and dimple much to the squad's amusement. But it showed us the way we had to go. Having said that, Neil was probably a better rugby player. So that was the challenge, getting the better players fitter and faster. The core of that squad probably never totally embraced the professional game, and they still held down their jobs outside rugby. Some of them were coming to the end of their careers so there was little point in them giving up careers and jobs to become full-time rugby players.

The Heineken Cup was also a big event for the supporters. They loved having these big teams coming to Sardis Road, and also loved the trips away to exotic places they had never been to before, although as we shall see later some of those places were more welcoming than others!

I had one major setback in my time with Pontypridd; I had a recurrence of the cancer. This time it was on my back, and when I was told what it was it hit me hard. The first time I just knew I would get through it. This time I was more frightened than before. I hadn't got rid of it, it had come back and if it had come back this time, how many more times would it surface over the rest of my life? As a result I now make sure that I keep well out of the sun, and when we go on tour and the players are topping up the suntan you'll find me with my shirt on sheltering in the nearest shade. Unlike the time when I was coaching at Penygraig, I didn't stop, and I didn't tell anyone that I was ill. Thankfully I went into hospital and they operated again, cutting out the problem, and I could return to coaching within a couple of days.

So for Dennis and I things were going well. With the new leagues in place there was something tangible to play for. Results meant something, and there was a table which showed players and supporters how well the teams were doing. In our first full season we won a dozen, lost eight and drew two of our league games, and reached the quarter-finals of the Welsh

Cup. The following season we won seventeen, lost four and drew one, and lost by two points to Cardiff in the cup semi-final. The season after that, 1994–95, we won seventeen and lost six to come second in the league. This was also the season we played the South African touring side. In those days the touring nation not only played international matches against the home nations, but played club and regional sides as well. We lost 9–3, but that was without Neil Jenkins, and Richie Collins, both on international duty, and Dale McIntosh who had broken his arm. In March of that season the club were invited to travel out to South Africa to play Northern Transvaal to mark the switch on of the new floodlights which had been installed. We were drawing 12–12 with ten minutes left and had Jenks kicked a penalty, admittedly from 55 yards, we would have taken the lead. We eventually lost 31–12 in a game spoilt by torrential rain, but we were not disgraced, and the club had been honoured by the invitation.

With the introduction of the European competition in 1995–96 almost every match had something riding on it. In Europe, the league or the cup, there were very few friendlies. What friendly matches there were gave us the opportunity to blood a few youngsters and have a look at new players. It was the time of arrival for the likes of Kevin Morgan, Gareth Wyatt, Lee Jarvis and another ginger-headed kid who would make something of a name for himself, Martyn Williams. Pontypridd were moving in the right direction. We had shipped out some of the less desirable players, and a new crop was coming through.

There was certainly a buzz around the place. The team was a good blend of the older experienced players and the new blood. It was a mixture of players from all around the Valleys, something that Ponty has thrived on, and probably still does. There was an inner belief among the squad that they just couldn't be beaten, and a feeling that it was Ponty against the rest of the world, certainly the rest of Wales. The organization was paying off, everyone knew their responsibilities, everyone knew what to do, and I felt as though I had contributed to that. It was an achievement.

Our progression in the cup got better year on year and in 1995 we got to the final. It was a special day, Pontypridd's first cup final, and the town turned out in force. Our team manager, Eddie Jones, had found someone who played the bagpipes and he arranged for him to lead the team from our hotel in the centre of Cardiff to the stadium. All very grand, but it was all too much hype really and I am sure it had an influence on the players' minds. We lost to Swansea 17–12.

It was just a matter of time, though, and that time came in May of 1996. The league season had gone well again, and for the second successive season we reached the cup final, this time facing Neath. This time we did things differently. No bagpipes, not even a night away in a hotel before the game. We got on the bus at the club just like a normal Saturday and, although we did have a police escort, it was down the road and straight into the stadium. At one stage in the game we were trailing and looked dead and buried. But the Ponty boys showed what character they had to come back and win 29–22. It just showed what we had built and what we were about, so much so that after the game in the dressing room I broke down and cried like a baby. Nigel Bezani led the team back out to receive the cup, and the majority of the 50,000 were still there. It was pretty emotional, but it was the culmination of everything we had worked at. We had given Pontypridd success but not only that, we had done it by playing rugby as we wanted it to be played. We had turned an unfashionable club into a respected team of winners. We were always the underdogs and no one ever gave us a chance. People had been against Ponty. Now we were something to be reckoned with. We had put the club among the elite of Welsh rugby. When I had walked into Pontypridd that first night as assistant to Dennis, I had had serious thoughts about whether I could do the job. Seeing Baz collect that cup and knowing I had been part of it, I knew that I could do it.

The two league games which followed were something of a

disappointment. We drew with Cardiff, and then travelled to Neath who scored the points and the tries they needed to win the league. We were third. The team had scored the highest number of points in the club's history, 1,583, with 211 tries at an average of five per game.

The following year we won the league title with Neil Jenkins as captain, losing two games all season. English and Scottish clubs came into the European competition, and there was a new competition, the Anglo-Welsh. We lost once in the Heineken, out in Dax, and came third in the group. In the Anglo-Welsh we lost to Leicester and Wasps. Again our tries and points per game average improved, no doubt encouraged by a bonus points system which had been introduced. If we hadn't done so already, we had finally put Pontypridd rugby on the map.

Seven great years coaching the biggest team in the valley I had been born into, and the team I had played for. Cup winners and league champions in successive years. Who would ever want that to end?

7

The Battle of Brive

I WROTE EARLIER how the Ponty supporters loved the European competition, as it gave them the chance to travel to foreign lands and watch teams they hadn't seen before. I think there will be one game, though, that will forever go down in the history of the club. In the 1997–98 season we were drawn in a group with Bath, once again, Scottish Borders and the cup winners from the previous season, Brive. Things didn't go well from the outset as we lost our first match at home to the English side, and then faced Brive away the following weekend.

We all knew that the atmosphere would be red hot, there would be intimidation both on and off the field, and there could be some traditional French tactics. All week we had been building up the atmosphere among the squad, determined that the French were not going to walk all over our team. For those who had been there in the days before Dennis John and I came on board it must have been back to normal. We impressed on them not to take a backward step, and if the rough stuff started, it was going to be one in, all in.

If we hadn't realised before, then the Brive warm-up left us with no doubts concerning their intentions. Their coach, Laurent Seigne, had a reputation for getting his teams really wound up. Neither the coaches nor the players could believe what we were seeing. He had them stamping on each other as part of the warm-up, and I don't mean gentle rucking. It was one on the floor and every one of them stamping on him as they went past. When they came out of the dressing room they had black eyes, cuts and bruises where Seigne had either had them hitting each other or he had been punching them.

The Chief and Phil John asked if we would let them have the last word, and certainly, for my part I had no problem with that. I think there is so much that the coaches can say, but when the rallying call comes from the captain or one of the players, especially players of that character, then I think it has a hell of an impact. It certainly looked like it had on this occasion. The players emerged from that meeting with ashen faces, they were pumped up, they were focused and it was impressive.

All was quiet early on apart from a few niggles which was nothing more than we had warned the players about. But then all hell was let loose as the Chief and his opposite number, Lionel Mallier, went head-to-head literally, as the Frenchman appeared to head-butt Dale. Just about all the players then went at it hammer and tongs, which took the referee Eddie Murray and the touch judges an age to sort out. As a result, Mallier and the Chief were red carded, but at least the players had stood up for themselves and for each other, which is what we had spoken about all week. That might have been the problem. Brive were used to having things all their own way at home and here was a team from the Welsh Valleys who were prepared to stand up to them and not roll over.

We were 16–6 down by half time, but fought back in the second half to lead 31–27. With moments to go the French side won a line-out near our line, won the ball from the throw and with just about the whole of their side in the driving maul they got over our line. Now the television cameras couldn't show who grounded the ball, if anyone, but with 4,500 French supporters clearing the wax from his ears, Murray (another Scottish referee to add to my black book) took the safe option and awarded the try. We lost by a point as the next whistle after the failed conversion was the final whistle and everyone ran for the sanctuary of the dressing rooms.

When we got in there one of the boys asked, "What's happened to you?"

"Nothing, why?" I replied.

"Well you'd better take your tracksuit off and have a look."

I had been absolutely covered with phlegm where they had been spitting at us. I just chucked the tracksuit away.

It was hard to take. The win would have made more history for Pontypridd as the first Welsh side to win in France. As it was history did come our way, but not the sort we wanted. It had been a battle on the field but at the end there were the customary handshakes all round and pats on the back. The nastiness seemed to have subsided, even more so when the players from both sides and the supporters, many of them from Pontypridd, were invited to Le Bar Toulzac. Now I wasn't in the bar, so I have relied on eyewitness reports of what went on, but basically it all cracked off. Apparently, Phil John thought he was being wound up by their captain, Philippe Carbonneau, and a few words were exchanged but nothing else. Then the players decided it was best to retreat while the atmosphere was relatively cordial. But then someone threw a bottle from an area where the Brive players were standing and it caught Jason Lewis on the head. Need I say any more?

Reports in the newspapers likened it to something out of the Wild West with blood on the floor and bottles, chairs, tables, the lot going through the air and innocent bystanders ducking for cover. The police arrived and apparently used tear gas to clear everyone out. We had been drinking with Eddie Butler and Jonathan Davies and a few others and someone came along and told us that there was a problem going on. We then met up with the Chief and Phil John who had decided at a very early stage of the riot that it might be a good idea to leave the bar.

We walked around the corner to be greeted by Jason Lewis, who was covered in blood, then Mike Griffiths, followed by the rest of the players. You could see their eyes streaming and their clothes were stinking of the tear gas. As we approached the bar another police van pulled up, and a police officer sprung out of the paddy wagon and you could see his intention was to sort it all out. His truncheon was waving above his head as he raced into Le Bar Toulzac like something out of the Keystone Cops. The next thing we saw was him being hurled out of the door, closely followed by the truncheon. I was pissing myself laughing, but also thinking 'Oh God! Here we go!'

Eventually they did get the thing under control and it all quietened down. There is one other lasting memory I have of the Battle of Brive. As we got off the coach which took us from the hotel back into town, the Chief was singing Sam Cooke's 'Working on the Chain Gang'. Every time I hear that now I think of Brive and what happened after the match.

Of course, versions of how it started depended on whether they came with a French accent or a Welsh one. The French accused our boys of coming into the bar determined to seek revenge for the defeat earlier in the day. What we can be certain of is that the Ponty boys came off better. Martyn Williams and Jason Lewis had some cuts, which team doctor Dave Pemberton had to dress, whereas the Brive halfbacks Carbonneau and Lamaison suffered broken noses, while several others who needed hospital treatment. Lamaison said that our boys had come in and been ejected, returning later intent on smashing the place up.

When we got back to the hotel, everyone had sobered up pretty quickly. We were lucky because we had Sam Simon with us, a solicitor, and he had a pretty good idea of what was going on and what to do. No one went to bed, we just mulled around the reception area. Six of the boys were taken in by the police for questioning: Jason and Steele Lewis, Martyn Williams, Phil John, Andre Barnard and, of course, the instantly recognisable Dale McIntosh. Now I know that the Chief and Phil John would never have taken a backward step in that sort of situation, but those in the bar said they had left very early into the incident, and we could confirm that as we met up with them. The Brive players who identified the six taken for questioning, it is thought, just came out with names and descriptions they remembered from the match.

It was a mess. We had to get the hotel to let us stay another night, and we had to arrange different flights home. As the night wore on people began to wonder about the rugby consequences. Would the club be fined? Would we be thrown out of the tournament or banned for future seasons? So much was discussed by various groups of players, coaches and backroom staff because we had so much time on our hands. Three of the players were released after what must have been a pretty frightening experience, but Phil, Andre and the Chief had to face further investigations into causing damage and violence. Needless to say, when we got home the interest from the local media was intense, and the event even aroused the attention of sports minister Tony Banks who called for "strong action to be taken if it were proved that Pontypridd players had brought the game into disrepute". And if it had been the Brive players who had started it? The respective unions got involved as well, with French rugby union president Bernard Lapasset saying that Pontypridd should be ejected from the competition if it was proven that they started the fight in the bar. And if it had been the Brive players?

The Welsh Rugby Union did nothing. As one of our former players wrote in his autobiography, 'From the Welsh Rugby Union there was only the sound of silence.' Roger Pickering, the ERC chief executive, asked for a report from the match commissioner, but that would only relate to incidents on the pitch. Pickering also suggested that both the relevant unions should begin inquiries, but again it seemed unlikely that the French rugby union would blame Brive. We feared the WRU might hang us out to dry. Whatever had happened, something had to be done before the following weekend as both Brive and Ponty had another round of European matches.

The Chief, Phil John and Andre Barnard were allowed home with the rest of us when we finally left France later on the Monday, but the investigations would continue in their absence, and they were told not to return to the area unless it was to face court action. It was also very interesting that the local administrator who was doing all the investigating, and who would eventually decide the punishments, was the president of the Brive rugby club! No wonder then that players important to our team would be banned from returning to the area. That fact, thanks to the way results in our group panned out, would cause problems later, but for now there remained a distinct doubt that the return game against Brive at Sardis Road would take place a fortnight later. By now, incidentally, others had come forward claiming injuries, including David Vindetti who said he had been bitten, and the bar owner who claimed to have suffered cuts and bruises. The duration of the brawl had also doubled from ten to twenty minutes, and doors were added to the list of objects flying around the room. What did I miss?

We had to go to Scottish Borders the following weekend while Brive reluctantly went to Bath, claiming that without the players who had been injured in the bar brawl it was unfair to ask them to play the match. Bath won by two points whereas Ponty, without Dale McIntosh due to his red card in Brive, won 23–16. We still awaited the decision of the ERC as to any punishment we would receive as they were due to announce their decision on the Monday. The Brive coach Seigne had said that he didn't want to play against the 'semi-civilised animals' at Sardis Road, and there was a very good chance that the ERC would impose an unprecedented decision to play at a neutral ground behind closed doors. It appeared that Seigne was as frightened of our supporters as he was of our players and would have preferred not to play the game at all. So we awaited news from the ERC headquarters in Dublin, which came in the form of a £30,000 fine for both clubs and a charge of bringing the game into disrepute for the Chief for his victory gesture to the crowd when he was sent off. They were not going to do anything about the bar brawl as this was the subject of an investigation by the courts. As for the return game, that was to be played as scheduled at Sardis Road, a decision which didn't please the French, but made ITV's *News at Ten*.

Team manager Eddie Jones assured Brive that there would be no hangovers from our trip to France, and that they would be accorded the best possible welcome. He warned us that any trouble could mark the end of the club, it was that serious. As for us coaches, we prepared the team just as we would have done for any other game, though we knew that if they wanted to play dirty then we could play the game that way. However, as we had shown out in Brive, we were capable of playing some quality rugby as well. I think what upset us most was that they were reluctant to come to Pontypridd. There was no way that any of their players would be threatened by our guys or their supporters threatened by our supporters.

Everything went as smooth as clockwork from start to finish in front of a large crowd, half the South Wales Police force ready to quell any riots which might break out, and just about anyone who was anyone in the world of the media. Everyone was expecting round two, but the game was a good one and there were no incidents on or off the field, even the score entered into the spirit of cordiality: 29–29. We outscored them by three tries to one, but took a pounding in the pack, and the French side kicked eight penalties. But the Brive captain did have the decency to say after the match that they had been given a fine welcome.

So from a rugby point of view that should have been the end of Brive, but as we beat the Borders again and lost to Bath again, that remarkably left a quarter-final play-off with none other than Brive... in Brive! Dale McIntosh, Phil John and Andre Barnard were banned from returning to the French region, so we were without them. By now, as well, the club had decided that this was to be a 'no-risk' occasion. We had to hire a plane to take us and get us back, and when we landed we were welcomed by armed police, who escorted us onto the bus! When we arrived at the ground armed police followed us to the changing room.

As soon as the game was over we were out as quickly as possible, once again accompanied by the armed police who never left our sides all the time we were in France. No Le Toulzac Bar that night for us. No wives and girlfriends came – it was like a football Champions League match: fly in, do the job, fly home. What a pity! I think it showed real disrespect on the part of the French authorities because we had already had the game in Pontypridd where absolutely nothing had happened. I just think they overreacted. Off the field Chief was cleared by ERC of bringing the game into disrepute, but Brive will always be remembered for events off the field as much as on it.

The following season there was another memorable trip to France but this one ended in humiliation, and in its way marked the beginning of the end of a golden era. We had broken even with three wins and three losses in a group which contained Colomiers, Benetton Treviso, Glasgow and us. That left us second behind Colomiers and therefore we qualified for the quarter-finals. This meant a trip to Stade Jean Bouin to face the awesome Stade Français. Sadly, Pontypridd's big chance had come the year before when those refereeing decisions had cost us dearly. Even though most of the players were the same, the team was now on the wane. They had been together a long time and were past their best.

It was 8–8 after half an hour, then Jenks went off injured and Gareth Wyatt moved to fly-half. Though it wasn't down to Gareth, our players spent the rest of the game behind our own posts. I wonder if people realise how players on the field influence the opposition. When Neil was on the field, I think the opposition realised that if they gave away any penalties he would punish them. Once he went off they thought they could relax and penalties weren't so important. Having said that, they played some wonderful rugby. There were periods in the second half when we went five, ten minutes without touching the bloody ball! Ten tries to two, 71–15, one of the biggest defeats I have ever been involved in, certainly with Ponty. It was a huge disappointment and a harsh lesson, but a lesson that we learned from.

There were still a lot of experienced players in that squad

but Phil John left, there were rumours that Jenks was going to Bath, and that Kevin Morgan and Gareth Wyatt were being courted by English clubs as well. By the end of the season the record books showed that we had used over 50 players, with a third of them playing just one game. New names were emerging who would eventually go on to make a name for themselves at international level: Michael Owen, Richard Parks, Ian Gough, Jason Forster and Jonny Bryant. The season, though, was a big disappointment as these lads were too young to make a real impact. We just scraped into fourth spot in the league, we had an easy run in the cup, until we met Llanelli, and the season ended with a load of injuries and a load of dissatisfied players.

Nothing was more obvious than major changes had to be made at Pontypridd. We had been smashed by Stade Français and the team needed to be rebuilt as many of the players were coming to the end of their time. It was time to assess where we were as a club, and some of the players knew that. I'm certain some of them began to wonder if that was the right time to call it a day. I also had a decision to make.

8

Down the Road to Cardiff

THE SUCCESS OF the past few seasons had convinced me that I had the necessary skills to be a number one coach. I must stress here that in our time together Dennis John had never made me feel, or appear to be, an assistant, a number two, a bit-part coach, call it what you like. We had discussed, we had planned, we had debated, we had even argued, but we had been united as a coaching team. Having said that, I don't think people outside the game realise how different it is being a number one from being an assistant.

I was now also part of the Wales coaching system under Graham Henry, and towards the end of the 1998–99 season the New Zealander had approached me and asked if I would be interested in going to Cardiff. My first reaction had been... as what? Was I going to be a number two again or were there different plans? He assured me that conversations he'd had with Gareth Davies, the Cardiff chief executive, and Peter Thomas the Cardiff backer, suggested that they wanted me as the number one. So, conversations had taken place involving me and about me.

On the Tuesday before we played Bridgend, I had a telephone call from Gareth Davies. It was an official approach. He firstly asked if I was interested and again I asked the same question: what as? He assured me that I was going to be the head coach and, of course, I told him I was interested. I put the phone down gently, and then jumped up and down punching the air. If anyone had looked through the window at that time, they would have sent for the men in white coats! I can't explain how chuffed, excited, proud, whatever you want to call it, I was. The words coming out of my mouth were like a pre-match team talk and not for the dainty ears of the Maerdy neighbours. It was not just because this was Cardiff, it was also because I had done it. I was going to be a number one. Just to be in the frame for a club like Cardiff was massive. After the dancing and the jigging had stopped I had to ring Dennis to tell him I had been offered the job. I felt I owed him that and he was totally supportive.

Gareth and I made an appointment to meet in his office a few days later. It didn't take long, I can tell you, not just because it was a move I wanted to make, but because I am not driven by money. I never have been. I wasn't then, and I am not now. I know some coaches out there go where the best deal is, where they can get most rewards financially. It's nice to be comfortably off, but money has never motivated me. My ambitions have always been motivated by whatever was the best move for me, and the best move at that time was to become a number one. To be asked by Cardiff was brilliant, but it wouldn't have made any difference had it been Pontypool, Ebbw Vale, Neath, Swansea or any of the other senior Welsh clubs. The position was more important than the money or the name of the club. The moment was right. If I delayed I might never get the chance again. I could see Dennis continuing at Pontypridd as long as he wanted to, although having said that, within a few months of my going, Dennis had gone as well. They wanted him to accept a director of rugby role; he wanted to keep coaching, so packed it in.

So I would have been crazy not to take the position I wanted at one of the top clubs in Wales when offered it, as it gave me that step up on the coaching ladder. It was going to be difficult, and again I had to talk to the family because I was an assistant with Wales, and now taking on this job would mean even more time spent on rugby and a lot of time out of the house. As usual, though, they were supportive and considered that I should do it. I was over the moon, to be honest, but then I sat down very early on and thought, oh shit – it's Cardiff. It is a valley thing and a valley mentality and I realised it would be difficult simply because of where I came from. It is just twelve miles from Pontypridd to Cardiff, but it has been harder for the people who have travelled those twelve miles than for players who have come from the other side of the world. I think there were about three games left in the season after the announcement had been made and the stick I took was unmerciful.

I hoped and thought that being the assistant coach with Wales would have some clout, unlike when I went to Ponty with Dennis with little behind me. Now I had a coaching record and a reputation. So I thought that would see me through. I was a little worried, though, that being part of Graham's team was something of a disadvantage as some of the players were thinking that it was just another method he was using to control Welsh rugby and control the clubs. I was flattered to be part of Graham's team, but there was no way I was Graham's lapdog. In addition, there was this Valleys thing, which I had to carry with me. Let me put it into context. A famous former Cardiff player once said to Jeromin, "Next time we meet we'll come to you and we'll have fish and chips." That was, and still is, the way people in the capital city perceive the Valleys. They are the posh restaurants; we are the fish and chip shops. Having said that, even though I had concerns about it being Cardiff, I never considered not taking the position, and the reason was that when I went into the job I told them that I was going to do it my way and if they didn't want it done that way then they could count me out. My way included getting rid of quite a few people.

Huw Bevan, the conditioning coach, went as I felt he was far too close to the players. Naturally, they didn't like me getting rid of Huw as he had also played for Cardiff, but it was almost as if that was part of the process; it showed I was going to be the new broom.

Peter Manning, the team manager, was dispatched as I felt he had been associated with Cardiff for far too long, and was another who was far too close to the players to have a professional relationship with the squad. I wanted to bring Bob Norster in as team manager and I felt that appointment was very important. I wanted my own way as much as possible, but frankly I was surprised I got away with as much as I did. Why Bob? Well he had played for Cardiff, and also I had been impressed with how Bob had conducted himself when he had been Wales' team manager under Alan Davies, especially with regard to his loyalty to Alan. I can tell you he took some persuading to give up a regular job, but I wanted to buy into that kind of loyalty. I wanted him to be both a link and also a buffer between the board and the rugby. He knew the job and he didn't let me down and because Cardiff was such a big club he wouldn't be assigned some of the mundane things that team managers normally have to do, like booking hotels and arranging transport. He could delegate that and concentrate on other matters.

It was going to be important that I made the right choice of assistant coach because an awful lot would depend on him during the first few weeks of the season. I had come across a guy called Geraint John. He had been a former Cardiff player, which wasn't a bad thing, and since retiring he had been involved with Gareth Jenkins at Llanelli and also at the University of Wales Institute, Cardiff (UWIC, now Cardiff Metropolitan University). We had been on courses together and also worked together in the Wales age group teams and I liked what I saw. I also brought in Alun Carter as the analyst. I knew Alun from the Wales set-up and he was also doing good work at UWIC.

In rugby terms Cardiff is perceived as the Manchester United of the Welsh game. They are known as a world famous name in the rugby world, from the southern hemisphere to the north. However, I had seen so many players with great potential go there and do nothing. A perfect example was Rob Howley. When he first went there he didn't progress and ended up going back to Bridgend to improve sufficiently for Cardiff to come knocking on his door again. Everyone can now see Rob's record as a Cardiff player in his second stint with the club and what he achieved with Wales. Cardiff had always been capable of pulling off results in big games, but they couldn't do it consistently. There were a lot of former well-known names off the pitch who just by their presence put pressure on being a Cardiff player. Great names like Jack Matthews, Bleddyn Williams and from a slightly later era, possibly the most famous of them all – Gareth Edwards. Not for one moment do I believe that they ever criticised what went on or even spoke to the players about the game "in my day...". However, many of them had seen glory days and famous performances, and now the current players felt it was their duty to be just as successful. A lot of the perception of what Cardiff should be came from the stands and the Arms Park clubhouse.

When I went to the Arms Park I inherited no less than 24 international players, but despite this, Cardiff's record over the past three seasons had been a tale of underachievement. Possibly that is down to their success in a way. The better the players in a side, the more likely they are to be selected for international teams, and therefore the fewer appearances they make for the club. Even when they return, it takes a couple of games for them and the team to adjust and they miss out on a lot of the preparation. A team with fewer international players often does better because it doesn't suffer the disruption. So players who had played for Wales in the previous three years – Derwyn Jones, Justin Thomas, Lee Jarvis, and Lyndon Mustoe – were all on the way out, while former Wales captain Mike Hall had to retire through injury. Why? Well when you move into a new club you have to make a statement that this is going to be your team and one way to do it is to get rid of senior names. Of course you don't often go to a club which has the finance to do that with such a group of players. Normally you have to keep players for as long as possible simply because the club doesn't have the money available to replace them. That wasn't a problem at Cardiff. But something had to change at the Arms Park as there hadn't been the consistency needed from a big club, and the defeat by Llanelli in the Swalec Cup semi-final the previous season had proved that point. We had to lift the standard.

When you go to a new club you have to make an impression, an impression on the players you want to keep and, in the case of Cardiff especially, an impression on the names in the clubhouse as well. Otherwise you lose it straight away. I must say I did it with a certain amount of trepidation; I was quite frightened about doing it. It was a time of uncertainty. I didn't know too much about how the club was run, about how it wanted to go forward, or what the intentions were, although I had discussed it a little when I was offered the job and I had a fair idea of what they wanted to do. So I met with people and talked to them, and was quite frank in saying that there were some people present who wouldn't be with us come the start of the season.

Derwyn Jones, the big second row, had 19 caps to his credit, but the game had moved on and rather left him behind. At 19 stone and 6ft 10in, he was too big to lift in the line-out. To me he was from a previous age. Apart from that I didn't rate him anyway. I replaced him with two players I rated highly, Craig Quinnell and Mike Voyle. Both of these guys were good scrummagers, good in the line-out, and what was an added bonus, they would front up to the opposition when the going got tough.

I also had a stroke of luck. Emyr Lewis had played 42 times for Wales, but because of a balance of numbers at number.8 I was prepared to let him go. There was no doubt in my mind that he was a good player and I rated him. Thankfully he stuck around and became an important part of the squad. I felt Mike Hall's best was behind him and was relieved in a way that he retired when he did as it saved me the task of bulleting him. Mike was great company and I am pleased to see that he has now carved out a very good job in the media.

Lee Jarvis was sacrificed to bring in Neil Jenkins. Lee was a good kicker and a good handler of the ball, but his defence was suspect. When the choice had to be made between Lee and Paul Burke, it was always going to be Burke who stayed. The clear out left us with twenty players which was never going to be enough, so we had to recruit, especially considering several players would be away with Wales not only for the Six Nations, as it was about become with the addition of Italy, but also for the impending Rugby World Cup 1999, being hosted on home soil. Some of our players could easily miss half the season so we had to recruit not just front-line players but players on short-term contracts to give us strength in depth. There was no need to take a risk and dip into the lower leagues to look for players. That didn't enter the debate at Cardiff. We could go for top international players. Also, I didn't have to get names who were just good rugby players, I could afford to be really picky and get players who I felt would fit into the style of game I wanted the team to play. I wanted the right attitude as well as the right playing quality. I went back to the English side Richmond, which had just gone bust, to get Quinnell's team mate, winger Nick Walne, who had a couple of Welsh caps under his belt.

When I had been at Pontypridd we had gone to South Africa and played the Bulls. I kept up my connections out there, and they were telling me about this youngster called Grant Esterhuizen. I spoke to Jake White and Ian McIntosh and they both confirmed his qualities and predicted that it was only a matter of time before he got a Springbok cap. I also had received good reports about him as a person and what he would bring to the squad, so as he was now the type of player I could afford, he was the perfect replacement for Mike Hall. When he came for the season he certainly wasn't a disappointment.

I knew little about the arrival of Pieter Muller, as Cardiff still had the habit of bringing in players without the knowledge of the coach. Looking at some of the failures attributed to Dai Young while he was coach at the Cardiff Blues it seems that system continued. Muller, though, was a great signing and someone I would certainly have gone for. He was a world-class player, and has contributed to Cardiff and the Blues well after my time there. Finally, in this group I added another Welshman, prop Peter Rogers. He had been playing out in South Africa and had built up a reputation as a very strong scrummager. He fitted my bill.

One other player I wanted, but we failed to get, was full back Shane Howarth. Shane, who was playing at Sale, was qualified for Wales (or so we thought), and was part of the national set-up, so I knew him well and liked what I saw. Unfortunately we lost out with Shane to the Newport Gwent Dragons.

There were still two players I wanted more than any other, and this meant going back and robbing Pontypridd. The first was Martyn Williams, and the other, of course, was Neil Jenkins. By now Dennis had left Pontypridd, so I didn't feel as guilty about ripping the two outstanding players from their squad. We were out in Argentina with Wales at the time and were joined by Peter Thomas and his brother Stan, Gareth Edwards, and Max Boyce on a round the world golf tour! I thought they had come out there because Wales were playing. Wrong, they'd just popped in to buy Buenos Aires airport, and the head of internal affairs just happened to be the famous ex-Puma fly-half Hugo Porta. They joined us at the team hotel and Peter inquired whether there were any players I would like to sign. I gave him the two names and he appeared quite surprised about my desire to get Martyn. But I had no doubt in my mind that, although he was still young, he was the best number seven in Wales at the time, and was destined to be a star. That was all that was necessary. Peter had the names of the players I wanted and so off he went to get them. It so happened that they were out in Argentina with us anyway which made his initial approaches no doubt easier, but when he returned to Wales he started negotiations with the clubs and agents. I didn't speak to either player about coming to Cardiff while we were out in South America.

It was very obvious to me that when the game went professional a transfer system like in soccer would appear on the horizon. Jenks was probably one of the most sought-after players in the UK at the time but that was the quality of player Cardiff needed, and could be in the market for. Eventually, at a cost of a reported £180,000, and with Lee Jarvis going the other way, Jenks took the same path down the A470 as I had taken and Martyn Williams was about to follow. I say a reported £180,000, as I had no dealings with the financial side of the club at all, and that was my shout. I felt that if I had been involved in paying money for players and deciding the value of their contracts, then I would be duty-bound to select them. I didn't want that restriction on my selection decisions. All I wanted to know was that the players were available. I believe those two signings, however, made teams sit up and realise that Cardiff were serious about their intention to become an outfit to be reckoned with.

I also asked Dai Young to continue as captain. I knew that he had thought a lot about taking the job when first asked by Terry Holmes twelve months previously. Now, though, he had settled into the job and I wanted him to carry on which he did.

Eventually we had a squad which included nineteen internationals to take us into the start of the season. All that now remained was to set out the stall. We hired a room in the Holiday Inn next door to the Arms Park and prepared to meet together for the first time. I brought a little of Pontypridd with me. And, as I had been impressed with something the former England soccer player Peter Reid had done when he had taken over as manager of Sunderland, I arranged for some cans to be stashed away under the table. The word had been sent out: get your wives or girlfriends to pick you up or order a taxi. I spoke about the way in which we would go about things and set out some ground rules which I considered important. But it was an exercise to get everyone feeling comfortable with each other, and I also wanted them to see me as I was, and the atmosphere that I wanted to instil around the squad. The best way to do that, I believed, was to relax and make the meeting as informal as I could. So I unveiled the cans and said, "Right, no one goes home until that lot is drunk!"

I thought it was a good idea to get everyone together, but in some eyes apparently I had made my first mistake. Some of the senior players didn't think we needed bonding. In addition, there must have been a feeling that this might have been the way they did it in the Valleys, but down here in Cardiff we don't drink bitter, we sip our gin and tonics. Finally, one of the players claimed to be annoyed because he had arranged to pick up his children from school and was forced to stay to drink beer. The whole point of the exercise was to show everyone involved that when you were with the squad, your team mates were the most important thing.

I also tried another team bonding exercise when all the players and I had a day off from World Cup training to watch the Cardiff side play Bristol in a pre-season warm up. I wanted the guys on the pitch to look and see their perhaps more illustrious team mates there in the stand watching them. The feedback I got was that the exercise worked and did help to bring the squad together, although probably there were mutterings from certain quarters which never reached my ears.

I was happy with our recruitment and I knew that we had good enough players not just in the first twenty, but as back-up as well. There were players like Mike Rayer, who took over the captaincy, and Irishman Paul Burke, who would be a more than able understudy to Neil Jenkins. These players were never going to be able to win you the Heineken Cup, but for the domestic season they were just what I wanted. This is no disrespect to these guys, because they were very good back-up players.

For a large part of the early season the club's internationals, and myself, were going to be away on Wales duty, which meant that Geraint would take over the running of the side. We agreed that I would turn up whenever I had a little time away from my international commitments. There was another problem for us to face at the start of the season as well. As Cardiff Arms Park was being used as a hospitality area for the Rugby World Cup, the pitch was going to be covered with tents and all the other trappings needed to host the functions. This wasn't going to do the grass much good after they had gone, either. So for the first nine games of the season the team played away, and it is testimony to Geraint and the players that they did as well as they did, with six wins, one draw and just two defeats, at Newport in the first game, and a thumping at Stradey Park by Llanelli.

After the opening day defeat at Rodney Parade, we then drew at Bridgend in what was a truly woeful performance. I thought carefully about what I said, but laid it on the line. We were Cardiff, we had to produce better, and if they, the players didn't, then the facilities were in place to ship them out. I wonder how that went down? We beat Neath by a single point, then came the thumping by Llanelli, the club's biggest-ever league defeat.

There was obviously complacency among some of the players in the squad who felt they had the divine right to get selected. I felt it was time to lay it on the line and circulated this letter:

A WINNING TEAM

We are going to have a rugby team. We are going to win some games. Do you know why? Because you are going to have the confidence in my system and me. By being alert, you are going to make fewer mistakes than your opponents do. By working harder, you are going to out-execute, out-tackle every team that comes your way.

I've never been a losing coach, and I don't intend to start here. There is nobody big enough to think he has made the squad or to think he can do as he wants. There are plenty of roads out of

Cardiff, and he will be on one of them. I won't. I'm going to find 32 players who have pride to make any sacrifice to win. There are such players. If they're not here, I'll get them. If you are not one of them, if you don't want to give that commitment, you might as well leave right now. I have been here for the last few months and I have learned a lot. I know how the supporters are and what they think of you and I know that in a city you need definite rules and regulations. Anybody who breaks the rules will be taken care of in my way. You may not be the best offensive player. You may not be the best defender. BUT YOU WILL BE A PROFESSIONAL.

I had often written a motivational letter to players before important matches, but I have never put a bollocking like that down on paper before or since. It must have worked, though, as everything clicked and we started winning our Celtic League matches.

I would be away again come the Six Nations, and perhaps some people thought my appointment odd given that I was going to be away for so much of that first season. But I felt that was Cardiff's problem, not mine. They knew I was part of the Wales set-up – if they were willing to offer me the job, I was willing to take it.

Our first home game was the opening Heineken Cup match against Harlequins which resulted in a 32–32 draw. A defeat in Montferrand in the second match left our campaign in tatters. Gradually, though, we got things together and produced the form I was looking for from our expensive squad, and we won four games on the trot to top the group and reach the knockout stages. The all-Welsh quarter-final at Stradey Park went the way of most Llanelli–Cardiff matches – they won 22–3 – but I was very satisfied with reaching the Heineken quarter-finals in our first year.

On the domestic front, the fixture list took on a more usual home and away format until towards the end of the season when we had a batch of home matches to catch up with, which was an advantage. Or perhaps not. The pitch was a disgrace, as it never had any time to recover from the damage left by the

World Cup hospitality tents. It was just a stinking cesspit, with very little grass and flooded by even the smallest amount of rain. We might have been one of the richest clubs in Wales, but we couldn't do anything about the weather.

We secured the Celtic League title with three games to spare after a 52–27 win against Neath, which was a bit of a bugger for poor old Dunvant. We were due to play them on the following Saturday in a game that the Welsh-language broadcaster S4C announced it would televise live. Only 1,500 bothered to turn up for a dead rubber being shown live on television and Dunvant lost a packet on bar takings.

With the Rugby World Cup done and dusted and the first season tucked away, I started to take stock of my career. There was a new young breed of coaches coming through and although I was very comfortable with my knowledge of the game and my ability to coach, I felt uneasy. They had one thing I didn't have, and that was the modern addition to the rugby knowledge and coaching ability: an academic background. The academics had got hold of rugby when the game had turned professional, and they were turning out coaches with qualifications. To be honest with myself I probably thought that my lack of an academic background made these new kids on the block a threat. From a more personal and inward point of view, I felt I was missing out on something, so I decided to get some letters after my name.

Huw Wiltshire was our conditioning coach at Cardiff and he had plenty of associations with UWIC, which had produced many a Welsh international player. Huw suggested I meet up with Lyn Evans who ran the masters course at UWIC. I met up with her and of course with Huw, who was to become my mentor, for some real soul searching. I was about to be examined in far greater depth than I imagined. I had no confidence in my academic ability, I was way out of my comfort zone, I was like a duck out of water and thoroughly intimidated by the academic environment, and we were only in the coffee bar!

Lyn thought that if I could write, if I could construct

a sentence and if I knew, or was willing to find out, how to research a topic, then I had a chance. She suggested I did an essay which she set me entitled 'Is coaching an art or a science?' Well, the title put me off for a start, but with, I can now admit, plenty of help from Huw, I jotted down a few words onto paper. That was my first mistake, as the lecturers liked their essays to be typed. I met Lyn again, after a reassuring coffee with Huw, and she gave me the option of her taking away my masterpiece and reading it, or going over it in front of me there and then with a red pen. Like a fool, I chose the latter, and as she went through my script the red pen flashed like a traffic light. Red here, red there, red every-bloody-where! I thought my chance had gone but to my surprise Lyn suggested that I could – with a great deal of help and hard work – make a fist of the course. Probably she saw that getting me through a master's degree would be as much of a challenge to her as getting through the bloody thing would be to me. We were both up for the challenge.

On the first night I met the rest of the students, after, of course, the now obligatory reassuring coffee with Huw. I felt quite intimidated meeting my fellow students. They were of student age; I was a grey-haired, gnarled and wrinkled valley boy by comparison. As it happened, after the first tentative steps by both parties, we were all good for each other. I was in awe of their academic ability, but they were in awe of the coaching experience I had under my belt. I could read the academic stuff, they couldn't read about the coaching experience I had and I had great access to players and coaches which they didn't have. Having said that, I was way out of my comfort zone with the academic work. I had to learn how to use the library, never mind what to look for. I found the academic language hard to understand, the terminology the lecturers were using was way beyond me, and then there was the problem of getting my thoughts and ideas down on paper. It was a fair exchange with my fellow students. I gave them various coaching resources and they helped me on the academic side. Huw helped me in many ways, showing me for instance how to get the best out of the library.

In the end it took me six years to complete the five-year course, but bear in mind that I was studying part-time, coaching at Cardiff, then Pontypridd, in Italy and finally Edinburgh, so it was hardly straightforward. In the end various people including Lyn, Huw and Jeromin persuaded me to finish the course and I am glad I did. It really has boosted my self-esteem and now I rarely feel overawed by anyone. Not only can I offer my coaching experience and skills, but no one can doubt my academic background either. Lynn Howells MSc has some clout, not that I ever add the letters to my name.

How did the course help my coaching? Well, I possibly got more out of it than the youngsters did. All the time I could relate exercises to incidents I had been involved in. It taught me to become very self-critical and also to think more critically. I analysed everything I did far more, and I also became more precise in the way I expressed myself. I started to put plenty of what I learned into practice in dealing with man-management issues. Before the course, when meeting with players to discuss their progress, I would start by asking questions, not knowing, to be honest, where the conversation would go, or what I was going to get out of it. Now, however, I give the player a questionnaire and ask them to rate themselves out of ten against a top-class player. How do they compare on fitness, ball handling, scrummaging for the forwards, even down to things like timekeeping, commitment and reliability. It's interesting that players always tend to mark themselves lower than I would, but the scores start the conversation, and questions can flow both ways. The players get far more out of it, I get far more out of it, but I would never have thought about doing things that way before doing the master's course.

My graduation day at St David's Hall in Cardiff was certainly special. I actually didn't want to go but Jeromin pushed me down the road and I am glad she did. There were hundreds of people there collecting certificates for things like catering, degrees in tourism, therapy, maths and sciences: they came up one after another for what seemed like hours. There were just a dozen of us receiving a master's degree. I was one of a dozen people who had reached a high academic standard and this brought home to me what I had achieved. If I hadn't gone that day I would never have realised that.

The fact that I was coaching at Cardiff did probably have something to do with my decision to do the course, but I would have wanted to do it had I been at Pontypridd, Treherbert or any other club. It was something I wanted to do if only to prove to myself that I could do it. It proved that I could study, that I could better myself, and that I wasn't just that dull boy from North Road School. Unfortunately, it probably didn't help me during the time I was at Cardiff. It was too late. By the time I graduated I am certain that some Cardiff players really rated me and others would never accept me.

In our second season in Europe we had an even tougher group, containing Saracens, Toulouse and Ulster. We knew all about Ulster from the Celtic League, but lost to them at Ravenhill, and also lost out in Toulouse. We won the other four games to top the group and reach the quarter-finals for a second time. This time we faced Gloucester at Kingsholm, a game we should have won, but lost 21–15. Several of the players came off the pitch seething as the referee Joël Jutge had crucified us in the scrums. Nick Walne and Gareth Thomas had scored tries but Gloucester had won by kicking seven penalties. Dai Young was up against Trevor Woodman and he was penalised time after time by the French referee. Interestingly the following week Woodman came on against Dai for England against Wales in the Six Nations. Dai minced him by doing exactly the same things as he had been penalised for the previous week, all of which were perfectly within the laws. I remember the former England football manager Graham Taylor saying that decisions made during a game by a referee could cost him his job and I honestly think the performance of Mr Jutge that day was the beginning of the end for me.

From then on, I think the pressure associated with Cardiff began to weigh down on me. At Cardiff we were expected to win the Celtic League and the most coveted piece of silverware was the Heineken Cup. That was the one that those in the clubhouse and those in the stands were after and if you couldn't deliver that trophy as a coach, your time was limited. Losing that quarter-final, I believe, was a huge turning point for me.

I realised over the summer that major personnel changes were necessary for the squad. Big-name players like Rob Howley and Jonathan Humphreys were coming to the end of their careers at Cardiff. I think those players actually recognised they were in decline. Paul Burke, too, was going to Leicester. What I had not envisaged were the exits of Leigh Davies and Gareth Thomas. They were to be shown the door as they had let the club down in a bar in Cardiff. Bob Norster alerted me to the problem and my first reaction was to think that we had all done mad things in bars. Initially I didn't think it was being particularly well handled by the committee, but when I saw the CCTV pictures of the two players urinating off the tables outside a bar in the centre of Cardiff it was a case of "Ah... yes... well, perhaps." So Alfie went off to Bridgend and Leigh joined Llanelli.

We had also introduced several young players from the under-21 side with considerable success. Rhys Williams had made such an impression at full back that he was capped after just 16 first-team games for Cardiff. His debut against Ireland in Dublin was a dream. Jamie Robinson was another, and I would later give him his first cap on the tour to Japan. There were others in the pipeline too: Ryan Powell, Gary Powell, Owain Ashman and a dozen others all under the age of 21. We had also improved the consistency of the team, things were looking good. But I had a two-year contract, and that two years was about to come to an end. I felt I had done well enough reaching two quarter-finals in my first two years, particularly considering the fact that we should have beaten Gloucester in that second season. I asked the natural question, "What is happening about my contract?" but the vibes I got back were sufficient for me to get the picture. Peter Thomas told me that I was going to have to re-apply for my job. That told me everything. If I had been what they wanted, I would have had my contract extended without any further discussion. I speculated that they were seeking a bigger name and that I was being kept in reserve in case that person didn't sign. It indicated to me that I was clearly their second choice. No thanks! Either I was good enough or I wasn't. I certainly wasn't going to re-apply for my job – they could stuff it.

I think that Cardiff, with all their high-profile players, their history, and their grand ambitions, wanted a big name as their coach. It didn't really matter how successful a guy from the Valleys had been. Unless he delivered the Heineken Cup he was history. Lynn Howells was never going to be a big enough name. Even if I had won them the Heineken Cup I doubt whether I would ever have been accepted there. But have Cardiff been a fantastic success since I left?

Looking back, now, I know I have been criticised for bringing too much of the Wales system to the Arms Park. I accept some of that criticism, but there were so many Welsh internationals in our Cardiff squad. What was the point of making them learn another system, another set of moves and another game plan? The one thing I would say is that you can't do the two jobs, that is coach Wales and a club or region. I think in more recent times Shaun Edwards has found it very hard working with Wales and still being director of rugby at Wasps. Having said that, I don't think that being involved with Wales cost me the Cardiff job – I just think that I was not a big enough name. I still think that there were too many people who held too much sway in Cardiff, and that the people upstairs listened to them too much and too often. Mike Hall was keen to tell the world that during the World Cup, when I was away with Wales, he should have been used to help out. Well, what would Geraint have thought of that if I had brought him in? He would have been quite right to think I didn't have any confidence in him or didn't trust him fully to do the job.

I had discussed players' contracts with those that dealt with those matters, only to find out that players we had agreed to sign for one year had been given a contract for three, just because he had been a loyal Cardiff man. And finally, there was the part played by certain other players. One of the board of directors, Alan Peterson, threw a barbecue at his home towards the end of the season. Peter Thomas was there, as were the coaches and backroom staff and of course all the players. Peter is reported to have mentioned to one of the senior players that things appeared to be going well and that my contract was about to be renewed, at which point the player informed him that if that was the case he would have a players' revolt on his hands.

There were people at Cardiff, on both the playing and coaching staff, who were loyal and whom I trust to this day. If Geraint or Huw had heard of any backstabbing or deliberately subversive disruption, I would have known about it from them. They tell me that whatever was going on was kept very low-key and very quiet. I know players like Dai Young were approached to join the group to try to oust me. Dai told them he didn't want anything to do with it. Jon Humphreys, on the other hand, would freely admit that he wasn't happy with the way things were being done. He doesn't admit to being party to any knifing in the back or whispering in corners of the dressing room, but he freely admits that he would not distance himself from those who wanted me out. I respect his honesty, just like I respect Dai's integrity. Other players have not been as honest as Humph, and have hidden behind complimentary comments about me. I know who they are, and who the main one was in particular, and I wish I could print his name here.

When I had driven down the road from home to Cardiff on that first day as Cardiff coach, I had been full of optimism, full of excitement. Driving back up after the last day I was full of bitterness. I was never given a rugby reason why my contract wasn't renewed. If someone had said to me from a coaching point of view you are not doing this or that, or my man management wasn't good enough or whatever, at least there would have been a reason. I might not have agreed with it but in this case I was never given a reason. For me it was time to move out, and at least they didn't push me.

9

The
Comfort of Home

WAS I SAD to leave Cardiff? Well, I was sad to leave most of the players and management and I was grateful to Cardiff for having given me the opportunity to become a director of rugby. But I was glad to be leaving the environment that Cardiff created and disappointed that I hadn't been given the opportunity to finish the job I had started.

I must have done something right on the club scene, though, because I had a call from Leicester. It didn't come direct to me but through my agent. Leicester was to English rugby what Cardiff was to Wales, with the only difference being that the Tigers were winning leagues and cups whereas Cardiff wasn't. My first reaction, rather like the approach from Cardiff was to wonder in what capacity they wanted me. Again the answer was as coach. To have a call like that just at that time really lifted my spirits. I didn't want to leave Wales, and was still involved with the Wales set-up, so a move up there would have been difficult. It would not have been the right move for me at the time so I backed off, but I was grateful for the offer.

It wasn't a bad position to be in. I was still employed by Wales. I had enough money to live on and didn't have to rush into anything. In October 2001, I had a call from Clive Jones, who had recently been appointed director of rugby at Pontypridd. We met up at the Rhondda Heritage Park in Hopkinstown, about a mile up the valley from Pontypridd. It turned out to be an offer to return to Sardis Road as coach, as things appeared to be slipping away under the current coach Richie Collins. Obviously returning to Ponty was appealing because it was my old club, and I had enjoyed success there with Dennis John; but I still wasn't in a rush to go anywhere.

Time was on my side, but I must admit I was impressed with the plans Clive had for the club with the academy, and the involvement of the valley. His thinking proved to be ahead of its time as this was the way the regions were expected to go when they were set up a couple of years later. Ponty, thanks to sponsors Buy As You View, already had a foothold in the Valleys with the development officers that were being put into place.

There was just something gnawing away in my head which stopped me jumping straight in and taking the job. The experience of coaching both club and country at Cardiff was telling me that this was not the right environment to put myself and my family into again. In the end, though, my heart ruled my head and I agreed to take up the offer, and I started back at Sardis Road in November 2001. Things had not gone well for the club. After winning the first game of the season at Bridgend, Ponty had suffered six straight defeats in the Celtic League, before a win over Caerphilly. In the European Shield they'd lost out in Beziers and then beaten Parma at Sardis Road. The Celtic fixtures then resumed with defeat in Edinburgh. That was the final nail in the coffin for Richie, his last game as coach.

There is no doubt that the club was very different from the one I had left two and a half years previously. It had two more years of professionalism under its belt, and Clive had done a good job putting into place everything a professional set-up needed. The players were training full time, but possibly the most important thing was that players were coming through the system. They were coming through the academy and being spotted in Valleys sides and brought to Pontypridd. Matthew Rees came from Tonyrefail into the academy in 2000–01 and became an important part of the first-team squad in 2001. Later he went on to captain his country and play for the British Lions. Players were being looked at with a view to the future, so that if we needed a second row in three years' time, we knew who would be the likely candidates. Ian Evans was another who fell into that category and was destined to play for Wales.

The more I think about it the more I realise that this was the future of Welsh rugby, and this was the model which should have been adapted instead of the way regional rugby was introduced a couple of years later. The smaller clubs in the area feed into the bigger club, with no great upheaval of the game, no great financial burden on the WRU and no feeling in the small clubs that they are being raped of their talent. If the player is not used he goes back to play for his club of origin, giving him the opportunity to play meaningful, regular rugby. If there were four, eight, ten big clubs in Wales, then that was because there were enough players coming through the system to sustain that number. As it is now I don't believe there is anything in place to encourage a progression of players. There aren't any goals for them to aim at; nothing to encourage them to try and better themselves. If a player isn't spotted and taken into one of the academies, then he appears now to be lost to the game.

The strange thing is that Clive was often asked to attend the Welsh Rugby Union to enlighten them as to what was going on at Pontypridd, so they appeared to be buying into the system, only to ignore it when the moment came to set up the regions. The system put in place by Ponty certainly helped me in my year as the regional coach at the Warriors.

Some people found Clive difficult to get on with, but he was very good at his job. So in the end the decision to rejoin Pontypridd was pretty easy. The club had ambition, and it had development coming through. There were still things to work on, but I thought, yes, let's go for it.

Looking at the team, things were promising. Several of the players who had been on the fringes of a first-team place when

I left were now established names on the Pontypridd team sheet. Others had broken through such as Duncan Bell, Gethin Jenkins, Michael Owen, Richard Parks, Rob Sidoli, and Ceri Sweeney, and Mefin Davies had joined from Neath. All those players were or would be Welsh internationals, apart from Bell who played for his native England. Gethin, or 'Mellon' as most people in rugby know him, had for some reason been sent out on loan to Treorchy, so I had to fetch him back pretty sharpish. Why he had been sent out I could never figure out, because even then he was a talented player. Some of the older names like captain Dale McIntosh, Paul John and Gareth Wyatt were still playing, and I also inherited a Fijian international fly-half in Nicky Little. What sticks in my mind about Nicky is his place-kicking. No matter where he kicked the ball from – from his 25, out wide, in front of the sticks or from the halfway line – every kick cleared the crossbar by the same distance. He did just enough and no more to get his kicks over, and what's more he could play the guitar and sing. We enjoyed his company. So with Nicky and Brett Davey we had two good goal kickers, and there was a nice mixture of experienced and fresh-faced players in the squad.

Everything was there, it was just a case of working on the game plan, and making sure that everyone bought into the same idea. My first game back as coach was the Parker Pen Shield game away at Leeds. Leeds were in the English Premiership, but were never up there with the likes of Wasps and Leicester. They were beatable, but we weren't helped by Gethin Jenkins and Nick Kelly receiving yellow cards. We lost 30–27, but the following week back at Sardis Road we beat them 28–16 to progress in the second string European competition. From there on things went well. We lost just seven matches between me taking over and the end of the season. One of those defeats came in the Parker Pen Shield final against Sale, who were second in the English Premiership, just a week after we had beaten Llanelli 20–17 to win the Welsh Cup.

We got to the Parker Pen Shield final having played a game

less than Sale, due to a farce of a situation involving a frozen pitch at Parma. Three-quarters of the pitch was fine, but from one 22 to the try line it was still rock hard. We said we wouldn't play, they said it was fit. I was adamant, as only the week before a player in the English Premiership had been badly injured playing on a frozen pitch, and in the end the game was called off. According to the rules the fixture then had be played on a neutral ground, but in their wisdom the organisers of the tournament came up with Kingsholm in Gloucester. Fair play to the Italians, how that was ever a neutral ground I will never understand. Parma had a couple of English boys playing for them, and they contacted some of our players and told them there was no way Parma were going to turn up. Nevertheless we still had to go through the rigmarole of going to Gloucester, changing into our kit, taking to the pitch and actually kicking off before the tie was awarded to us.

I think we would have beaten Parma wherever we had played them, but it put us through to a match against Francois Pienaar's Saracens which we won, and then a semi-final against London Irish who the week before had won the English Premiership title. Winning there 33–27 was a fantastic result for us, but as with our cup game against Llanelli, the semi-final might have come too close to their big win. One thing which sticks in my mind about that game was the tackle Jonny Bryant put in on the South African centre Brendan Venter. When their talisman was pole-axed in that manner it changed the game. At times a tackle of that magnitude at a particular time in a match is as important as a try. I don't think many people expected us to beat the English champions, but it put us into the final against Sale.

The win over London Irish came at a cost. Our squad was good, but we didn't have enough strength in depth to withstand the big games which were now coming thick and fast. We were so thin on the ground that we had played scrum half Gareth Baber on the wing against the Irish, and fourteen of our starting team had played the whole game. It was no surprise to me that we lost our next two Celtic League games against Neath and Newport. We did manage to beat Edinburgh, and our Welsh Cup win was only the second in the club's history. But you can guess how much that took out of the players. They were buggered.

For the Parker Pen Shield final we went to the Kassam Stadium in Oxford to play Sale, the team second in the English Premiership table, with a game plan which I must say raised a few eyebrows. One of the biggest names in English rugby at the time was Jason Robinson or Billy Wizz. Our plan was to kick the ball to him, which people thought was suicide. Why kick the ball to the opposition's biggest threat? Well, that was just the point. If we could pin him with the ball, it cut out Sale's most potent weapon. If we let him run at us off a pass he would do damage. It worked well, and we led 15–3 at half time. However three quick tries by Sale allowed them back into the game and while Brett Davey kept us in touch with his kicking, as the game wore on you could see the boys were tired. Unfortunately we gave away too many penalties, and Charlie Hodgson punished us to see his side home 25–22. After the game we went back out from the dressing room to find almost the whole Pontypridd contingent in the 12,000 crowd were still there. They started singing 'Always look on the bright side of life', which was absolutely amazing.

It would be nice to think that on my return to Pontypridd I worked a miracle, but it wasn't like that really. I inherited a team with little or no belief in themselves, and one that lacked any kind of organization. I arrived to find there were good players, and there were people there who played their part, such as Steve Richards the conditioning coach, Mike Griffiths was the scrummaging coach and Steele Lewis the backs coach. I kept all of those guys on and added Gary Jones as the team manager. There was no game plan. It was all very bitty. But nothing really changed apart from the belief and the organization. Some of the Valleys commando mentality – the relationship between the team and the supporters – had gone and I think that was down to the team losing. But it didn't take an awful lot though to get that back, and the scenes after the Parker Pen final against Sale showed that it was there again.

I felt I was back home. The difference between Cardiff and Pontypridd was that at Cardiff you got people in to clean the stadium, to mend the seats and do those kinds of jobs. At Pontypridd this was done by former players or older members. You could go there in the morning, have a cup of tea with them and learn that they were doing it for nothing. That was the way the club was. These people were Pontypridd members and I think all that adds to a club. They feel part of the club, and mingle with the players, and for me it was a comfortable feeling.

So I was home and ready to embark on my first full season in charge. Little did any of us know what was around the corner. The first big bonus of that 2002–03 season was the return of Neil Jenkins. I think he had had enough of the new regime at Cardiff Arms Park. Rudy Joubert had been appointed as my successor, and from what people have told me, just six months after my departure those who opened the exit door for me were wishing they hadn't. Jenks didn't need much persuading to come back up the A470 to feel the comfort of Sardis Road. We had a good foundation to build on: the Welsh Cup win and the defeat of three English sides on the way to the Parker Pen final. We felt good going into the season but defeat out in Leinster soon knocked us back. After that though we went on a run of nine unbeaten games in the league and the Parker Pen. We were playing in two domestic competitions as the Celtic League and the Welsh League were run as separate competitions. We lost two games between the start of the season and the turn of the year, then the WRU dropped their regional rugby bombshell.

We continued to do pretty well in the leagues, and in the Parker Pen we reached the semi-final where we came up against Wasps. Once again the depth of the squad, or the lack of it, cost us, as injuries started to mount. Sonny Parker broke his arm against Connacht, while Paul John was injured and missed the home and away legs against Wasps. In previous meetings he had always had the upper hand against Rob Howley, but I am sorry to say this time Howley had little trouble, which upset me after what had gone on in Cardiff. At Pontypridd we just didn't have the money to build a strong squad and when our success was reflected in eight of the squad being included in the Wales squad – Mefin Davies, Gethin and Neil Jenkins, Michael Owen, Sonny Parker, Richard Parks, Ceri Sweeney and Rob Sidoli – our resources were stretched. How did we have so many players of that quality? Simple, they wanted to play for Pontypridd. Most of them could have gone elsewhere and been paid far more money than we were paying them, but they turned their backs on the riches, because they were local boys, and playing for Pontypridd was worth a great deal more than finance.

By the end of April it was confirmed that regional rugby would signal the end of Pontypridd as we knew it. That made the remaining league games rather meaningless and, coupled with our injuries, the season came to a messy end. We sat down and decided that as the senior players had their minds on other things, we would chuck in some youngsters. Any player from the academy or the under-21s who we thought had a chance of making it we would put into the team. Some of them played well enough and grasped the opportunity to grab a contract with a region. Ian Evans was one, Richard Fussell was another, as was hooker Duane Goodfield, but for such a close-knit club which had seen such fantastic results it was a sad end.

From just about the turn of the year onwards the talk on everybody's lips was the debate about regional rugby. I am certain it affected Pontypridd more than any of the other teams. The reason I say that is because the likes of Cardiff and Llanelli were going to stay as they were. There never at any time appeared to be a chance of Pontypridd standing on its own or being one of the regions. It is fair to say there was a feeling of, sod it, we won't be here next season as players and management, and there won't be a Pontypridd as we know it. There was certainly a different attitude and a different feeling, and as much as you tried to motivate things, it was nigh on impossible. During that time it would also be fair to question my own attitude and my commitment. In any other season the results and performances we were getting would have hurt. Now it didn't hurt.

As much as I tried to hold things together there was always that worry at the back of players' minds about a contract for the next season. Who would the regions be? Where would the regions be? Once it became obvious that regional rugby was going to happen then people started to worry, and not just the players, the coaching staff as well. I was thinking about whether I wanted to be a regional coach. Was there going to be a job for me at the end of the season? And the fitness coaches, the medical staff and the team managers were all thinking along the same lines. Minds, including mine, were not on what they should have been focused on, no matter how hard I tried. The dressing room wasn't the same, the preparation wasn't the same. You can't just turn up on a Saturday and expect to play like the old amateur days. There has to be a build-up through the week for the game on the Saturday.

Once everything was sorted out then we had the problem of where the players were going to go. Who was getting a contract with our region? Who was going to have to look around and hope they got something somewhere else? Then there were those who weren't going to be given a contract at all, and all the time I expected them to be giving 100 per cent to Pontypridd. It was not a good time.

I suppose I was grasping at straws, but I thought there had to be and always would be a Valleys side. I clung onto that for as long as I could until they came up with the way it was going to be split up. Off the field the club committees discussed the prospects. For us on the playing side, I don't think we ever had a chance of altering the way things would go. I don't think we could have influenced anything.

I will freely admit that I found it difficult to focus; it was difficult not to think of other things. I still had the family to consider, and my biggest thought at this time was whether I wanted to stay with Pontypridd. Would I be happy not coming up against the Leinsters, the Munsters, the Cardiffs, the big sides from Europe, and the quality of the players they brought with them? No one thought that Pontypridd would cease to exist, but we all knew deep down that Pontypridd was going to change; the standard of the game was going to go. That was the biggest thing I had to come to terms with. Obviously I wanted a region.

I shared the belief of Henry, and Hansen and the others who pushed the case for regional rugby, who were saying that if you got the best players into a smaller number of teams, it would benefit Welsh rugby. It would give us a better chance in the Heineken Cup which had become the main northern hemisphere competition, and would also benefit the national side. Where I disagreed was the way they were going to do it. It may seem daft to say it, but there is far more to a region than just the team. You need the market, you need the support, and you need the structure. So once I had made that decision I started planning my future. Just like everyone else around the place, I wasn't giving 100 per cent to Pontypridd either. It was a difficult time for me, but I keep coming back to how it must have felt for the players. They must have been in bits.

Did Cardiff have the same feelings as us? Did they hell. They were staying as Cardiff; they had got what they wanted whether it was by negotiation or bullying the WRU. Cardiff were meant to be called the Blues under the new regional regime, but it took them a bloody long time to drop the Cardiff and call themselves the Blues. To be fair, plenty of people still call them Cardiff despite the years which have passed. It was the same in Newport. The Dragons were the regional team in Gwent, but it took a long, long time for the Newport to be dropped as they insisted on calling themselves the Newport Gwent Dragons. At least Pontypridd and Bridgend were called the Warriors from the outset, as the Neath and Swansea amalgamation was called the Ospreys from the start.

Another thing which hurt the Pontypridd fans was that they had stayed financially viable throughout all the years of professional rugby. They had lived within their means. The same could not be said of Llanelli. They had been forced to borrow money from the WRU but they were being allowed to remain as a single region. It was a strange feeling going to the other clubs at this time. I felt sorry for Caerphilly. They had no idea which region they would be in. Just a couple of years previously Swansea had been playing in England during the rebel season. Neath were very much akin to Ponty. They felt the same as we did.

We had two final games that season. The final home game against Llanelli, which we won, and the final game of the season at Cardiff. The Llanelli game was the worst as we knew we would never play as Pontypridd as we knew it at Sardis Road again. The changing room was pretty dull, I don't think there was much celebrating of the win over Llanelli that night. With a new era on the horizon you might have expected people to be relieved and excited, but they weren't. Even those players who had got contracts and whose futures were secure were not excited. I had a contract, I had my region, but I certainly wasn't happy and celebrating.

Looking back I think a big mistake was made and I think there might be quite a few people in the blazers and on the committees of the Welsh Rugby Union who would agree, if they were honest, that a mistake was made. It has not worked out the way people expected or hoped it would. The debate surrounding overseas players still rumbles on. There is no development in place after almost a decade of regional rugby. Has the standard improved? I think not. Cardiff got to the first ever European Cup final where they were beaten by Toulouse, and have since won the Amlin Cup. Pontypridd got to the Parker Pen final where they lost to Sale, but these have been the only occasions when Welsh teams have reached European finals and no one else has been close. Tell me that is an improvement.

10

Making History with Wales

No matter what a coach achieves with his club or region, coaching at national level has to be the highlight of his career. It certainly was for me. I suppose my coaching career was something like the progression of a player from the smallest club right through to the international scene. It was a tough road from Tylorstown to Osaka but, God, was I proud. Players will tell you that when you stand in line at the start of an international match and hear 'Hen Wlad Fy Nhadau' then the hairs on the back of your neck start to bristle. Well, believe me, for a Welshman standing there as a coach it is exactly the same feeling.

I have never been lucky enough to do what some people have done and that is go straight in at the top. My coaching career has been a series of progressions, and I have had to work hard at whatever level I have been at to move up to the next level. There have also been sacrifices, mostly on the family front as I have had to spend a lot of time away from home with squads and matches.

I started to become involved in the Wales set-up when I was coaching the first time at Pontypridd in the 1996–97 season. I had done my apprenticeship, I suppose, with the district teams, and their under-21s against New Zealand had been a success. I had also done some of the elite player and coaching courses, so I was starting to become noticed and recognised in the coaching establishment. Terry Cobner made the call, and I was chuffed, to say the least, to be asked to become involved in the Wales set-up at any level. It was another punch-the-air moment.

Back then I was working with Mike Gossling, and it's interesting to look back at how we worked compared with the set-up today. It was simply Mike and I plus John Perkins, the team manager, and a committee man. These days there must be a cast of dozens looking after the age group teams. Not then.

When I coached the Celtic Warriors I had to up my level and standard of coaching, just as I had done when I joined Dennis at Pontypridd, and when I joined the under-21s. When you coached at club level it was Tuesday and Thursday evenings, and then you came in for the game on a Saturday. With the under-21s we would meet up on a Friday night before a game and it was a case of how you used that extra time. Players were obviously from different clubs, so we had to mould those individuals into a team and a unit. We also had more time to work on tactics and patterns. On the night before a game we got stuck into the flip charts to make sure everyone remembered their jobs, and then there was the captain's meeting.

It was an interesting period because it was the first stage at which the age groups, the schools and the youth came together in one team, and for us it was fairly successful. One game sticks in my mind more than the others and that was the game against France in Paris. We played at the old stadium, the Stade de Colombes. It was here that they filmed the soccer match in *Escape to Victory*, when the players including Pele and Bobby Moore all escaped through a hole dug in the bath. It was also the first time I had been involved in a game on foreign soil with the national set-up. It was an experience to say the least. The French police escorted us on the coach journey from the hotel to the stadium, and the outriders were ruthless. They were kicking and bashing cars out of the way. There was no 'excuse me' with them. They were on a roll and nothing was going to stop them.

The following season I stepped up again, this time to the A team, and now I was the head coach so I was certainly progressing. I had coaches working under me, one of them being Geraint John. It was a relationship which was going to last a good few years. Again it was a successful time, culminating in the win over England at Leicester's Welford Road. It was the first time a Wales A team had beaten their English counterparts on English soil, and something sticks in my mind from the journey home. I was in the car with David Pickering, and it was just a throwaway line from Dai when he said, "Now you have done that I bet they will be onto you to join the national set-up." It was only a tongue in cheek comment, and little did either of us realise that within a couple of months the call would come.

Wales had a terrible Five Nations in 1998. The Arms Park was being demolished to make way for what was to become the Millennium Stadium, so Wales' 'home' matches were played at the home of English soccer – Wembley. Whether that had any effect on the results, I don't know, but Wales lost 60–26 to England at Twickenham, beat Scotland at Wembley and Ireland at Lansdowne Road, before getting thrashed 51–0 by France back at Wembley.

Record defeats by England and France in the same season meant the writing was on the wall for coach Kevin Bowring, who was promptly sacked. At that point Dennis John was asked to take the tour to South Africa, and I had a phone call from Terry Cobner to go as his assistant. Even though I was coaching with Dennis at Pontypridd, it was Terry who phoned me as everything to do with coaching went through him. Dennis knew they were going to ask me, in fact he may have had something to do with it, but he was pretty good at keeping the lid on things and making sure they were done the right way.

It was a thrill to be asked to join the national team, and to go abroad was something special again. So far there had been exciting moments but being asked to become one of the coaches with Wales was the biggest thing that had happened to me. Working with Dennis would be the easy part, as we were coaching together at Ponty. But, as he said, we were now going to have to lift our level of performance again. Dennis had some experience of coaching at national level as he had moved ahead of me from the A team to the senior team, but little did we know what was in store for us. Some players quite frankly took the decision that with the way the recent results had gone, and with South Africa being at that time probably the best side in the world, this was a good tour to miss. I can imagine quite a few players thinking this tour would not do their careers any good at all. That is something I just cannot comprehend. It was a chance to go on tour with the national team, a chance to play for Wales. After all, why do we start to play the game if the ultimate goal is not to play for your country? Rob Howley, who had been Kevin Bowring's captain in the championship season, wrote an article in the *Wales on Sunday* in effect saying that he felt it was crazy sending out a Wales team on a tour of that intensity.

Some players had genuine injuries. Howley, Scott Gibbs, Neil Jenkins and Ieuan Evans had all toured with the Lions the previous season, and all had suffered injuries. But some were afraid to go to South Africa, it's as simple as that. Others realised it was a tour to avoid. Players were dropping out in droves. It is easy to make up an injury. Who is going to say that a player is lying? It had been a long, hard twelve months for some of the senior players, but you can't just ring up a nation's rugby union and say, sorry, we've had a few hard months, we won't be coming.

There was another problem as well – payment. Arguments took place between the players and the WRU, and those weren't resolved until the moment we left. The players would be getting £1,500 per man and that was it. There were bonuses but, with the squad we had, the players didn't feel much chance of hitting the £500 extra if they beat Zimbabwe, Emerging Springboks, Natal and Borders. There was even less chance, they thought, of pocketing the £1,000 for beating South Africa for the first time ever in the one-off Test match. Rob Howley, if I recall the situation correctly, was less than excited about the appointment of Dennis and myself as coaches. He was the one to push the discussions with the WRU. Well, fair enough, he was one of the senior players going on the tour, and he was the captain, so maybe it was right for him to speak for the squad. Rob has never been one to sit back and keep quiet if he thinks there is a cause to fight for. Andy Moore, Garin Jenkins and Arwel Thomas were other players who I believe said their penny's worth, but believe me there were players on that tour who would have played for nothing.

We were due to meet at the Copthorne Hotel just outside Cardiff and discussions were still going on as departure time approached. Dennis and I didn't know when, or even if, we would be leaving. In the end the players were persuaded by Terry Cobner and team manager Trevor James to get onto the bus. With the promise that the WRU committee would discuss their concerns, and a fax would be sent out with the committee's decision, we set off straight for the airport and the flight to Zimbabwe, our first destination. Something similar happened in 2003 when a dispute over payments for a tour to New Zealand resulted in the squad missing the plane, and having to catch a flight the following day. For our tour in 1998 it was just another setback, another frustration, another upset. It didn't bode well. It would have been difficult enough for established coaches, but for Dennis and I, having to put other things in place like training programmes, styles of play, etc., it was virtually an impossible task.

Even when we got out to Africa the problems weren't over. Following our win over Zimbabwe the fax arrived and, as expected, the offer hadn't been improved. Also there was a loophole in the contract and some of the players were astute enough to spot it. Once a player had taken part in three matches on the tour he was automatically entitled to the maximum £1,500. Well, once players had reached this 'target' the treatment table was busy again and there were more flights home. One of the forwards' parting shot was, "See you when you get home. I'm off, you can stay and fight." We knew what was going on, but what can you do? You can't tell a player he isn't injured. It doesn't sit with me that you would give up the chance of touring with your country and fake an injury. There were players on that tour, and players who pulled out of the tour, who thought more about themselves and what they could get out of it than the benefits to the national team.

I can look back now and admit that I missed the messages that were coming from some of the players, but this was the professional age when money mattered. This was my first tour as part of the national team. I was in a rugby-mad country like South Africa, and I was just overawed by it all. They really looked after us. There was the usual round of functions and off-the-field events to attend, and for me it was just an amazing experience.

The difference between Zimbabwe and South Africa was immense. There were a lot of poor people in Zimbabwe and even then it was a shambles of a place. Before the game, people who were living in the dressing rooms had to be moved out. There was something else which stuck in my memory about the build-up. Two of the paratroopers who were to hang-glide into the stadium before the game missed the field and smacked into the concrete wall at the end of the ground.

We beat Zimbabwe 49–11, so at least we won the first game, but from there on it was downhill. We lost to the Emerging Springboks, Borders and Natal, so our chances against the full Springbok side were slim.

By the time we played in Pretoria we were down to the bare bones of an already thin squad. We had lost Rob Howley with a genuine hamstring injury in the Natal game, and we took the field with a XV which was little better than a decent club side, albeit one that could not be criticised for lack of effort. They just were not good enough to take on the world's best team. Paddy O'Brien, the referee, didn't help much either as some of his decisions didn't do us any favours. Just for comparison I have listed below the team which played against France in the last game of the championship season, and the team we put out against South Africa.

Wales 0 France 51	South Africa 96 Wales 13
15 Kevin Morgan	Byron Hayward
14 Wayne Proctor	Dafydd James
13 Neil Boobyer	Mark Taylor
12 Leigh Davies	John Funnell
11 Gareth Thomas	Garan Evans
10 Neil Jenkins	Arwel Thomas
9 Rob Howley capt.	Paul John
1 Andrew Lewis	Mike Griffiths
2 Garin Jenkins	Barry Williams
3 Dai Young	John Davies
4 Mike Voyle	Ian Gough
5 Andy Moore	Andy Moore
6 Rob Appleyard	Nathan Thomas
7 Colin Charvis	Colin Charvis
8 Stuart Davies	Kingsley Jones

Replacements: Darrill Williams, Stephen Jones, Darren Morris, Garin Jenkins, Geraint Lewis, David Llewellyn and Chris Wyatt.

Some of those players went on to have decent international and club careers, but at that time they were young and inexperienced. Stephen Jones won his first Welsh cap as a replacement in Pretoria, and he went on to win 103 more. Colin Charvis and Andy Moore have captained Wales as well, but others like Paul John, John Davies, Mike Griffiths, John Funnell, Byron Hayward and Kingsley Jones, wouldn't be seen around Wales' squads any more.

Dennis and I knew we had little chance of winning, but we

tried to give the players the idea that they had a chance. We were 30-odd points down by half time, but humiliation wasn't on the cards. We thought we could keep the score to reasonable proportions. But when they just ran in tries at will we felt sorry for the players. As a coach you don't feel for yourself, as you will get over it, But for the players it can have a lasting detrimental effect on their careers.

That 96–13 scoreline is etched in Welsh rugby history. Never before or since has a Welsh team conceded so many points, so as a coach you definitely think your chances of staying in the job or progressing have gone. I didn't believe I had any chance of becoming the Wales coach even before we left for South Africa; I thought Dennis might, but not me. Mike Ruddock was being mentioned as the next coach, and there was even a thought that they might go outside Wales to appoint someone. You never knew with the WRU what they were thinking or which way they would jump.

As I was going on to New Zealand on a fact-finding mission after the South Africa tour, I didn't kop the full force of the media reaction when the boys got home. The WRU sent myself, Leigh Jones, who was coaching at Newport, David Pickering and Geraint John with the task of finding out how New Zealand rugby was run, and in particular the Auckland Blues as they were the top team at the time. We had to pinch a few ideas and bring them back to Wales.

The journey to Auckland involved a stopover night in Australia. Determined to see as much of Sydney as I could, I dragged Leigh around to the opera house and a few of the sights. Then it was time to find something to eat, so we had a walk around the harbour area, as you do, looking for a decent restaurant. We wandered into one to have the shock of our lives. There, sitting around a table, were WRU chairman Glanmor Griffiths, secretary Dennis Gethin, Terry Cobner, and Graham Henry. What happened next was like a scene from the circus. Dennis put his hands up to his face and said, "Oh no!" Glanmor tried to hide by putting his hands over his eyes and pretending that if he couldn't see us we couldn't see him. Terry Cobner just jumped up and called us over. Graham Henry didn't know who we were. We were introduced to Graham and then sworn to secrecy by Terry, Glanmor and Dennis, as we knew what we had stumbled onto. Graham was being sounded out to become the next Wales coach. The temptation not to ring home and tell everyone was immense I can tell you.

Leigh and I did obviously discuss what we had witnessed, although at that point we didn't know whether Graham would accept the offer, but we both agreed that something had to be done in Welsh rugby, and all credit to the WRU for exploring every option. As it happened, when Leigh and I flew to Auckland the next day, Graham was on the same flight, and came over to chat to us. He showed his witty side by reminding us that South Africa had beaten Wales 96–3: "A little bit unfortunate, mate," was his take on the result. He explained that he would be out of Auckland with the New Zealand development team for the first week we were over there, but we did arrange to meet up before we went back.

When we did meet up again Graham asked what questions we had for him, so I went in like a bull at a gate. "Where have you found a house in Wales?" I asked. Geraint, Leigh and Dai Pick said I shouldn't have asked that, but Graham, fair play, replied, "Where would you suggest?" and we knew then he was coming to Wales.

We learnt a lot in New Zealand, both from the guys in Auckland who looked after us remarkably well and from the people who ran New Zealand rugby. I didn't go to all the meetings but the others told me that they sat around the table with four other people who were accountable for what went on – that compared with the WRU which was run by Glanmor Griffiths and about 27 committee men. When someone asked who would carry the can in the event of something going wrong, all fingers pointed to one man, the chief executive, he was responsible for running New Zealand rugby. Fair play to the WRU, they took on board a lot of the ideas we went back with and Dai Pickering was instrumental in pushing through what he had seen in New Zealand.

So Graham Henry arrived in Wales on 31 July 1998, surrounded by massive media attention. I had a little chuckle, of course, because I had known for several months what was going to happen. Was it the right thing to do? At the time I think it was. There was no stand-out coach in Wales to take on the role and take Wales to a new direction. There were very good coaches in Wales, and Graham never fetched anything new to the table as far as coaching was concerned. Those coaches could coach rugby as well as Graham could, but it was the different things he brought with him which stood him apart from the Welsh coaches. It was the analysis, the man management, and also his ability to handle the WRU. When you bring a coach in from outside you have to accept what he is bringing with him as well, and the different ideas he's got. If a Welsh coach had been appointed at that time, he certainly would not have been paid that amount of money, reportedly £250,000 a year, and he would not have been given the same leeway as Graham was given in changing things.

He admits that he knew hardly anyone in Welsh rugby apart from some of the senior players he had heard about, and probably only those by name. He had never met them. He didn't waste much time in getting some of them together to ask various questions, and to make suggestions about who should be on his coaching team. I suppose the senior players at that time would have been people like Dai Young, Scott Gibbs and Rob Howley. My name must have come into the conversation, and I don't know if it had been an advantage meeting Graham in New Zealand, but I got the call to be one of his assistants. I was excited, naturally. That 96–13 scoreline hadn't done me that much damage after all, it seemed, but also I was excited because it meant working with someone different. What he was bringing to the role of Wales rugby coach was his organization, his man management, the analysis and the way he wanted to take it forward.

We met up several times as a coaching group in Graham's house. Alun Lewis, who was then coaching Newport, had been appointed as a selector, and Dai Pickering had been taken on as team manager. Trevor James, who had been involved in Welsh rugby in various capacities, was appointed administrative manager, and there was one other appointment which showed just how different the Henry regime would be. He had heard from several players across the world of rugby about a Geordie called Steve Black. Blackie was the conditioning coach at Newcastle, who were at the time the top team in England. Henry found out that Blackie was more than just the team's conditioning coach, he was the players' motivator.

The first time I met Steve I couldn't quite believe what I was I was seeing. He was huge, well overweight, with a big round face and black beard. Many people have made the observation that he is a double for Friar Tuck, and it's a good comparison. My first thought was how the hell could someone this size be a conditioning coach? It must have been a case of do as I say, not do as I do. Blackie and I hit it off immediately and became good friends, and we have remained good friends ever since. When we went away and the rooms were being dished out, Blackie always liked to have a room next to mine which was fine for him, but a bugger for me. Steve has a sleeping disorder, sleep apnoea, which meant he breathed so slowly while sleeping that he could die. Blackie had to sleep with an oxygen mask on, and the oxygen was supplied from a machine which made such a noise you could hear it in the next room. So while Blackie slept safely and soundly, those on either side were kept awake by something resembling a jumbo jet taking off!

Reading about sleep apnoea it is surprising that Blackie did the job he did so well. It causes all sorts of problems when people are awake: fatigue, judgement and short-term memory loss, and decreased motivation. Well, Blackie never struggled for motivation, not that I saw anyway. I had never seen anyone work the way he did. He preferred to work with individuals, he said, because each individual needs a different motivation.

Blackie was more than a conditioning coach, in fact some would say he was more of a psychologist. He got into a player's mind, and he motivated them to do things they wouldn't normally do. In any case, he maintained that it was not his job to get the players fit, that was down to the club and regional fitness coaches. His job was to get them fit to do what Graham and Wales wanted them to do.

As a coaching and management team we discussed the way things would be done. Graham's theory was that you won the ball and got over the gain line as quickly as possible. Then you went into the sequences, and in certain parts of the field you played in a certain way. Later Graham introduced the famous pod system which had been invented by Australia's Rod McQueen, but more about that later. At this time Graham produced a game playbook in which he formatted certain moves from certain situations. During his hours of analysis, he would then work out which plays from his book would suit likely weaknesses in the opposition.

Another thing Graham brought with him was a structure. It wasn't that other coaches didn't have a structure, it was just that Graham's was finely detailed. Each player and each position had a precise role and if it didn't work then there would be another plan to put into action. If Plan A didn't work, then there was always a Plan B, and a Plan C. If we could see that something wasn't working, then we would send on instructions to change to a different plan. Every player knew the book and it was just a case of turning to a different chapter. Critics would say it was too regimented, but at the time I think it was the right way to be going. In the past I felt that if Plan A didn't work then there wasn't an alternative. Messages were sent onto the pitch with the water carriers or Mark Davies the physio. Once we became more successful there would be an opportunity to let it free up a little and allow players more freedom to play a bit more.

We met up with the squad for the first time for the South Africa game at Wembley, and immediately Graham had made changes. We had a headquarters, the Copthorne Hotel at

Culverhouse Cross on the outskirts of Cardiff. Graham insisted on having the players for a week before an international and although not everyone stayed there for the full week it was our 'home' for the preparation period. Previously international players had met up on a Wednesday night in Cardiff, had yet another training session to add to the ones they were already doing with their clubs, and then gone home. Graham ditched that as he thought it was only adding unnecessary sessions to an already overcrowded training schedule. We met on the Monday and immediately went to work.

We had just started our build-up to the game when a rumpus broke out. The WRU marketing department had come up with an idea to launch the new era of Welsh rugby under their new and very expensive coach. They wanted to stage a picture of Graham standing in front of the squad. The picture was going to be taken at the top of Snowdon where Blackie would deliver an inspirational speech to the squad about being at the top of Wales. The problem was that when the time came you couldn't see your hand in front of your face on top of Snowdon, let alone take a picture. So the photo was taken in a car park and superimposed onto a background with the words 'Guide Me O Thou Great Redeemer' plastered across the top, words from one of the great hymns sung in the chapels of Wales. That was where the backlash came from. Religious groups thought the poster was blasphemous; it even went as far as the Advertising Standards Authority. The poster was seen on billboards across Wales and helped in the build-up to the big game against South Africa.

There was one other problem: we didn't have a ground to play on. In preparation for Rugby World Cup 1999, the National Stadium had been demolished and Millennium Stadium was being constructed in its place. Hence the move to Wembley.

It was a quirk of the fixture list that we should play South Africa so soon after they had stuffed us in Pretoria. Graham thought that would work in our favour. He thought they would be complacent. They were also coming off the back of a hard Super 12 series, and we had most of our missing players available again. For us as a coaching team, and Graham in particular, they were ideal opponents. After that 15-try mauling, who ever expected us to come even close to winning? The level of expectation among the Welsh public was pretty low. The bookies were giving Wales a 36-point start! As it happened we came close. Very close. A couple of debatable refereeing decisions went against us and there were a couple of silly moments like when Gareth Thomas had a scuffle with one of the South Africans after we had been awarded a kickable penalty. The penalty was reversed and with the score at 20–20 inside the last five minutes, who knows what might have happened.

Another significant moment came when a streaker ran onto the pitch and completely disrupted the flow of the game. Graham was convinced, and I would share his optimism, that before his appearance we were in a winning position. The whole flow of the game changed after the stoppage which gave the South Africans an opportunity to regroup. They won the game 28–20, but some of the pride had been restored to Welsh rugby. Graham's analysis of the Springbok three-quarters was typical of his approach. He discovered that they were going to play their fly-half Franco Smith at inside centre, and after assessing the situation, decided that Smith would be their weakness. Hours spent watching videos paid off, very nearly.

After the South Africa game it was back to Wales to play Argentina in Llanelli. Here our forwards got 'tuned' big time. I'd had big discussions with Graham about the role of Garin Jenkins. At the time Swansea had a good pack, and I felt that Garin at hooker was the main man in that scrum. Garin didn't fit the bill as far as Graham was concerned. He didn't think he was a good enough rugby player and preferred Barry Williams from Neath. Apart from that, Garin tended to speak his mind. I still believe that for a scrum to do well, as much as the props might do well, the main man is the hooker. I argued with Graham that the success of his Auckland team had been built on Sean Fitzpatrick, the hooker. Eventually he came round to my way of thinking, Garin came in and luckily for me it worked.

We saw off Argentina 43–30 thanks to some sparkling tries and I think that was as important a win as any under Graham Henry. On the back of the improved performance against South Africa maybe the 'Great Redeemer' tag wasn't that far wide of the mark. Graham had influenced the players' thinking. He had already shown his man management skills and had talked to the players and influenced their way of thinking. Not just the 22 involved in the games, but the wider squad of potential Welsh internationals. He had projected himself. You could tell he was used to standing up in front of players and talking to them in ways they understood. He made them feel that they were something special, that they could do it, and going into the game against South Africa he made them feel that way again.

By the start of the Five Nations, Graham had set a programme in place which meant that we would meet up with the players on the Sunday evening before an international and work would start straight away. We'd start by dissecting the previous match, then we would study the opposition and look at the strengths and weaknesses that Graham had spotted in their plays. We didn't watch whole matches, just the points Graham had picked out. He only showed the players what he wanted them to see. All the coaching staff took part in the analysis and if necessary we pointed things out to Graham. That seldom happened as Graham had always spotted the point before we had. Later in the day, and going into Monday we would introduce the players to the systems we would be using, in my case in the scrums and line-outs. Then we would break up the plays into little blocks.

Graham initially did two sessions on a Monday but Blackie persuaded him that one was better and he agreed. Anyone popping down from the WRU might have wondered whether they were getting their money's worth out of the new coach, but one high intensity session is better than two of less quality.

Tuesday was another video day, spent looking at the opposition, their strengths and weaknesses. This is where Alun Carter the analyst came into his own. Alun was an expert with the video machines, and having been a former international himself he could go through the videos with Graham and dig out the pieces he wanted to emphasise. It's interesting looking back at how the game turned professional. People might wonder what we did with the players all day. Well, this was the new stuff. Despite having access to the players 24/7 during the week before an international, there was no way we were going to have them running around a field for eight hours at a time.

Among the things we'd study in this analysis would be the opposition's line-out variations. If they had a three-man line-out, what did they do off it? What about their five- or six-man line-out? Where did they throw in attack and in defence? Then in a similar way we would have a look at their scrum variations.

You can spot patterns and tactics from video analysis. Graham spent 30 hours watching England games before we played them at Wembley and gleaned that they liked to attack by driving from attacking line-outs. This meant he and I would have to come up with a defence.

On the Tuesday after training Graham sent the players home, with instructions not to return until the Thursday morning. This was a great idea as the players came back refreshed and relaxed and with an extra bounce after a night at home. He felt that it was beneficial to have a midweek break, and for the boys to spend a night in their own beds. As Wales is such a small country and most of the players lived within a short drive of Cardiff they could make the journey home and back for the Thursday morning quite easily. In places like New Zealand, South Africa or Australia that wouldn't be possible. There was no break for me, however. I had not long been appointed

Cardiff coach and so would be off down to training to try and sort out the problems there.

On the Thursday we re-enforced the game plan and had an intensive session with a complete game run-through the way we hoped to play it. We would both be on the pitch watching what went on, and if I spotted anything I wasn't happy with then I would mention it to Graham. I would never stop the session. Graham would do that as you couldn't have more than one person controlling the session, as it would cause total confusion. After a training session we would set off for the venue. Thursday was travel day.

On Friday we would have a session at the ground, walk around, maybe run through a few moves but nothing too strenuous. The only exception to this would be Jenks. Neil would kick and kick and kick. He would learn every eddy, every trick the wind or breeze could play on a ball. His dedication was amazing. Long after the rest of the players were on the coach, Jenks would be banging balls through the posts. Sometimes someone would pipe up, 'What are we waiting for?' But as soon as the players realised that it was Jenks still practising his kicking no one complained. They knew full well that Neil Jenkins' kicking could win games. In the evening Graham would talk to the players before leaving the captain to talk to them.

On Saturday morning you might see the forwards running through a couple of line-out moves in the hotel car park or, when we stayed in London, Hyde Park would prove handy. Nothing too physical, just a loosener. Graham always gave me time with the forwards to have my say and I liked to do that just after breakfast. I felt I had a big part to play in what went on and that I had control over the forwards and he never ever questioned it. My talk at this point would be quite technical: instructions for the tight head prop, a reminder to put pressure on certain positions, line-out signals, defence and attack from the line-out and so on. When I started talking I would be calm and controlled, but as the emotion got to me I would begin to lose it completely. I know some of the boys even ran a sweep on the number of swear words I would use.

A quarter of an hour before the bus left Graham would have his final chat. This was something else I learned from the master: how he set up the room. The players would be seated in a semicircle in number order, starting on the left from 1 through to 15, and then the replacements. That way he would know exactly where everyone was, and if he wanted to make a point to a prop or a centre, a flanker or a full back, he would know exactly where to look. If everyone had been gathered together randomly in a group he would have lost impact looking for them. It was a ploy that I would later use in my final team talks when I coached clubs and regions.

In his talk Graham would make general points. He'd talk about the game plan he was looking for, and maybe pick up on one or two players and the part they would be playing. Graham also got pretty wound up in these meetings, but being a former headmaster his language was a lot better than mine!

On our arrival at the stadium Alun and I had an important job to do which believe it or not involved singing a song in front of the crowd. The number we usually chose was Nat King Cole's 'Mona Lisa'. Not many people can say they have sung in front of full houses in London, Edinburgh, Dublin, Paris, Buenos Aires, and of course Cardiff. Not many people heard us, it must be said, but the idea was to test the coaching team's talkback system from various parts of the ground. Still I can dine out on the fact that I have sung at some of the biggest venues in Europe!

We kicked off the Five Nations, the last Five Nations incidentally before Italy made it six, against Scotland at Murrayfield. If we were still learning about Graham Henry, then Graham Henry was about to have a memorable introduction to the Welsh support of their team. Max Boyce wrote a song about the trip to Scotland; about the coach loads, and train loads of fans who made the journey. Add to that the dozens of extra flights that took off from Cardiff airport that weekend, and it seemed to Graham as if half the population had de-camped to the Scottish capital. If there were 20,000 fans with tickets, there was an equal number who just wanted to be in Edinburgh to taste the experience and watch the game in pubs or hotel bars, before enjoying a night out on the town.

We were staying in a hotel which looked right down Princes Street, and Graham couldn't believe what he was seeing. Looking at the sheer numbers of red and white shirts, scarves, hats, he just could not believe how much it meant. It made little difference in the end, though, because we lost to Scotland, and the also at Wembley against Ireland. But rather than demoralising everyone, if anything those defeats refocused us. Graham was good at pushing the disappointment to one side and concentrating on the next task. I would have dwelt on those defeats, but he never lost sight of what he wanted to achieve.

Our next port of call was Paris, where Wales hadn't won for 24 years, so you can imagine that the odds were not in our favour. I had won my little battle, and Garin Jenkins started at hooker, but it was Scott Quinnell who had a massive game for us and we won 34–33. I think it was the biggest game as far as Graham's influence was concerned. The players bought into the way Graham wanted the game to be played. From then on the confidence came and we believed we could beat teams.

There was quite a feeling of relief among the coaching staff. The game plan had worked. We could see it had worked and, more importantly, the players could see it had worked. No one mentioned the 24 years in the build-up. Actually no one realised it until the press conference afterwards.

A single point victory over France lifted our stock for the final game of the Five Nations back at Wembley against the old enemy, England, who were going for the Grand Slam. Graham had got an idea up in Scotland what the Five Nations meant to Welsh fans, but he still didn't have any comprehension of what a game against England meant; and also what it meant to the players and coaches. No matter what else you do, beat England and the season has been successful.

At first Graham thought it would be just another Five Nations game. There was nothing to compare with this out in New Zealand. I think it started to dawn on him on the bus trip from the hotel to the stadium which took about 20 minutes. It was probably the only team bus ride I have been on where absolutely nothing was said. Total silence. No player spoke at any point on the journey. I think everyone involved puts pressure on themselves, we've got to beat England, we've got to beat England.

Graham soon joined in the antagonism towards England, though, when we got off the bus. Clive Woodward had arrived before us and pinched the home dressing room, which as the home team should have been ours. It didn't take much to wind up Graham but well done, Woodward, the slippery road to defeat had started.

The marketing people had been working overtime to make the game feel like a home match even though we were something like 200 miles from the Severn Bridge. They enlisted Tom Jones and Max Boyce to whip the Welsh supporters before the game, and of course we had the usual choirs and the hymns. The aim was to bring the old Arms Park to Wembley.

Inside the dressing room, if anything, it was quieter than normal. There is no doubt that going to Wembley affected everyone. Here we were at the home of English soccer, and who had sat in this very seat while changing into his kit? We were using the same dressing room with the baths and seats which great names had used, and our players were in awe of the place.

There was always a feeling that we could beat England on this occasion, and the players couldn't wait to get at them. Anyone who was there, or who has watched the game, should be honest enough to agree that we should have been dead and buried by half time. But the maestro, Jenks, kept us in the game with his kicking. We were in with a shout. One of the many things I learnt from Graham was, in a situation like that, you speak to the players at half time and make a maximum of two or three points to them. Three things in this half I want you to do. This is where we are going wrong. Any more than that goes over the players' heads as they are so wound-up about the game. Graham made his three points, bang, bang, bang, and that was his half-time talk.

As we took the long walk from the tunnel around to the benches we had to pass the Five Nations trophy. Woodward, who was in front of us, went up to the guy standing by the cup and said to him, "You can put the white ribbons on that now. We've got that." I was there. I actually heard the arrogant man say it. The moment to savour came in stoppage time. We had a line-out following a Jenks penalty kick which had found touch just outside their 22. Garin Jenkins threw in, Chris Wyatt won the ball, Howley to Scott Quinnell, and Scott Gibbs came on a tremendous angle to smash through Tim Rodber's tackle, dance through two more attempted tackles and touch down for the try. Looking now at the television pictures Graham is expressionless in the stand and I am alongside him trying to look as unconcerned as our leader. No chance. Inside I was churning because despite the try we were still a point behind with the conversion to come. I said to Alun, "We haven't won this yet. We still have to get the kick." As Neil Jenkins stepped forward, the BBC's television commentator Eddie Butler asked, "Who would you want to kick this in world rugby? That man." The ball went straight between the posts. The Scots must have been as happy as we were as England were denied the Grand Slam and Scotland took the championship.

If it hadn't dawned on Graham before the game how big a game against England was, it certainly dawned on him now. Having said that it was nowhere near as big for him as it was for the rest of the Welsh coaching, management and playing staff. For me it was immense. To walk around Wembley stadium and see people crying, it was huge. Woodward never came near us after the match. John Mitchell, the assistant coach, great guy that he was, came and spoke to us, but from Woodward there was nothing at all.

I was flattered and proud that Graham paid tribute in his press conference after the game to the progress made by the pack, "which shows Lynn Howells' ability as a forwards coach". He was always quick to give credit to others. Here was Lynn Howells, first coaching job Tylorstown, now part of the Wales coaching set-up who had just been involved with a win over England. Could that ever make up for not having played for Wales? After a long pause for thought I would have to say yes. Realistically I was never good enough to play for Wales, but to be involved in coaching a side which had gone out and beaten England was pretty good. Back home Wales was awash with pride, singing pop group Catatonia's refrain, 'Every day when I wake up, I thank the Lord I'm Welsh'. They even made car stickers with the phrase on.

Despite three wins on the trot over Italy, France and then England, a trip to Argentina is seldom something any side looks forward to. But as a forwards coach I thought it was one of the countries you should want to tour, mainly because their game is forward-orientated and always a battle up front. So for me it was a good tour to be going on. With the recent wins under our belts I thought we had a good chance going out there. I enjoyed that trip because the people were nice, and it was a very different country to Australia, South Africa or New Zealand. The Argentinians were a little bit laid back but enjoyed their rugby and the forward confrontation in particular.

Having been together for the best part of year by now, I was getting used to Graham's ways. There is a totally different mindset to a New Zealander compared to a Welshman. He is more abrasive. That is not to show any disrespect, but they will call a spade a spade whereas a Welsh person will be a little bit more reserved. We don't like to tell people what we think of them. Graham's thinking on rugby also differed. He was used to winning and he brought a winning mentality to Wales.

The forwards had started to play well which Graham had

acknowledged after the England match, so I felt going to Argentina, whatever else was going on, my department was doing it right. He didn't interfere too much with the forwards, but at that time there was a new ploy in rugby – the drive from the line-out – and we weren't very good at stopping it. His only instruction to me was a defensive one: stop it. There is only one way to stop a driving line-out and that is sheer hard work and attitude. Good attitude, good body position and everyone working together. On a positive side, Graham wanted us to employ the driving line-out as well, but again he just said, "Make it work". At one stage in training I even had team manager David Pickering in the opposing line-out because I wanted to make it harder for the pack by overloading the defence, or the attack.

Graham knew the structure of a line-out, and he knew where he wanted the ball thrown in in certain positions on the field. We had worked a lot on using Martyn Williams at the back of the line-out and that had been one of the ways in which we had beaten France. They hadn't marked him at the back of the line. So Graham had plenty of ideas about the line-out options, but as far as the mechanics were concerned he left that to me as he had plenty of other things to occupy his mind. That has to be better than someone trying to dabble in your territory all the time.

We needed a pack of forwards capable of competing with the Pumas and not taking a backward step, and during the tour I think we achieved that. Going into the matches we knew we had strength in the right places despite the fact that we had discovered problems. We didn't have a proper scrummaging machine and couldn't find one in Argentina. The reason for that was that they didn't use them. They would do most of their scrummaging live and against each other. We couldn't do that as we didn't have enough players to do it. When you are on tour there are bound to be injuries and there were not enough spare forwards to pose a meaningful opposing scrum. So we had a machine shipped out to us. The machine was an aluminium sledge type which posed a problem in Argentina. Because the grounds were so dry and hard, the machine just slipped over the top of the surface. The press boys were very keen to see the scrummaging power, so we used that to our advantage. We piled everyone we could muster on top of this machine to provide some resistance, including the press. There must have been going on 15 people providing the weight, and it gave the Argentine people watching something to think about. They must have thought that if our scrum could drive all that weight, what might they do to the Puma's eight.

There was one moment with that machine that our kit man John Rowlands will never forget, and he has never forgiven me for it. Rather than just scrum, get up, then scrum again and so on, I always got the boys to do a move off the machine. Sometimes this involved spare people holding a tackle bag for the ball carrier to run into. On this particular occasion John was holding a bag and big Craig Quinnell was the ball carrier. Craig hit the bag and took out John, who ended up with numerous stitches in a head wound and concussion. So we had a kit man for the day who didn't know whether he was in Argentina or Aberdare.

Our scrummaging work gave the right impression to the local watchers but didn't help us in the first warm-up game against Buenos Aires which we lost. We did, however, win up in the hell hole that is Tucuman.

In the first Test we certainly out-scrummaged the Argentine pack. We knew we had the talent behind our own pack to beat Argentina and so it proved. We knew if we got parity up front, at least, then we would beat them. In the end we did better than that, we out-played their forwards where it mattered. That laid the platform for Dafydd James to score one try, while forwards Brett Sinkinson and Chris Wyatt scored the others. Jenks added points with his boot and Shane Howarth dropped a goal for a 36–26 win.

The win was even more pleasing because before the game we had had to put up with some non-existent tour organization.

When a team tours a country it is the task of the home union to sort out all the arrangements like hotels, coaches, travelling, etc. The Argentinians gave us a bus you wouldn't have found on a route up the Valleys. It was a well-worn model, slow, bumpy and smelly. There was no police escort, and as the traffic in Buenos Aires moves at snail's pace anyway, it took us well over 45 minutes to get to the ground from the hotel. After the game it only took us fifteen minutes to get back to the hotel, so we realised that our driver had taken us on the scenic route, determined to keep us cooped up for as long as possible.

Getting to the ground hadn't been the end of our troubles. At the Ferro Carril Oeste Stadium we had been told we were not allowed to go onto the pitch and given an indoor basketball court to warm-up on. We couldn't wear boots, it wasn't big enough for us to run through moves, there was no height for the kickers to practice, and no chance for the players to get used to the humidity, the ground or the atmosphere generated by the crowd. Needless to say the lack of welcome afforded to us by our hosts featured strongly in Graham's pre-match speech.

Between the two Test matches we had a game against Argentina A in a place called Rosario, about five-and-a-half hours from the capital. This was another coach ride from hell in a bus which had seen better days and to make matters worse we lost 47–34.

The second Test was totally different. Team manager Dai Pickering had sorted out the ride to the stadium and the warm-up facilities for this one. But on the pitch it was literally a battle. At one stage there was a massive 31-man punch-up, the 31st man being our doctor, Roger Evans, who was trading punches on the touchline. One of their players had stuck a punch into the back of Craig Quinnell and floored him. That sparked off the punch-up, and the player whose name I can't remember had Craig on the floor looking for seconds. Roger jumped onto him to pull him off Craig, and landed one on him at the same time. It was a matter of standing toe to toe with them and the feeling in the camp was such that not even the doc was afraid to do that.

Winning the second Test 23–16 we became the first British side to win a Test series out in Argentina. On our return Graham's credibility among the Welsh public had rocketed. He could have been given the freedom of every city, every town, every village in Wales. He could do no wrong, and I think it enabled him to get more and more freedom to go down his own path without the WRU questioning his reasons or his motives. The big thing with Graham, though, was that he included all of us in the praise being heaped on him and the squad. He made everybody feel part of it. I knew I had contributed a lot towards that series win in Argentina, and the wins over France and England. No team goes to Argentina and wins Test matches without a good pack of forwards, and I was the forwards coach. Whether the man in the street knew what part Lynn Howells had played, I don't know, and to be honest I don't care. I knew, and I knew that the people close to the team knew, and to me that was the important thing. My friends were a bit uptight because my name was seldom mentioned in the media, but it didn't bother me then, and never has. Having plaudits in the press is never a big concern for me at all. The thing for me is that I have always been a players' man and as long as the players felt I was doing right by them then I was happy. And of course a side which is winning is usually a happy bunch.

There was no time to sit back and take stock of what we had achieved over the past few months, no time to savour the euphoria of beating England or winning in Argentina. We were about to embark on the biggest event to hit Welsh rugby, hosting the 1999 Rugby World Cup, but before that came an event which ranks at the very peak of my coaching career.

11

The World Cup

IT WAS 1999 and the year that Wales hosted the greatest competition in rugby union. I say that, but the crazy thing was that games took place in Wales, England, Scotland, France, and Ireland. This was the first World Cup of the professional era, and only the fourth to take place, so no country, certainly not Wales, had the facilities to stage the entire competition. But I know that several of the players who started the tournament out in Ireland or France didn't feel part of it at all until they reached the latter stages and actually came to Wales.

The centrepiece of the tournament was the magnificent new stadium which was used for the opening ceremony, the first game, and the final. It was down to the chairman of the WRU, Glanmor Griffiths, that the place was built. Glanmor has had his critics. I found him insecure, sometimes difficult to get on with, and certainly difficult to get decisions from, but that stadium will forever be his legacy to Welsh sport and Welsh rugby in particular.

Under normal circumstances we would have gone our separate ways and taken a well earned rest from rugby after the summer tour of Argentina, but not this year. We had a week off, then it was back to the Copthorne Hotel and the start of preparations for the four warm-up matches which had been planned, the first of which was against our old friends South Africa. Graham had decided that this hotel on the outskirts of Cardiff would be our World Cup base. There were no pitches or fitness facilities at the Copthorne, of course, so we had to get a bus to Sophia Gardens to do the teamwork. It was only after a conversation Graham later had with the owners of the Vale of Glamorgan Hotel that it became the new headquarters and training centre for Welsh rugby, with its superb indoor facility, the barn, offices, treatment rooms, fitness areas, gyms and outdoor pitches.

Our match against the Springboks was to be the first to be played at the partially-completed new stadium. If someone said I could only have ever had one game on the Wales coaching staff, the game against South Africa would be the one. Beating England is always special, as was the first series win out in Argentina, and going on tour to Japan as the Wales coach a little later on. But this was different because it came almost a year to the day after they had beaten us 96–13, and South Africa coach Nick Mallett had called us the worst international team he had even seen. There were still a lot of the Welsh players who had suffered that mauling lining up against South Africa in Cardiff that day, and for them and Welsh rugby, the result made it the number one game in my book. I had never lost 96 anything in my life, so to have the opportunity to go at them so soon afterwards, and this time with a team we felt was good enough to win, was sweet. We had been in with a chance in our last game against South Africa, at Wembley, but that match had come early on in Graham Henry's reign. By the time we faced them on 26 June 1999 at the Millennium Stadium, things had begun to slot into place.

Since that fateful day in Pretoria, we had beaten France, beaten England and won the series in Argentina, so our confidence was high; much higher than coming back to Wales on the back of a 96–13 thrashing. There was another factor as well. Even though there was still scaffolding in places and the roof was held up by pillars of metal, we could see that the new stadium was going to be something special. The workmen in their hard hats watched the training session on the Friday, and got free admission to the game on the Saturday, watching from their spots high up among the girders.

There is no doubt that the Millennium Stadium is a fabulous place and the atmosphere in it is intimidating because the crowd is really close to the field. When the roof is closed the noise level shoots up even further. It makes you proud to be Welsh when you can talk to people from other countries about that stadium.

One thing which wasn't right, though, and I feel still isn't right, is the pitch. Where scrums had taken place and the turf had lifted you could actually see the pallet on which the grass was meant to rest on. These days the grass is laid in long strips rather than the squares, but there are still times when the turf moves under the pressure of a scrum.

Another missed opportunity was the lack of a warm-up area. There is nowhere to run through line-outs, do sprints and go through routines. That said, there are advantages in having the teams warm-up on the pitch. The Welsh players begin to get the support and the feel of the crowd, while the away team can start to get nervous. As the players go through their pre-match preparations the choirs are singing, the crowd is chanting, and the atmosphere is building. I think that is a massive benefit for any Welsh team, even though I still don't think the singing these days is as good as it used to be in the old stadium.

The Wales players and management did have some part to play in the design of the changing rooms and how they look today, but on the day of the South Africa game the dressing room area wasn't completed by any means, and the players didn't have the individual lockers and cubicles they have now.

As well as giving the team a valuable warm-up for the World Cup, the South Africa match had been arranged to serve another function. The builders and safety people needed to check on the flow of the crowd into the stadium before a game and out of it afterwards. Few could have guessed that the game would be remembered as much for its scoreline as for its significance as the first to be held at the Millennium Stadium.

It all worked like clockwork both on and off the pitch. Wales played well and took South Africa on in the forwards.

The question had always been whether we could get parity or match them up front, as in my opinion it always starts up front. After what we had done out in Argentina it was obvious that our forwards were good enough to take anyone on, while in the backs we always knew we had the capability to take teams on. In the end Mark Taylor, who had been on that losing side in Pretoria, wrote his name into the history books as the first player to score a try in the new stadium, and the team became the first Welsh team to win against the Springboks. It was a good opening for the new home.

After the game Blackie and I just walked around the pitch looking at the place, imagining what it would look like when it was finished, and soaking up the atmosphere as well as what we had achieved. Blackie realised what it meant to me personally to have beaten them so soon after that disaster out in Pretoria, and what it meant to the rest of the players who had taken part in both matches. It was another example of the skill of the guy that he realised that. That was exactly why we were walking around, just to make that moment last a little bit longer.

The players and the management team went off for their shortened summer break before meeting up again in mid-July. We had decided that as the World Cup was coming to Wales, we should take the tournament out into Wales. So Graham arranged a series of camps and training sessions around the country to get the public involved. The camps took place in Brecon, Bangor and Pembrokeshire. In the end we didn't need much to generate interest, the crowds that came out to watch us train were huge. They wanted to meet the players, to get autographs, and photos. It was Graham's idea and it shows again how he thought outside the box. No one else had thought of taking the national team away from Cardiff. It worked because the players really saw who they were representing, while the supporters appreciated the chance to get up close to their heroes. The change in venue and the special arrangements made us realise what the World Cup was about, that it was something totally different to a Six Nations game or an ordinary international. The World Cup was being hosted by Wales, and people were beginning to feel pretty pleased with themselves.

In our next warm-up game against Canada, Graham picked a team with the idea of getting the players to show how much they wanted and deserved to be part of the World Cup. He also wanted to give players who hadn't been part of the South Africa match some game time in which to state their case. I think it is fair to say that before the Canada game, Graham and the rest of the coaching team knew pretty much which players would feature in the first match against Argentina, and which was the strongest XV. I think there were still one or two places up for grabs, but the majority of the team was there. The build-up to these matches was different. The intensity was different. We had the players for longer than usual. It was the summer, and the players didn't have to go back to their clubs. We were in charge of the conditioning, so Blackie had another role to play, and given the amount of time we had all those players, it was important that we had the carrot of some matches to dangle in front of them. Given the nature of the World Cup we knew it was unlikely that every player would stay fit or available for the whole tournament. The fringe players, who might not have toured Argentina or been in the squad against South Africa, were going to be needed at some time or another. So we had to create atmosphere in which every player would think he was needed. We had to make sure that everyone was included in everything we did, and avoid creating a first team and dirt trackers mentality. It was probably the most difficult thing we had to deal with but inevitably Steve Black came to the fore with his ability to make everyone feel special.

We also wanted to use our World Cup game plan in the game against Canada to give us a chance to see whether we were getting things right as a coaching set-up. We won 33–19, and as coaches and players we now knew our game plan could work. The result reinforced the idea that we were going in the right direction, and that every player in the squad was capable of settling into that environment.

Next up was France and here Graham wanted to see what he thought would be the XV to start against Argentina. In this game, as with all three of the warm-up matches, we wanted the team to play with intensity, because we knew that somewhere along the line in the World Cup we would have to play against at least one of the top nations. To do that we had to keep everyone buzzing and excited; we had to keep everything interesting. We wanted everyone lively and realising that they were moving up to another level. We were also coming off the back of some good results, so confidence would be high anyway. As it turned out no one played themselves in or played themselves out. In fact the warm-up games just reinforced what we were thinking, which was excellent from our point of view. We beat France 34–23, and although it was good to keep the unbeaten run going, that wasn't the important factor.

Finally we had visitors from the USA. By now of course we knew our strongest XV, and the players had a fair idea as well. This game, though, gave all the remaining players a chance to show their capabilities in an international match and show that they could play to the system, because it was almost certain that at some time over the next month they would be needed. The good thing was that the back-up player knew that the player ahead of him was better than he was. A good example was at fly-half where Steve Jones knew that Neil Jenkins was the better player, and Steve was happy with that. The USA were comfortably beaten and our progress, just like that of the stadium, was a stage closer to the finished article.

Looking back on those three games, we played poorly against Canada, but that was probably because it was very much a team that hadn't played together and we had worked the players hard and they were tired. Against France we had a poor first half which was down to some apprehension. I think the pressure had got to the players. They were playing for a place in the World Cup side. As for the coaching team I think we felt we had it right, not only the right team but the way we wanted to play. By now, thanks to Graham's work, it was easy for everyone to change the game plan because people were used to what we were doing.

In naming our World Cup squad of 30 we knew we had a few positions where there was little depth in terms of selection. One was scrum half, another was full back. What worried us was making sure we selected players who could play in more than one position, which would give us the depth we needed to get through a World Cup. That played a big part in Graham's selection for the final 30.

The final piece in the preparation jigsaw was the camp in Portugal. Out there we knew the weather would be good and also the facilities. More importantly, after having invited the public to the camps in Wales, we now wanted to work away from prying eyes. There is no doubt that coaching teams send out spies to make sure you haven't got any new plans or tactics up your sleeve. The Portugal camp was about making the players feel important. It was a quality environment with all the facilities we needed, and it was away from all the World Cup hype going on at home. There was quality relaxation time when the players weren't working, and we did work them hard, three short sessions a day of high intensity in the heat. With my fear of the sun, that was a bit of a problem for me. I was the only one in the group with a long sleeve shirt, hat and tracksuit bottoms on, while the others were quite happy to be topping up their tans as well as doing the workouts.

Returning home we broke camp to allow the players some rest, before meeting up again six days before the opening ceremony and the game against Argentina. We tried to do everything as we normally did for any international, but it was impossible. Six Nations games are massive, the England game is always bigger, but this was on a different level again. It was just the buzz. To be involved in the World Cup was massive. The pressure was immense and continuous, and what made it worse was that we were in Wales and there was no escaping it. The media can't always afford to send correspondents to far flung places like Australia and New Zealand, but when we are in Wales we are within easy reach of even the smallest local radio station and the smallest local newspaper. There is so much expectation of Wales among the Welsh people, and in the World Cup there is also the expectation the players put on themselves as well.

Eventually the day of the opening ceremony dawned. It was touch and go whether the Millennium would be ready. There was a problem over the safety certificate right up until the last day which threatened the opening ceremony, but that problem didn't get through to us or affect our preparations in any way. The opening ceremony was to take place on the pitch but as far as we were concerned it was just something which was going on outside the game. I think a lot of credit should be given to the players here who just switched off the hype of the opening ceremony, and focused on an international match against Argentina.

Eventually the ceremonials were over and we were ready to get the tournament started. There is always a special feeling going out to play an international. Although I had never experienced it as a player, of course, I had experienced it in a coaching capacity, but this blew my mind. It was the first time we had walked out into the new stadium with a full house. The crowd had been hyped up by all the goings-on for the past hour or more. The World Cup had come to Wales and the noise and atmosphere generated by a crowd of 72,500 excited fans was trapped in by the closed roof. If that didn't send a tingle through the body nothing would. And that was the problem.

In the first half against Argentina we were awful. I wasn't surprised. It was only to be expected given the size of the occasion. At half time Graham issued a bollocking although in his usual style it was a controlled bollocking. Individual players were given a bit of a roasting, but then it was a matter of saying what needed to be done in key areas. It wasn't about ranting, he was clinical about what he was saying. As for me I took the forwards to one side as a group and said, "Boys if you are going to play like this we are going to lose. You have been

229

out there (to Argentina) and got a result, you have let them come here and dominate us on our own field."

The records show that we did win that opening match 23–18; 13–9 up at the break thanks to a try by Colin Charvis converted by Jenks who kicked a couple of penalties. In the second half Mark Taylor scored another try and Neil added the rest of the points from the boot. The Argentinian fly-half Gonzalo Quesada was the only points' scorer for the visitors, kicking six penalties to keep edging his side closer and closer.

After the game however the brown stuff hit the fan. Colin Charvis was cited for punching Roberto Grau and ended up being banned from the remainder of the pool matches. It was going to be a massive loss for us as Charvie was a big part of our pack, but because of the pre-tournament work we had done with the likes of Martyn Williams, he would slot into the number six shirt quite comfortably. During the game Peter Rodgers, our prop, had had his ear bitten, and the photographer Huw Evans has a brilliant picture of Garin Jenkins with an Argentinian finger about to rip his eye out. Pleasant bunch!

We also suffered another loss. Unbeknown to us, during the second half Blackie was taken ill and rushed off to hospital. We didn't find out about this until after the game had finished. I was in my usual place up in the coach's box with Graham. During the game I would have the headset on and Graham would give me the instructions to pass on to the guys at the side of the pitch. One of his messages which I could never understand was, "Tell them to get f*****g excited" but I passed it on all the same. Thankfully Blackie made a full recovery and came back to the Copthorne in his usual jolly style as if nothing had happened.

The Argentinians had been determined to get one over on Wales after what had happened out in Buenos Aires. They came to Cardiff to rough us up, but found that we were ready to battle with them just as much, and they came out second best.

Our next game was against Japan, who we felt were the

whipping boys in our group. The feeling was that the other teams would pile on the points against Japan and we had to do the same to build up our own points' difference. Japan have never had many big players so they would never be able to dominate against us in the scrums and line-outs, but if I remember they had a very fast winger in Daisuke Ohata, so we had to keep the ball away from him. As it happened, of course, both wingers, Ohata and Patiliai Tuidraki scored tries.

Everyone expected us to beat Japan comfortably, including the players, and that can be a problem. The way we told the players to approach the game was to get the points, then imagine it's 0–0 and start again. The 64–15 scoreline handed us the win and the points we wanted.

There were two significant events in that game. First Neil Jenkins equalled Michael Lynagh's international points total of 911, then we lost Craig Quinnell through injury, in what would be another big loss from the forwards. We were virtually certain of qualifying for the quarter-finals, but the game against Samoa, and Argentina's result against Japan would determine who we played.

Back in the 1991 Rugby World Cup, Wales had been beaten 16–13 by Western Samoa in Cardiff in what had been at that time the most embarrassing defeat in Welsh rugby history. The piss takers, mostly in England of course, had said it was just as well Wales hadn't played the whole of Samoa. Of course by 1999, Western Samoa had indeed become the whole of Samoa and they were our next opponents. Samoa had Brian Lima at full back, winger To'o Vaega, fly half Stephen Bachop and at flanker the brilliant Pat Lam. For Wales Gareth Llewellyn came in to replace Craig Quinnell, and Chris Wyatt joined him in the second row.

Losing once again to the south Pacific islanders, this time 38–31, left the whole squad devastated. What was more devastating for me as the forwards coach was that we lost a line-out on our own try line and lock Lio Falaniko went over for a try. It was a game we all knew we should not have lost, but we didn't play as well as we could have. In sport you know that now and again you come up against a team who on that particular day play better than you do. On this occasion there wasn't any time when we thought we played better than Samoa did. We thought they were the better team. Pat Lam was the reason, no doubt about that. He knew Graham, he had played for him in Auckland and knew the way he would be thinking and working, and of course knew Wales after the game in 1991. Graham took the defeat personally. He went very quiet. It hurt Graham, not just because Wales had lost, but also because he had probably been out-thought by Pat Lam. It became personal to Graham, he was that kind of man. I don't think he blamed anyone else for not doing their jobs right. He blamed himself for not getting it right. What also made it difficult was that it was the first loss for ten games, when you don't expect it to happen. They knew what we would do, and whatever we changed they came up with the answer, and they were capable of stopping it. They simply out-thought us. The forwards hadn't played well, I don't think anyone had played well, and for my part I was like everyone else in thinking that it was my fault.

Against Samoa Jenks broke the international points scoring record with a penalty. The crowd knew the significance of the kick, but to Jenks it meant nothing. What bothered him was losing. Now we had to sit back and wait for the result between Argentina and Japan to see where we would play our quarter-final. If Argentina beat our points total then we would go to Murrayfield to play Scotland. If they didn't, then we would get to stay in Cardiff, but play Australia.

Although it may surprise some people to know it, we wanted to stay in Cardiff and play Australia, and that is what we got. We felt the Samoa result had been a kick up the backside, and if we could play at our best we could beat the Wallabies; if we went to Murrayfield then beating Scotland would have been easier than Australia in the kind of form we were in. To win the tournament you have to play the big sides somewhere along the line. When you play them doesn't really matter.

There is a story that someone found all the Australian moves on a piece of paper in a toilet in a fitness centre in Cardiff. Well, nothing of that kind was ever sent to us. I think the story is just one of those which have gone down in folklore. Some paperwork was left there, but it contained no moves and was of no use to us in the game preparations. In the build-up there was a feeling that the performance of the forwards would be of more importance than ever in determining the result. That put added pressure on me, especially as the forwards hadn't played very well against Samoa. Also in John Eales, Australia had the best line-out jumper in the world at that moment, but I felt that Chris Wyatt could give him a run for his money, in the line-out anyway. I also felt that we were more than capable of taking the Australia scrum on, and in that area we could compete. It was thought at the time that Australia was a complete team that was very good in all aspects. So yes, it put pressure on me as a coach, but that is international rugby. You have to front up to that. I enjoyed that, anyway, and I think the pressure came mostly from me. Up until the Samoa game the forwards had been going well enough and that was part of our game plan, but I wanted a bit more out of it all.

When the game kicked off things went wrong for us from the start. Dai Young was injured early on and that had a massive, detrimental effect on the scrum. Dai was a very good player and people didn't give him enough credit for what he did. He wasn't a ball carrier, and we knew that, but his stats showed that he was probably first or second to every breakdown. He would hit rucks all the time and we would win the ball, his line-out support work was very good, and his scrummaging was second to none. He was replaced by Ben Evans who was a very different type of player. Ben was a ball carrier and didn't do the close contact work that Dai had been doing, and it definitely influenced the game. Ben was penalised at a scrum and when Rob Howley, as captain, asked the referee why, the ref would only say that the touch judge had alerted his attention to a foul. When Howley asked the touch judge he denied having said anything to the ref.

There had been concerns about Colin Hawke the referee before the game. There appeared to be something of an issue between Hawke and Graham Henry. It was pretty obvious when we had the meeting with him before the game that there was little love lost between the two of them. Graham told me before the meeting that there had been issues with Hawke in the past, and during the meeting it was obvious there was an atmosphere. Whatever Graham asked, there was a negative answer. Most people agreed after the game that the referee hadn't done Wales any favours. George Gregan scored a try after Stephen Larkham had kicked the ball into a player in front of him, and this accidental off side should have resulted in a Wales scrum at least. Gregan got the benefit of another missed infringement by Hawke when he failed to punish a knock-on in the build-up to the final try, but by then we were probably a beaten side anyway.

The records show that we lost 24–9. We were out, and in front of our home crowd. For me, however, the biggest disappointment had been losing to Samoa not Australia. When you play the top nations there is always that fine line as to which way the game will go. Looking back, I think our build-up to the World Cup had been superb. I wouldn't have missed the tournament, and everything that went with it, for the world. It was a great experience, with a totally different intensity to anything I had ever experienced before. Playing in Wales added both to the pressure and the enjoyment. It was good to be part of it at home, though you couldn't escape from it. I enjoyed every minute of it. It put you on an edge for longer than a Six Nations tournament, and as the competition went on you had to scale back because it was so intense that you couldn't keep going at the same pace. I found it a massive learning curve. I just found everything about it exciting. It was also interesting to work with someone who wasn't Welsh, with Graham and his winning mentality and the way that he thought about the game. The one thing I did find strange, and hard to understand, was the way he felt it was his fault that we lost, and nobody else's. It showed another side of him.

When we broke up from the camp I had a feeling of disappointment that we hadn't gone further and not won it in front of our own crowd. After the high of competing you have to come back down to normal life and it was difficult, but I had the benefit of going to my new coaching job at Cardiff. Graham had nothing to look forward to until the next Six Nations, but as usual he didn't waste his time lying on a beach.

12

Leading the Nation

THERE WAS ONE thing you could never accuse Graham Henry of doing, and that was standing still. He was always looking for the next development in the game, and was always ready to adopt the latest methods. The Australian coach Rod McQueen introduced a system which became known as the 'Pod System'. Graham latched on to this and when he returned from his break Raewyn, his wife, informed us that he had spent hour after hour studying and working on this system. That, knowing Graham, I can fully believe.

The 'Pod System' has been a mystery to many people who watch Welsh rugby. Basically it involves a group of players who operate in a certain area of the field. If it's from a line-out you have forwards working the far side of the field, and forwards working the middle of the field, and the remainder plus a handy three-quarter operating the near side. Those were the only areas they covered, and it saved the forwards tracking about all over the field, from one side to another, from one situation to another. It should have conserved their energy. To confuse things even further, if you take the line-out as an example, depending on where you throw the ball the personnel change in each of the pods because of the work they have to do in the line-out.

In McQueen's plan you only worked the system in attack, because it enabled you to keep the ball for long periods as defences came steaming up and you could keep the ball. Graham's plan was to work it on any part of the field, and I believe that was a bad idea. My reason for thinking that is that when you are playing from your own areas of the field you sometimes need to send more players into a situation, and also in defence there can often be more players trapped at the bottom of rucks, which means a pod is short of numbers somewhere.

Let me try and make it a little simpler. There was a group of players who covered from the far touchline to the far fifteen-metre line. Another group covered from the far fifteen-metre line to the near fifteen-metre line, and a third group covered from the near fifteen-metre line to the touchline on the near side. Does that make it any easier to understand? The answer should be no because that was the problem for the players. Under McQueen's system the plays were all the same and each player knew what to do. Under Graham's system there were so many alternatives that the players became confused. When Graham came to this country his playbook was simple, and that was what brought success to the Welsh team in the form of wins over France and England, then the tour to Argentina and the win over South Africa. Now it was a heck of a lot more complicated, too complicated for the players to put into practice without there being gaps. I believe the 'Pod System' hastened the downfall of Graham Henry as the Wales coach. It became an obsession with him as he couldn't see at times that it didn't work. He spent a hell of a lot of sessions developing this system with the national side when realistically you don't have that amount of time. At club level, where you have the players day after day after day, then it is something you can work on. But when you only have the players a week here and a week there, you don't have the time to develop it. Graham went full-on with the pods and would have done anything to make it work.

During the next Six Nations we had beaten Italy out in Rome and Graham, Dai Pickering and I were sitting around a table in the hotel mulling over the result and the way things had gone. Everyone knew that Graham had been appointed coach of the 2001 British & Irish Lions going to Australia while Wales were going on a tour to Japan, and it had crossed my mind several times who would be coach on that tour. Well, in the hotel that night Graham answered the question. They wanted me to take the tour. Needless to say in front of Graham and Dai I controlled my emotions, with a gentle smile and a thank you very much. But when I got back to my room in the hotel it was, you've guessed it, another punch-the-air moment. I couldn't wait to tell the family who were naturally as overjoyed as I was. It was the culmination of everything, really. You don't get much higher than coaching your national team, and the family were as pleased for me as I was for them after all the sacrifices they had made, all the times I had been missing when I should have been concentrating on them.

After telling me that I was taking the tour, Graham made two stipulations. Firstly he wanted to see how several of the younger players who were on the verge of the Wales set-up would cope in international rugby, and secondly there were also a couple of untried coaches, Leigh Jones and Geraint John, that he wanted to look at in the same way. Of course I knew both of them very well. I had been to New Zealand on the fact finding mission with Leigh, and Geraint was my assistant at Cardiff. So there was no problem there. Together with Clive Griffiths, a very good defence coach, we made a good team. Apart from the coaching side we had Trevor James to do his usual administration job, and they always send a committee man with these tours. My luck held as it was going to be Sam Simon who I had known for years from Pontypridd.

As a coaching team we then had to sit down and look at our selection. Bearing in mind Graham's request that some of the young players be included, we also had to consider who would be going on the Lions tour and so were out of the frame. After that we had to decide which of the remaining senior players we wanted to take, and which we wanted to leave at home to rest. The mixture had to be right so that we weren't going out to Japan with a team which wasn't strong enough to compete. Of the youngsters Graham wanted Jamie Robinson, Dwayne Peel, Andrew Lloyd, Alix Popham, and Gavin Henson, plus a couple more, to go, to see how they coped with international rugby.

Graham made no more demands on us. He did not instruct us to use the pod system, or play to any particular style. After discussions among the coaches we decided for obvious reasons that we didn't want to move too far away from the way the national team had been playing. I, however, wanted us to put our own particular style on the tour. I felt that the players should have a bit more space than they would be given back home, especially as the type of opposition we would meet on the tour would give us more time on the ball and more time to play with more freedom.

The build-up was virtually non-existent because of the players' club commitments and also Wales had agreed to play a match against the Barbarians, so we had a week to prepare. We had the players together for a couple of days in the week before we flew out, and I had to explain to them that there might be a limited amount of field time for some of them. So it was up to the individual whether they took advantage of that time or not. The ball was well and truly in their court.

We knew that the Japanese game was always frenetic, it is the way they play, but we also knew that we could dominate the line-out and all aspects of the forward play. We also had to play a structured game as they would be very happy to chase around the pitch all day, so it was a case of us taking control. So the plans were in place.

It's a long flight to Japan and having landed in Tokyo, we spent the first four days at the Nihon Aerobics Centre. The players were not impressed, but from my point of view it was a good place to prepare. The very first thing that hit us was that we would have problems with the heat and humidity. In fact that hit us as soon as we got off the plane and that stayed with us throughout the trip. The Japanese looked after us superbly, the hotel was great, and so was the food, although Trevor James made sure that we ate our kind of food rather than too many local delicacies. One of the times we did go out for a typical Japanese meal the boys were not that impressed. We were all sat as they do on the floor and they served up thin slices of beef which you warmed up by tossing them one at a time into a vat of boiling water which they placed on the table. Well it was OK if you were one of the first to toss your slice in, because the longer the meal went on, a film of fatty scum settled on top of the water. Less and less of the slices were consumed and as soon as the meal was over and the party broke up most of the boys were off to the golden arches, because McDonalds had made inroads into Japan like everywhere else in the world.

Japan is a lovely country, but what struck me most of all compared with non-English speaking places like France or Italy, was that because of their writing you never had a clue where you were. With most languages you get a letter or two which are the same, but with the Japanese writing there's no chance. We were lucky that our liaison officer from the Japan RFU came with us everywhere we went, no doubt well aware that there could still be people missing from previous tours. They could still be out there somewhere trying to get back to their hotel; it's possible, believe me. Another thing was the number of people. When you walked along the pavement you would be confronted by a line of people four abreast coming towards you, then another and another, there never seemed a way through a crowd. Jim Blair came up with a warm-up routine called the 'Magic Square' where players from different sides of a grid criss-cross each other running across the grid. I'm certain he devised that drill after watching Japanese people on a zebra crossing outside a station in Tokyo. How they didn't all bump into each other and end up in a heap I will never know.

Naturally on trips like this there is a need now and again to don the number one's, as they are called, the collar and tie and best blazer. We were required to pay a visit to the British Consulate. This was in Kobe, where only a few years earlier there had been a devastating earthquake. We went there and back on the coach, but there wasn't a sign of a building which had been destroyed or a collapsed road or any evidence of devastation. I wonder how long, or short a time it will take the country to recover from the problems they encountered in 2011.

I will freely admit that being the coach of Wales on a trip abroad like the one to Japan, was fantastic. There were differences being the number one to being an assistant. Pressure, for one. It all stopped with you and you were the one who had to face it all up. The media demands were another difference, and the fact that you had to make that final decision about things. When you are an assistant you just went where you were required to and when. If you are the head coach you have to arrange when things like training sessions, media sessions, etc., will take place. I knew it all had to be done, but as head coach you have very little spare time. You would be talking to players, or talking to coaches, talking to the media, or talking to management. You have very little time to yourself. The good thing, of course, was that instead of having a small room next door to Blackie or someone else making a racket, as head coach you had a suite. Now it may be my upbringing, it may be where I am from, but why does the head coach get a suite? For me a bed, and a table and a decent bath are all I need. It's ridiculous to get a suite, and I can't get my head around it.

So our first match was against Suntory, a team owned by a major drinks company in Japan. Most of the clubs out there are owned by companies, and Suntory won the All Japan championship in 2000 and 2001. We lost 45–41 when we had been in total control of the game and that was down to one factor: the humidity. If we had been playing back home, or in temperatures we were used to, then we would have won the game comfortably. I had to pull Duncan Jones off the field as he was staggering because of the humidity and dehydration. Duncan was so badly affected that he didn't play again on the tour, and only once did we even risk putting him on the bench.

As much as you may talk about getting fluids inside the players, it was a learning curve for us and them. We knew we had to get more inside them. They realised they had to take more fluids on board. Such was the heat and humidity that the players' shirts were five to ten pounds heavier at the end of the match than when they started. We had learnt a lesson.

There was disappointment in the camp because we had talked about going the whole tour without defeat, but under the circumstances what we had learnt was more important to us. We discovered that the local referees were poor. So poor, in fact, that as a management team we sent a letter to the Japan Rugby Union explaining our concerns about the next game, which was against the Japan Select XV, which would again be refereed by a Japanese official. It was not that we were bad losers, but we could not come to terms with some of the decisions that the ref had made in the Suntory match.

We were careful in our wording: 'The team management were disappointed with the standard of refereeing in the match against Suntory.' We then went on to cite certain areas. Diving over the tackled player, off side at the ruck and maul, and the fact that Suntory conceded seven penalties during the whole match, to Wales' 25. During 67 minutes of play Suntory were penalised just once. Now with all the will in the world no team goes for 67 minutes without conceding a penalty. We closed the letter by saying: 'We have brought this matter to your attention privately as a matter of courtesy. We hope Mr Iwashita, [who was to referee the next game against the Japan Select XV], will be more consistent.' We didn't mention our letter to anyone outside the party and as far as I am concerned this is the first time it has been made public. Did we think the referee against Suntory had been biased? Well, we hoped that our letter to the Japan RFU didn't hint at that, but behind closed doors that is exactly what we thought.

Out in Osaka we had our second midweek game against the Japan Select XV. We played this in the Nagai Stadium which also hosted England's game against Nigeria in the football

World Cup matches when they were played out in Japan in 2002. It held 50,000, but on the night we played there were more like 500 watching. The thing that struck me when we arrived was that they were laying turf around the corners of the pitch where a running track cut into the field. There was one bloke there giving the orders and about five or six women laying the turf. Sexual equality had gone a long way in Japan! We were proud of our Millennium Stadium in Cardiff, but the quality here put that into the shade. Everywhere in the Millennium where the breeze blocks are exposed, they might be painted decorative colours, but in the Nagai all the walls were covered with plastic sheeting. No expense had been spared, and this was only a provincial stadium.

Also that was the night when I saw one of the funniest things ever on a rugby field. It was the policy that some of the squad who were not playing, and the replacements, were used as water carriers. Again the humidity, even in the night time, was pretty high, so at every stoppage on went the water boys. Well one stoppage occurred right on the far side up in the corner of the field, so off set Craig Quinnell, who had been substituted. Halfway across he had to stop to take a swig of water out of one of the bottles, and we even thought of sending on a water carrier to refresh one of the water carriers! No problems with dehydration this time, we had learnt our lesson from the first match and we won quite easily 33–22. An up-and-coming wing called Shane Williams scored two tries.

That result put us on track for the first of two Tests against Japan, the first one coming up at Hanazono Field in Osaka. This was another afternoon game, so we had to make sure, even more than the game against the Select XV, that the players took on plenty of fluids. We also brought in iced packs that fitted around the players' necks and shoulders to cool everybody down. We won, of course, 64–10, with Shane scoring four tries on his eighth appearance for Wales in an international. I wasn't surprised that we won or that we won so comfortably. The biggest surprise was how well some of the younger players who Graham Henry had stipulated had to go on tour had developed. Shane, obviously, was one. Chris Anthony and Jamie Robinson won their first caps, likewise Gavin Thomas, Adrian Durston, Andy Lloyd, and Jamie Ringer. To have so many players making their international debuts and to win so convincingly was a great effort and with so many senior players with the Lions it showed the depth we had in Welsh rugby.

There was one other player who made his debut that day, and although he was always going to play for Wales one day, I regret that it was me who had to give Gavin Henson his first cap. Gavin is not a team man, and it became quite obvious very early in the tour that Gavin does what Gavin wants to do. He doesn't conform to a squad mentality. There is nothing wrong with being your own person, but when you are part of a team, you have to become a team member, you can't be an individual. You can, to a certain extent, play as an individual and express yourself, but there has to be a time when you become a team member and he wasn't capable of doing that. A lot of people might think this is childish, but this is how it became obvious to me that Gavin didn't mix. Within a team situation, especially on a tour a long way from home, you try to get things going and build team morale. On this tour we had a T-shirt which was never washed but anyone who was due to win their first cap had to wear the shirt for a designated time during the day. It stank. Well there were plenty of candidates with such a young squad and everyone bought into it, everyone that is except one person. Gavin Henson completely refused and just threw the shirt down, saying, "I'm not wearing that." He therefore alienated himself from everyone in the team. It appears that he has continued to do just that throughout his career. He plays a game or two for Wales, then goes off and does a reality television show. His time at Saracens was short-lived; there were words spoken about his team mates and Jonny Wilkinson at Toulouse. It's just what Gavin Henson wants to do to the detriment of everyone else. He is a fabulous rugby player, I would never decry his rugby ability. But I would never have him in any squad of players that I coached. I am glad from a rugby point of view that it was me who gave Henson his first cap, but as a person within a team environment he can cause problems to that team environment. Out in Japan everyone else was tight as a group except for one person, but he didn't mind that. As long as you as a coach can handle that, and are happy with that, then that's fine, but I certainly wasn't happy with it. It's not Gavin's fault that he plays two games of rugby and then gets selected to play for Wales as he did against the Barbarians in 2011. That is the Welsh selectors' problem, not Gavin's problem.

So after the games in Osaka it was off to the capital Tokyo for the final two matches. We travelled on the bullet train which just took my breath away. The speed was one thing, but if the timetable said that the train would depart at 12.30, it departed at 12.30. When you purchased your ticket you were given a seat and zone reference. You lined up at that zone and after travelling as far as it did and the speed it did, it stopped precisely at the allotted spot. It was something they could do well to learn about on our railways back home. Our hotel in Tokyo was a skyscraper built in one of the few areas of the city where they could construct tall buildings due to the risk of earthquakes, and also the rock foundation. We had just about everything we needed in the hotel and if I thought Osaka had been hot and difficult to navigate, then Tokyo was as bad if not worse. I didn't stray far from the hotel as I could have been lost in minutes. Everywhere looked the same, and again there was the problem of not being able to recognise where you were. Also we had major problems getting around from the hotel to the training pitches and back again, and then going to the matches, just because of the density of the traffic.

Our game before the second Test was against the Pacific Barbarians, which meant another team to select and another round of media calls to announce the team and explain the whys and wherefores. I announced the team, and also that we would rest the tour captain Andy Moore who had played in the last two matches. In his place I named Bridgend lock Chris Stephens as captain, but that caused a problem. Chris had been involved in an incident with the Cross Keys full back Ioan Bebb. Chris had punched him during a match damaging Bebb's eye and there had been a major row about it. That had been in 2000 and here we were, six months later, with me picking him to captain a Wales XV. Trevor James took the phone call from the WRU back home, basically asking what the hell Howells was doing picking Stephens as captain. I stuck to my guns, because with such a young squad, resting senior players who had played in a Test match and would be required to play in another one in a couple of days, I felt we needed someone to front up to the opposition, and Chris was the man. Fair play to Trevor, he stuck by me, so much so that when we allowed Chris to talk to BBC Wales, Trevor sat alongside him during the interview. The interviewer was warned about the line of questioning to avoid, but sure enough went straight in with one about the incident with Bebb. In stepped Trevor, ending the interview. The players were also incensed by the questioning and boycotted the reporter for the after-match interviews. I felt as coach that I was duty-bound to talk to the BBC so I talked to them, but the players kept out of the way. The row ended there and then after the game. Everyone got on well after the match, but I still think it was the right decision.

We were up against it in this match because this Barbarians side had some quality players in it. At the time a lot of New Zealanders and other nationals had decided to earn a few bob playing out in Japan, and I don't think there was one Japanese player in the side we faced. Instead the Barbarians had a total of 160 All Black caps between them, so you can see the strength of the opposition. Before the game I caught our scrum half Ryan Powell asking Walter Little for his autograph. I wasn't amused, I can tell you, and I told him so. It just showed to me the immaturity of our squad. To play against Walter Little for Ryan would have been huge, but you don't do that before a game. Needless to say it was men against boys and a 36–16 defeat was no shock to me or the rest of the party.

So to the final game, the second Test match against Japan, at the headquarters of the Japan Rugby Union the Prince Chichibu Memorial Stadium. Much smaller than the other stadiums we had played the big games in, it was open to the sun and again we had to be careful about liquids. There were more debutants, some of whom have gone on to have fantastic careers with Wales. Dwayne Peel made his debut as a replacement, but it was a first start for a centre named Tom Shanklin. Now if Henson was a player you wouldn't want in your squad, you can give me a dozen Tom Shanklins any day. Here was a complete team person who would do anything for his team mates. Tom was so keen and committed he wore the T-shirt when it was his turn, and was so enthusiastic about making his Wales debut that he shaved his head. His father Jim had played four times for Wales in the Seventies, and he came out to watch his son follow in his footsteps. What he thought of his shaven-headed offspring I have no idea, but Jim would be able to see his son go on and win no less than 70 caps, and score 100 points on the way, with two tries coming in this game. If there was a player I was proud to have given a debut to, it was Tom Shanklin. On a tour, and a tour so far from home, you need that tight-knit group environment. I am sure that for some Japan was a lonely place, and these were young lads so I bet there were one or two who would have been quite homesick. That is when you need that team environment around you.

It was a winning debut for me as Wales head coach as we again comfortably beat Japan 53–30 to win the series two-nil. When we returned home I had to report to Graham.

Every coach has to produce a report on his tour, or his season, and the trip to Japan was no exception. As a management team we put our heads together to make certain recommendations about the tour and the players we had taken on it. In logistical terms the first thing we identified was that more time was needed to prepare before the squad set off from Wales. Also advanced intelligence was essential. More information had to be given to the management team about training facilities, playing facilities, and simply what to expect when you got out there. Problems with climate, or in other countries it might be altitude, travelling, etc., it all makes for a smoother operation.

After our experience in the first game another recommendation was that all games had to have neutral officials. It was unfair to ask local referees to remain unbiased when officiating in matches that involved players they might know well, and coming up against foreign opponents. I mentioned the problems we had encountered in the match against Suntory.

We also recommended that a full-time analyst be taken with a tour. I found it very difficult to give feedback to the squad or any individuals with the analysis to back it up. As this had been a development tour, I felt it important that the young players knew what they were doing right and where they were going wrong. As far as the tour went, though, we all thought, and I put in my report, that development tours were essential for the development of young players.

As a coaching team we also did a résumé of every player on the tour: how they had developed, their strengths and weaknesses and recommendations for the future. For example I recommended that three players were ready to be included in the squad for the forthcoming autumn internationals: Jamie Robinson, Iestyn Thomas and Gavin Thomas. Graham Henry must have taken notice of the report as all three played a part in the games whether it was starting or coming off the bench. I also looked further ahead to the 2003 World Cup, and suggested that four more players should have made the grade by then: Andrew Lloyd, Alix Popham, Dwayne Peel and Adrian Durston. I am pleased to say that the first three of those players not only went to the 2003 World Cup, but all had decent international careers. The only exception was Durston.

The report which went to Graham and the WRU had a decent

résumé of every player, except one. I have already mentioned at length what I thought of Gavin Henson, and by the end of the tour I had seen nothing to change my opinion. I have watched Gavin since, and of his rugby there can be no question. I feel sorry in a way that he never made a World Cup with Wales. His half an hour in the warm-up match against England at the Millennium Stadium before the 2011 World Cup, showed exactly how good he can be, and if he had stayed on the field, I am certain Warren Gatland would have had a difficult decision whether or not to take him to New Zealand. But back in 2001 I had seen enough to convince me that Henson was not a squad man, was not a team man and was only interested in one person: Gavin Henson. His keenness to take part in reality television programmes when he should have been concentrating on his rugby career proved the point.

I mentioned all my misgivings about him to Graham, but I did not include him in the list of reports which I handed in at the end of the tour. That would be seen by committee members, members of the WRU, and could end up being seen by I knew not who. I felt my personal opinion about Henson should be made known to the coach, but that was enough. He could then decide whether he wanted to include Henson in further Wales squads or not. Graham never commented to me about my observations on Henson, but I know he took them on board.

We returned home and I pulled up outside the house back in Maerdy and, God, it was good to be back home. After a tour like that, and there was a lot of travelling involved, that is honestly how I felt. Also because I had done it, I had coached Wales. No one could ever take that away from me and when I sat down and thought about it, it had been a successful tour. I think we developed players and coaches, including myself, and it is important that you feel you are improving yourself all the time. When you look at the players who gained their first caps, a lot of them have gone on and had big international careers.

After returning from Japan I was quite happy that things

would return to their normal routine. Graham would be the boss and I would be one of the assistants. There was never any problem on my part about having to go back to being a number two. Japan had been a great experience. I had achieved what few other people in Wales can say they've done, coached their country, and we had been unbeaten in Test matches. I was satisfied. Then the phone rang.

"Do yer wanna come over for lunch, mate?" he asked in that familiar New Zealand tone. Well, who could refuse an invitation like that from Graham Henry? Of course I said yes. "I want to discuss one or two things with you," he added. So off I went to the Coach House in Marshfield which was the ironically named place Graham and his wife Raewyn rented when they were over here.

I expected to discuss my report on the Japan tour a little more, perhaps look forward to the forthcoming games in the autumn, or maybe he had cottoned onto another revolutionary scheme like the pod system.

We sat down and had food and after we had finished he said, and these were his exact words, "There's got to be changes, mate, and either I am going or you are going, and I'm not going anywhere." That, for me with the way I am, was just the way to do it. There was no preamble, no beating around the bush, no flannel, just straight out with it. Fair play he did add, "Lynn, there is nothing wrong with what you have been doing, there just needs to be a change. Things are going along, things are not happening, we need a change." As a coach I could well understand that every so often you need to freshen things up. You need a new face, a new voice, a few new ideas and a different way of putting things before the players. As Graham said, it needed to be him or me changing, and he wasn't going anywhere, so it was me. In time everything was sorted out and I would leave after the final game of the 2003 Six Nations.

I have nothing but good thoughts about Graham, and the time I spent with him and Wales. The Wales we have now owes a great deal to his methods, his foresight and his ability to get things done. I know earlier in this book I have said that too many foreigners had too much control over what happened in Welsh rugby. I know that regional rugby was in Graham's mind when he found out the state the game was in when he arrived. But it wasn't him who killed rugby in the Valleys, nor was it him who disbanded the Warriors in the disgusting way it was done. If Graham had stayed a while longer, then things might have been done very differently.

Graham Henry identified that there were many people in Welsh rugby who were working in different directions. "Wales," he said, "needed theme missions sold through the media, clubs schools etc., so that everyone was working in the same direction." How right he was. He recognised that success was needed at the level below the international team and that Wales didn't have that. For example when we went to Argentina on that successful tour, 30 of the 37 players had come from four clubs. We needed the best players playing in teams who could compete in the European competition. He also saw a place in his scheme of things for London Welsh which needed to become a development centre for Welsh players in England.

He also looked at funding, which would include having the best Welsh players playing in Wales. The top players needed to be on tripartite contracts involving themselves, the WRU and the clubs. We needed a domestic league of about 16 semi-professional clubs, and below that no money should be given out to pay players. The game should be amateur.

As for the game itself there needed to be a development plan to produce coaches as well as players, in a development culture rather than just a winning culture. The training facilities in place at the time were inadequate, there was no indoor training area of any size, and the country needed a centre of excellence. It was Graham who got that, with the development which took place at the Vale of Glamorgan complex.

Let me say here and now that I have nothing but the greatest admiration for Graham Henry, both as a coach and a man. To say I enjoyed working with him is an understatement. To do what he did with Wales was nothing short of a miracle, turning a team which had been beaten and had conceded 96 points into one with a record-breaking run of 10 wins, needed the skills of rugby coaching and man management. To do what he has done with the All Blacks since he took over has been nothing short of amazing as well.

To be in his company was often illuminating and amusing, there is more behind that impish smile than you get to see in his public appearances. But there was one time when I have to say I could not agree with what he was planning and doing. 'Grannygate' has gone down as one of the most embarrassing moments in Welsh rugby history, and there have been a few other contenders over the years.

Graham wanted to get the best possible players representing Wales, and he would have left no stone unturned in rooting out any player who was capable of pulling on a red shirt. The problem was that in the case of two players, Shane Howarth and Brett Sinkinson, he didn't turn over the stones.

At the time, and we were only five years into the professional era, there appeared to be either total confusion, or total ignorance of the eligibility rules regarding international players. I think Graham could see that there were several dodgy international qualifications doing the rounds, and that the International Rugby Board, the game's governing body, was doing nothing about it. So why not join the trend? A Bristol prop, David Hilton, was playing for Scotland on the pretence that his grandfather was born in Edinburgh, but it turned out he was born in Bristol, and Hilton, who gained over 40 caps for Scotland, should never have received one.

There were also things going on between the Pacific Islands and New Zealand which raised more than an eyebrow. So Graham knew of two New Zealanders who he felt would strengthen Welsh rugby. One was a full back playing for Sale, Shane Howarth, the other was flanker Brett Sinkinson. Both became part of the Wales squad in the 1999 World Cup, and both played in the Six Nations, before the *Sunday Telegraph*, digging into their past, discovered that neither of them had the Welsh ancestry they claimed.

When questioned Howarth claimed his grandfather was born in Cardiff but when a reporter in New Zealand went to the births, marriages and deaths records building in Wellington, he discovered that Howarth's relations were New Zealand through and through. He couldn't find anything which linked him to Welsh ancestry, and certainly if the reporter couldn't find anything where he was looking, then Howarth didn't have anything to present to the WRU to prove that he was qualified. As for Sinkinson he didn't know whether his grandfather was born in Carmarthen or Caernarfon, but it was found out he was from Oldham in Lancashire. The newspaper reporter apparently telephoned Sinkinson with the news and that they were going to run the story with a copy of the grandfather's birth certificate. There was a deafening silence at the end of the phone until Sinkinson asked the reporter if he could hold the story for a while. That's not how they operate. He admitted that he never had Welsh qualification, but insisted he never knowingly breached the rules. It was felt that Sinkinson had been taken along for the ride, but said that he had never been told to claim Welsh ancestry by Graham, while Howarth had more about him and probably knew what was going on.

The IRB didn't help in these matters. Apparently their take on the eligibility rules were that the players had to present evidence of their eligibility to their union, but the IRB never asked to see documentation, claiming that it was the union's responsibility.

Graham had ideas about other players as well. There was an Australian centre, Jason Jones-Hughes, who he fancied would help Wales's cause. This set Australian backs up as he had played for Australia at every junior level and they weren't for letting him go to Wales without a fight. His grandfather came from Colwyn Bay, which gave him perfect qualification to play for Wales. Australia then complained, urging the IRB to scrap the grandparent rule for qualification.

As a result of the *Sunday Telegraph's* investigations, people started to sit up and take notice. Howarth was withdrawn from the following Six Nations game the next Saturday, Sinkinson was injured and couldn't play anyway; but the WRU was squirming. At a hastily arranged press conference team manager David Pickering said that an investigation would be held and that the qualification of these players would be looked at again. Secretary Dennis Gethin said it had been "a salutary experience". The IRB held an investigation and said that they would not impose any bans or fines on Wales or Scotland, but would leave the respective unions "to bring to task the players and officials whose actions caused the breach". As far as I am aware no action was taken against anyone in Wales, but the union had to find £10,000 for the costs of the hearing.

I think when all this blew up we had a fair idea that there was something dodgy and neither Shane nor Brett were Welsh. There was always a grey area around it all and when the news actually broke that they had no Welsh qualification, I don't think anyone was really surprised, certainly not me.

Howarth never played for Wales again. Sinkinson did gain legitimate qualification through residency and took his place in the Wales team after a few months.

So what part did I play in all this? Thankfully none. I often discussed what was going on with Allan Lewis and other members of the backroom team. I knew that things weren't being done properly. There was no point in me saying anything to Graham as he seldom changed his course once the compass had been set. He was probably right to try and get the best players he could for Wales, and as the IRB had done nothing to stop or even investigate other breaches of the eligibility rules then why would they investigate us? It's rather like playing the referee in a match. You push the laws until the ref blows his whistle and penalises you, then you know where the line has been drawn in the sand. Unfortunately for Wales it was us who copped the bad publicity.

I was disappointed, I have to say, but there was nothing I

could do about what was going on. Graham, Trevor and David Pickering took themselves off and made all the decisions about the players and their eligibility. What was more upsetting was that there were perfectly qualified Welsh players capable of playing for Wales who lost out because of Grannygate, such as three of my former Pontypridd players, Martyn Williams, Kevin Morgan and Brett Davey. Martyn was denied fourteen Welsh caps by Brett Sinkinson's appearances, while Kevin lost 19 to Shane Howarth.

It was a sad time for the squad. We had put this squad together, we had experienced some good times together, and both Brett and Shane were quality guys who were liked by their fellow players and the backroom staff. It wasn't as if they were ostracised or disliked by the rest of us because they had been dragged into this mess.

Needless to say the whole thing stirred up a hornets' nest, and now Colin Charvis's eligibility was doubted. Thankfully he and others such as Matt Cardey, another player with New Zealand links but a genuine Welsh ancestry, aroused no suspicions. The damage had been done to Welsh rugby, but Graham kept his head down and the storm blew over.

There is no doubt that Grannygate goes down as one of the darkest days in Welsh rugby. Who was to blame? I think blame can be apportioned to several areas. I think Graham bears a certain amount of responsibility, but having said that he was only trying to get the best for Welsh rugby, and I don't for one moment think he thought they were not qualified at the start. He had obviously heard from somewhere that these two players had Welsh qualifications.

The players must have known that they didn't have any credible Welsh ancestry. Did they say to Graham and the WRU, "We have Welsh ancestry" or did Graham and the WRU go to them and ask them if they had Welsh ancestry?

Agents could see pound notes fluttering before their eyes and had no regard for the damage any fall out would have on Wales, Welsh rugby, or probably the players either. And finally there were people within the WRU who didn't do their jobs properly in making sure that the documentation was in order before a player pulled on a Wales shirt. One thing is certain, it wouldn't happen these days. The lesson was learnt. I will put my hand up, as well, here. I now feel that if there were people on the fringes who had doubts, and I was one of them, then we should have come forward and said more than we did.

So two very important players, who we had all got used to, were taken away from us. And no one could ever say that those two players didn't give everything for Wales when they played, when they trained, and when they did anything with the national set-up.

Graham had brought over Steve Hansen, a former Auckland policeman who had been coaching with the Hurricanes out in New Zealand. Hansen was a forwards coach and we were told initially that he had come to observe, and that is what he did. Gradually, though, I got the impression that he was itching to have a go. Now there is nothing worse for a coach than to have someone breathing down his neck.

After we came back from Japan the next match on the horizon was the Six Nations game against Ireland, the final game of the 2001 Six Nations tournament which had been postponed until October due to the foot and mouth outbreak and the restrictions on travelling during the spring.

I could see that Hansen was on the touchline, but gradually as the days went on he began to come onto the field and have an unwelcome input. I didn't say anything to him at the time because I didn't want a row in front of the players, but I certainly made my feelings known to Graham. Apparently Graham had given him things to look at, such as the contact area, but there had been no word from him for me to expect an input from Hansen, no word that he could come on to the training ground and start putting his point of view forward, he just did it.

With this going on it was obvious to me that Hansen was going to be my successor as forwards coach. Well, that would have been fine had he just come along and observed. I can see a lot of sense in the guy wanting to see how things had been done previously. But he couldn't or wouldn't wait until my time was up at the end of the Six Nations. So I went to Graham and discussed what was happening and decided that I would call it a day after the match against Ireland. Hansen was in, which was just what he wanted.

My relationship with Hansen was never good and I can imagine people saying that was because I disliked the fact that he ousted me as Wales' forwards coach. I will say yes to that for one reason, because of the way he did it. That showed the manner of the man, chipping away and not being up front. Eventually, by the time the regions had arrived and I was with the Warriors, Hansen had replaced Graham as the Wales coach. I could never work with the man. I could never have any time for someone who put the performance before the result which was one of his often repeated phrases. Had he waited until my time was up after the 2003 Six Nations, my relationship with him and my feelings towards him would have been far better than they were.

I was upset at leaving Wales, as it was not the way I would have wanted it to finish. I had enjoyed working with Graham Henry, with Trevor James and the rest of the management team, and with the core of the players who had been with me over the three years. It was very different to working with players at a club because the turnover at international level is much greater.

This was a low point in my coaching career. Things had gone sour at Cardiff and I had finished there before going to Japan. Not long after the heights of coaching Wales came the depths of losing my club job and my job with Wales. Thankfully Ponty was about to come to the rescue.

13

Foreign Lands

THE SUMMER OF 2003 was just about the lowest time of my life. Several years before I had received the news about the cancer, and that was scary, but this was depressing. Everything I had worked for, everything I loved doing had gone – killed off this time by Moffett and the WRU.

The Warriors had gone, and despite Leighton Samuel saying he was going to fight against the closure and take back the region and all the other big talk he came out with, I knew it was the end of the region, and the end of me coaching in Wales.

Moffett had assured me that I would be looked after. Stuff it. To say I was disillusioned with Welsh rugby is probably an understatement. OK, you have to move with the times, and you sometimes have to do things which you don't want to do, but I could never come to terms with the way the structure of rugby had gone. The region had gone. Pontypridd had gone. The game in the Valleys had gone in. There wasn't even a development side in the heartland of Welsh rugby, and I couldn't come to terms with the way that it had been handled, the way they had handled the players and the coaching staff in particular. Every decision that Moffett was making was a financial decision and there was no thought about the rugby implications and I couldn't understand that.

I would come home and sit in my favourite chair in the house and wonder what had happened. I was angry, no doubt about it. Angry at what *they* had done to me over the years.

First Cardiff, then Wales, now the region. It had ruined rugby for me. In many ways I could relate what had happened to me to what had happened to friends and relations less than a quarter of a mile down the road from my house. Their livelihoods had been taken away when the mines were shut in the same ruthless manner for the same reasons: money. I felt just as they felt when the pits were shut, chucked on the scrap heap. You are no good to us anymore, you are in the way, we don't need you or what you can do, go away. The one big advantage I had over them was that I had my health. At least the job I had done hadn't left me wheezing and coughing my way from one staggering step to another.

Later I began to question what I was going to do. I wanted to stay in the game. I loved coaching, it was my life, but one thing was certain, I didn't want to remain in anything connected with the WRU or even Welsh rugby. That isn't easy to say being a Welshman from the Valleys, who had coached at just about every level in Wales, and even coached the national side. If they had come to me and said, 'Lynn, we want you to take over another region,' I would have said no. If Wales had played an international match the following day, who would I have supported?

It appeared to me that I had two choices. I either looked for a job outside rugby and maybe coach somewhere on a part-time basis, or I looked for a coaching job outside Wales. There was a third choice, as I mentioned earlier, and that was taking the job offered by the Blues going around the Valleys trying to persuade them to support the region. How could I go around and persuade people to support something I didn't believe in myself? That idea was scrubbed at an early point. It was an insult, anyway.

It was while I was deliberating my future that the phone rang again and it was Clive Burgess. Budgie had played for Ebbw Vale, and for Wales, and had also played for an Italian club called Leonessa. The job really came about almost by mistake, because the conditioning coach at Pontypridd, Steve

Richards, had been approached by Leonessa to fill the job as coach. Something must have been lost in translation as Steve realised it was a rugby coach they wanted not a conditioning coach, so Steve mentioned my name to Clive and said that I was looking for a job. I was on holiday at the time in Scotland and I was lucky enough to be in an area with mobile reception and got the call from Budgie: was I interested?

Of course the answer was yes. I came back immediately to arrange a trip to Italy. It was pretty impressive, I must say. They put me up in a top-class hotel in the town of Garda, with a balcony overlooking Lake Garda. The club was seven minutes away from the lake, and the area was fabulous. The hospitality was amazing; the food out of this world and everything away from the rugby was very tempting. The club was impressive, too. They used a brand new stadium which they had built and the whole place was far superior to anything we had in Wales on the club scene.

My problem was I knew nothing about Italian club rugby. I knew all about their national team, but from what they told me and from what I understood, it became pretty obvious to me that I could have had a big influence on the club by simply organising the place. There was another problem, as well, and this was something I had to think about when I returned home. The distance. There was no way I could travel home after the game on a Saturday evening. It was a two-and-a-half-hour flight from Bristol to Venice, then another two-and-a-half-hour drive after that. So with the drive from Maerdy to Bristol it made a round trip of something like seven hours. So travelling wasn't an option, which meant a complete move out there and a change of lifestyle.

The majority of people I was talking to spoke good English which was fine. The worry was when they weren't talking to me, they were talking in Italian and I didn't understand a single word. I realised pretty quickly that if I went there would be long periods when I would be isolated. Did I want that? Could I stand it? Then of course there was the most important thing, the family. There were a lot of things going through my mind at that time. Looking back now, I think even at that early stage of negotiations, they had sold the place to me, but was I thinking straight, or was I just wanting to get away from the WRU and Welsh rugby? I think the latter was a very strong influence in my decision. It was a chance to break away from everything. It was also a chance to stick two fingers up at the WRU and say, 'You see, someone does want me.' But the major consideration had to be the family. That was the biggest consideration in all this, so before I made any decision I had to come back and discuss everything with them. Was Jeromin going to come out there with me? We had to look at the kids and the grandchildren. There was my daughter Claire and her children Caitlin who was nine at the time, and Dale, six. Also there was my son Lee and his child Kia who was seven, and what we didn't know at the time was that there would be an addition, Kian, who was born while we were out in Italy.

What people might not realise, unless they have been in the same position as me and been away from home a lot, is that because of rugby I had missed my kids growing up. I had spent so much time coaching, so much time with the Wales squad, so much time on tours, that I had missed huge chunks of their lives, and I didn't want to do the same with the grandchildren. Jeromin was a practice nurse in a doctor's surgery. It was a good job and a job she loved. That would have to go. So all these things had to be considered before I even started to think about the rugby aspects of the move.

Jeromin made the decision easy, as she has always done, and I can't emphasise that enough. It's a great opportunity, was her take on it. The people at the surgery she worked at were great. They said she could come out for a month and then come back to the job for a month, or would she move out permanently?

It wasn't an easy decision. The rugby side was. That was easy, and had I been single I would have been out there like a shot. Lots of players go out to France and Italy these days and they love it. For a player it is much easier because most of them are single, but also when they get there they mix with the other players, but a coach can't do that. Outside the rugby environment a coach doesn't socialise with the players or the management. There were so many other things to take into consideration. I would think about it and decide, yes, I'll go, then a few hours later something would happen to change my mind. Then something else would have me thinking differently, and so it went on. Everything they say about us Welsh is true. We don't want to move away from home. It is not an easy thing for a Valleys person to leave. How does the expression go? You can take the boy out of the valley, but you can't take the valley out of the boy. Well, it's the same with us men as well.

Fair play to the people at Leonessa, they could see how difficult a decision it was for me to make, and they gave me time, all the time I needed. It took me about two weeks to finally decide to go. That was also encouraging because they were obviously keen on having me there and with me taking so long to make up my mind they could have decided to get someone else.

Eventually, of course, the decision was to go and we started by commuting. Things were helped by the structure of the Italian season. They completely close down for two weeks over Christmas, so I could come home then. Easter is another big shutdown time. Also the Italians are great for their Saints. It would be Saint somebody's day so no game, another week off and another weekend at home. There was more time off in Italy than anywhere else I have worked in rugby.

When I got out there I kept on the assistant coach, Phillipe Dabuse, who was French but spoke perfect English and good Italian. The team manager, Alberto Merrigoni, a former Italian international hooker, spoke very good English, and there were players there from England, Argentina and New Zealand. Also several of the Italian players could speak my language, so communication was no problem. I had asked them to send over some videos of games involving Leonessa which I studied, only to find when I got out there that most of those players had moved on, so I knew little to nothing about my team, or my players, or the opposition.

I arranged a meeting with the players and the management, and set out rules which I thought were important, the disciplines which I expected of them. It was the usual things a coach demands of his players: punctuality, dress code, etc. So I was ready for my first session. I broke things down into small groups and did small group skills to try and find out more about each player. Also we were into the conditioning part of pre-season, so the conditioning coach was doing most of the work and I could observe. Then after training it was barbecue time. I have never had so many barbecues as I did in Italy. The Argentinians were always up for a barbecue and it proved to be a good way of integrating and getting to know the players.

The club was well run. It was run like many clubs over in the UK. They had a secretary, a team manager, the facilities were good and the place ticked along very nicely. They were in the Super Ten in Italy, but I would probably say the standard was lower premiership in Wales, lower championship in England. Italy was coached by John Kirwan and had been in the Six Nations for three seasons, so as yet there wasn't any real benefit from that coming into the Italian club game. John wasn't looking at the present club players as the future of Italian rugby, more at the players in the junior sides and the coaches who would come through in a couple of years' time. And so it has proved because Italy have certainly become a stronger outfit in the Six Nations having beaten Scotland, Wales, and France so far, and now give everyone a much harder game. We had the Italian outside half of the time, Rima Wakarua, needless to say a New Zealander, and John told us that we could tap into anything he had available to him as back up and support from the national side.

Leonessa had a big local rivalry with Brescia a few miles away, but apart from games against them, crowds were poor. Only about 500 would be watching most games. The money for the club came from a group of former players who were businessmen and they financed the operation. That was different to the other Italian clubs like Calvisano where, rather like in the UK, one person put up the money. It meant that if one of the Leonessa backers pulled out they simply replaced him with another one. That appealed to me after my dealings with Leighton Samuel. No longer were all the eggs in one basket. Payment wise it was probably worth in total to me about the same as I had been earning in Wales. The actual cash was less, but they found me a house, gave me a car and so the difference in financial terms was made up of perks, and they paid the tax as well.

On the field things went pretty well. We never had the resources of the Calvisanos or the Trevisos, but Leonessa could hold its own as a mid-table club. We never had the financial clout to compete for players with the top clubs, and if the smaller sides like us ever produced a good player, he was soon tempted away by the big name clubs, which the national selectors spent most of their time watching. They must have been happy with what I was doing as just after Christmas in my first year they offered me a twelve-month extension to my contract, taking me to the end of a second season. Alberto Merrigoni persuaded Italian prop Massimo Cuttitta to come and play for us which was a big boost. Since Leonessa, Massimo has been with me at all the other clubs I have been at as my scrum coach, and he also went with Scotland to the World Cup in New Zealand.

I wanted to spend some of my time with the young players and the young coaches who I hoped would leave a legacy for Italian rugby. The young players were fine, but the coaches were set in their ways. Their idea of a good session was big on contact. Fly at a tackle bag fifty times and you had done a good work out. The trouble was their players couldn't pass the ball from A to B, and neither did they have the skills in other aspects of the game, and that is the problem with Italian rugby now. But it was very difficult to change the coaches attitudes.

It was then that I became a Welsh spy. Mike Ruddock had been appointed Wales coach, and he asked several Welsh coaches who were working in France, Ireland, and myself in Italy to do a bit of research into how the players in respective countries might play in the Six Nations. Mike phoned up and asked me, and I didn't have any problem with it as Mike had been a good friend for many years. But I did go to the Leonessa board and ask them if they had any problem with me doing it, which they didn't. Mind you, I didn't tell John Kirwan. I sent Mike reports on players' strengths and weaknesses, but I never saw the Italian team train so I wasn't reporting on them. If I saw anything which I felt was useful, I passed it on. I was quite happy to do that. My antagonism towards Welsh rugby was towards the WRU not the Welsh team, and certainly not Mike.

A typical example of how Italian rugby was run came one match day when we had done our warm up, and I had done my final chat to the players. The referee had been into the dressing room and done his bit, and we were about to go out onto the pitch when the referee, an Italian, came up and said the game was off! I looked at the opposing coach, who happened to be a New Zealander, and he looked at me. We both looked at the referee, and asked why. The Pope has died, was the reply. Being a Baptist boy from up the Valleys my first reaction was to ask what that had got to do with a game of rugby? No, said the ref, the game was off. And not only was the game off but the bar closed and the clubhouse closed. Rivarto, like the rest of Italy, went into mourning and everything just closed down. I can understand it, really, as they were fierce Catholics, but to me and the New Zealand coach it was a bit over the top that everything including a game of rugby stopped. But stop it did.

Religion also dictated the training schedule. I would post out the days' training for the forthcoming week and then after the match tell the players that we were training on Tuesday, Thursday and Friday that week. No, we can't train on Friday, they'd say. What do you mean? We have a game on Saturday! No, we can't train Friday. It's Saint someone's birthday, and sure enough the whole place would stop. It pleased the New

Zealanders, and the other foreign players in the team. They became instant Catholics and enjoyed a day off.

Things were going well with Leonessa, and at the end of the second season, they asked me to sign for another year. In fact I think I may even have signed the contract, but then had to ask for a release. There was nothing wrong with the club, and there was nothing wrong with Italy or the rugby. How could you not enjoy it when you were watching your team play under the shadow of Vesuvius one week, Mount Etna the next, and finishing a run of fixtures in Rome? Not bad for a boy from Maerdy. But an offer came in which gave me the chance to return to the Celtic League and pit my coaching skills against the Welsh regions. It was just as well that I did choose not to stay as the year after I left the club folded when the money men pulled out and it no longer exists. A real shame, as it was a good outfit.

When the phone rang it was my agent asking if I would be interested in the director of rugby job at Edinburgh. I said yes straight away. He arranged an interview, and I went over and I was lucky enough to get the job. I then had to explain the situation to the board at Leonessa, who were good enough to give me the release, though I had a clause in place which gave me a get-out if a big enough club from the UK came looking for me.

Edinburgh gave me the opportunity to coach again at a higher level, but also at the back of my mind was the feeling that I was putting myself into a window where the WRU could see me. I had the confidence in myself to make a success of the job and thumb my nose at them; to show them what they had missed and make them feel they shouldn't have chucked me on the scrap heap. The other big appeal was that Edinburgh had been taken over by the Carruthers brothers, Alex and Bob, and it wasn't being run by the Scottish Rugby Union. I had no reason to doubt the integrity of the SRU at that time, but after my experiences with the WRU, I didn't trust any governing body in the game. I soon learnt my lesson on that one. I suppose there was a danger in that individuals were running the club, just as Leighton had done, but surely there couldn't be more than one Leighton Samuel – could there?

Bob and Alex Carruthers were rugby men. Both had played at the amateur level but both had empathy for the game. Alex had a recruitment and personnel business, while it was a little more difficult to pin down how brother Bob had earned his fortune. Let's just say he was an entrepreneur. He was in the music business, I think. He managed a couple of small bands and staged music concerts and produced music videos. The story goes that they were sat in the stand at Murrayfield watching an international when the idea struck them that they could help Scottish rugby by pumping some money into the capital club. Scottish rugby was in turmoil at the time as the SRU was desperately short of money. They had about half the turnover of the WRU and they had to fund three professional teams at this time as they were still running the Borders. There was no Tony Brown or Peter Thomas who were financing teams in Wales with open cheque books. The Carruthers brothers offered to buy the Edinburgh franchise, which appealed to the SRU as it would off-load one of the teams into private hands. I don't think they ever expected to make money out of Edinburgh, but they would get the lifestyle of rugby owners – international tickets, the best seat in the house – and there was some thought that they would recoup some of the running costs by using Murrayfield as a concert venue.

On the playing side I knew the players pretty well, having coached teams to play against them with Ponty, the Warriors and Wales, and I also knew the coaching team. Frank Hadden had moved up to be the Scotland coach, but his assistant Rob Moffett was still at the club.

I didn't feel it was necessary with Edinburgh to have the 'drink all the beer session', or the barbecues which I had held as the introduction at Cardiff and Leonessa. These guys knew the level I had been coaching at. But I did hold a meeting with the senior players, like Hugo Southwell, Chris Paterson,

Scott Murray and Ali Hogg, when we talked through what they thought the problems were with Edinburgh, what I hoped to bring to the team and so on. They thought the recruitment of players and the finances were the main problems, but also that their play wasn't physical enough. They appeared pleased that I was on board as my reputation at Pontypridd and with the Warriors was that I brought a physicality to the table. I don't think they appreciated just how much physicality was going to happen, mind. Apparently their sessions before I arrived had been pretty gentle, and I felt they needed that physicality to come into their game. It was a case of taking on board what they thought and adding what I thought.

I must say that I found more resemblance to my experience of the players at Cardiff than with the Warriors. This was the big city team in Scotland just as Cardiff had been the big city team in Wales, and just like Cardiff everyone wanted to beat us. What didn't help was that we were using Murrayfield, the home of Scottish rugby, as our headquarters and our base, and there was a dislike of Edinburgh. Playing at Murrayfield certainly wasn't a big advantage to us; in fact it probably had the opposite effect. The ground can hold 50,000-odd, so playing in front of the sort of crowd we generated, 2,000, meant the place was soulless. There was little atmosphere and what atmosphere there was soon drifted away to the rafters with the crowd being so spread out in the stands. To make matters worse there is a running track down in front of the main stand, so everyone ended up even further back from the touchline. Some of the players, especially the Scottish ones, were excited because they were playing at the home of Scottish rugby, but it certainly didn't help us.

Of all the clubs I have coached, Edinburgh was the most difficult. Out of a squad of 35, twenty or more of those were Scottish and most of them were part of the Scotland squad. So when Scotland had a squad session or were preparing for an international, the squad I was left with was nowhere near strong enough to compete in the Celtic League. That is why

Edinburgh never seem to be able to compete in the tournament, because the demands on the players from the international team are so great.

There were one or two players who didn't help the situation either, because they thought they had made it big time when they came to Edinburgh. There weren't many of them, and certainly not as many as there were at Cardiff, and there was a fair nucleus of the players who believed they were there to do a job. Certainly there weren't the same problems within the dressing room that I'd had at Cardiff. I suppose like any group of players there were those who didn't like my way of doing things or saying things, but I never got the impression that there were players stirring up things behind my back. When things don't go according to plan and a team isn't winning often enough, there will always be a group of grumblers, and we had those on and off the field.

We started the season with a mixed bag of results until the autumn internationals came on the scene and then we struggled. Chris Paterson and the other guys had been right, there was a lack of grunt. You can't coach grunt. You can buy it by getting bigger and better players, but you can't buy it if you haven't got the money, and we didn't have the money. Also when I went to Edinburgh the recruitment for the 2006–07 season had more or less been completed, so we had to go with what we had. The rest of the club was brilliant. There was a good structure in place, there was a good academy and, needless to say, as we shared the Scottish international facilities, they were first class. The problem was the exodus of players to the Scotland squad when the international calls came. The only way around that, and it is still the case today, is to bring in a good number of overseas players, or to make a statement by saying that the Celtic League isn't important and it doesn't matter if the Scottish sides come bottom, as long as they produce players for Scotland. Everyone would know then what the situation was.

That season we lost too many games at home, and too many

games in general to finish eighth in the table with eight wins, a draw and eleven defeats. The results would have an impact on what would happen at the end of the season. Having said that, we needed quality non-Scottish players and towards the end of that season we had signed Stephen Larkham, the Australian three-quarter. He would not only have been available during the bulk of the season, but he would also be a perfect example to the rest of the players, a leader. Players like that are players who fans want to come to watch. They put bums on seats and can teach young players and develop them, so you win all round.

Only a few months into the agreement between the Carruthers brothers and the SRU, things started to go wrong. The first problem surrounded the bar takings after matches. The brothers said they should be receiving that money to put back into Edinburgh rugby, while the SRU said that was never in the deal. People tell me that it's likely the SRU were right as they had franchised out the bars, so there was no way that they were in a position to promise to give the takings to anyone else. This caused the SRU to wonder whether the new owners had in fact got the money to run the club at all. You can't imagine some of the modern football owners, or even the money men in British rugby, fighting over the after match bar takings from a crowd of about 2,000.

The problem was that because the SRU were so desperate to get Edinburgh off their books and hand it over to Alex and Bob Carruthers, the deal was completed in about six weeks. There is no way that proper negotiations had taken place on either side, and that the legal situation had been nailed down.

The SRU, it was claimed, were also slow in handing over money to Edinburgh from the Celtic League and Heineken Cup deals. This was supposed to help all the clubs in the various countries survive.

The Carruthers brothers had said they would take over the running of Edinburgh providing the SRU maintained the three Scottish professional regions in Edinburgh, Glasgow and the Borders. In March 2007 the SRU announced that it was closing the Borders and, what was more, all the money saved would be pumped into Glasgow. None of it would come to Edinburgh. Naturally those running Edinburgh were pretty upset that Glasgow would have a distinct financial advantage, and believed the money should be divided between both the remaining regions.

The longer the season went on, the more unpleasant the situation became. Because of what had happened to me at the Warriors, I could see the writing on the wall at Edinburgh. I could read the signs and see the scenario developing.

On the financial front some of the good players were being sold off to cut costs. Scottish international forward Simon Taylor was going to France. Other big earners were being touted to reduce the wage bill. That wasn't going to help me.

As a result of the financial wrangling, the Carruthers brothers decided that they would stick to the letter of the contract regarding release of players for the Scotland squad going to the 2007 World Cup in France. Frank Hadden had expected to have all his players together, but the Edinburgh boys weren't released until after a week and a half into the squad's preparations. Naturally it wasn't long before one side was threatening the other side with lawyers and legal action. That was likely to cost thousands of pounds which neither side could afford. Eventually the lawyers managed to keep the whole thing on a sensible level and negotiated a deal whereby the SRU handed over to the brothers the amount of money they had put into Edinburgh over the season, and took back control of the region.

The majority of the staff, including the players, were to be included in the deal, except for three people, and guess who was one of them? My contract was simply terminated. It bore all the hallmarks of the end of the Warriors. No one from the Scottish RFU said anything. I think I found out from Alex Carruthers. Frank Hadden, the Scotland coach, said he hadn't seen what was coming, but I believe he knew what was going on although other people have said he didn't know. Gordon McKie, the chief executive, and Raymond Heggerty, the financial director, certainly knew, as did the board, but no one bothered to tell me.

Once again I had lost a job, not for rugby reasons but because of a row this time between an owner and a union. I was caught in the middle, and I was one of the ones to get the worst end of the stick. I suppose the results didn't help, but that was hardly the fault of the coaching staff with the way the players were being taken away for international duty. Others were critical of my methods, saying I was too 'old school'. Well it had worked everywhere else, and would work again. Have my successors had much more success than I had during that one season? I think not, and that is because of the system, not any failing on their part.

I was sad to leave Edinburgh as, despite what had happened and the way it had happened, Jeromin and I loved the place. It was certainly the best place I have ever worked in, and the best place Jeromin and I have moved to with my work. It is certainly a temptation to move back there permanently, and who knows what might happen.

I was lucky again because when all this was developing with Edinburgh my agent came on to me about another offer. Tim Lopez from Essentially Group was my second agent. I had asked Mike Burton to act for me towards the end of my time at Cardiff when I thought that I might be offered a new deal. But how wrong I had been, as in the end there had been nothing for him to negotiate.

Tim told me that he had received a call from Doncaster rugby club. Now I had heard of Doncaster rugby league club, I had heard of Doncaster races and Doncaster football club, but Doncaster and rugby union had not been on my list of results to look for. I drove down not knowing what to expect. I didn't know whether to expect the usual tin shack of a stand with a tiny clubhouse, or something more grand. I pulled up in the car park and I was just totally amazed. Gobsmacked might be nearer the mark. I could not believe what I was seeing. The main field was in front of a brand new two-storey clubhouse. There were four other fields around the clubhouse, a stand on one side and terracing on the other side. I was completely thrown by it all. This was a Championship side, in the second tier of English rugby, that I had never heard of, and the facilities just amazed me. Here I was going once more into something completely new. I didn't know the town as I had never been there before. I didn't know what the people were like. It was something totally new but, with the facilities I saw before me, it looked exciting.

My predecessor at Doncaster had been another Welshman, Clive Griffiths. He had gone off to rejoin Mike Ruddock who was coaching at Worcester. Before he left he had brought an Irishman, Justin Bishop, to Castle Park, and because it was already into the pre-season by the time I arrived, Justin had been looking after the coaching. Thankfully Justin and I hit it off straight away and he was able to give me a rundown on the players, the club and thankfully something on the English Championship of which I knew little. We also had a couple of Welsh players there, as well, so that helped. I had a meeting with the players and told them what I was looking for. I asked for the usual commitment, effort, and quality of work, and assured them that we would be alright.

There were several things which struck me about the Championship that I had not experienced with the other big clubs I had coached. First, we played every Saturday. There was no week off for internationals. We played from the beginning of September through to the end of the season without a break. The second thing was that every week it was a war of attrition. Every game was a battle, because of the way the games were played and the size of the players was huge. I know in the Celtic League we had to have squads to cover for international games, and to rest players for the bigger matches, but at Doncaster we had to have big squads simply because of the demands on the players.

During the first two years we were fine because we had the budget, but later we didn't have the finances to run with a big enough squad. We were helped because we could take players on loan, and also there was the dual registration system. Teams in the Premiership seemed to work closer with teams in the Championship than clubs in Wales did. We linked up with our nearest Premiership club, which was Leeds, and had seven of their players on dual registration, which helped. So if a player or two got injured I had to go looking for a replacement.

There was a different kind of pressure going to Doncaster. Pontypridd, Cardiff, Leonessa and Edinburgh had all been in the highest leagues they could get into in their particular country. Even the Warriors couldn't go any higher. Here there was a league above to gain promotion to, so there was something to aim at. True, at all the other clubs I had coached, even at Tylorstown, results were important, and the aim was to finish a season as high up in the particular league as possible. At Doncaster there was another goal: the English Premiership. What level were we at? Well, a good example is the British & Irish Cup where teams from England, Ireland, Scotland and Wales played each other. We beat Pontypridd and Llandovery from the Welsh Premier League so I would say we were probably somewhere between Ponty and the regions. I don't think we would have beaten the likes of a Celtic League side on a weekly basis.

There was also a method, for want of a better word, to playing in the Championship. There were three parts to the season. First of all the aim was to get to the middle of the table where you were safe. Then you had the British & Irish Cup, and then you pushed for the play-offs among the top eight. There you were playing for promotion to the Premiership, so even if you were top of the league it didn't matter, because following the league season you had the play-offs home and away. I'm not sure whether it is a good thing. It certainly extends the season, and you did get a slight points advantage by finishing as high as you could in the league, but surely the best team over the whole season finished top, and they should be the ones to go up? Also the British & Irish Cup was a devalued competition. Those weekends were the only time you could give your top players a break because they played week after week, so clubs tended to put out weaker sides.

Another thing I noticed with the Championship was that as soon as you started winning games and your name was about, people started to take notice of you as a team. For all the four years I was at Doncaster we lost players either to Premiership clubs in England or to Celtic League sides. We were constantly losing our better players to bigger clubs, even though most of them only became bit-part players and none really made a name for themselves. Losing those players made it more difficult to make any progress. I hadn't experienced this before because the teams I had been coaching *were* the bigger clubs.

After I got there the owners, Tony De Mulder and Steve Lloyd, sat me down and asked me a simple question: how much would it cost to get into the Premiership? About £5m. was my answer and that was just the wages, but I quickly added that despite what they already had in place the ground wasn't good enough anyway. So I suggested that before they started talking about getting players to the club they should get the infrastructure right, because at that stage Doncaster would not have been allowed into the Premiership with the facilities they had. Fair play, they fronted up. They forked out about £3m. and had a 1,600-seater stand built along the length of the field on one side, which also housed bars and hospitality boxes. It was a fabulous facility, and would certainly have matched anything most of the Premiership clubs could boast. So that was how much they wanted to be up among the big boys.

On the playing side we played our part and the results were good. The problem in England is that there is always a yo-yo club which is not good enough to stay in the Premiership but is far too strong for the Championship sides. Leeds have been up and down over the past couple of years. Mighty Harlequins came down one season and went straight back up, and Worcester have been down and up again, so the only side to get promotion from the Championship recently, and stay there, have been Exeter, who have spent millions on facilities and players.

For the first two years I was at Doncaster we were in the mix, but couldn't quite make it. The first year we ended up third in the table. The following year, despite having to play a crazy nine games in 27 days, we reached the semi-final of the British & Irish Cup and got a play-off place, only to lose to Bristol. Then came the cut backs. Like everything else, money became tight and with it the money the owners De Mulder and Lloyd spent on Doncaster. For the last two years I was there we had budget cuts followed by budget cuts, but there was an honesty about it all. They realised that promotion to the Premiership wasn't an option by now. There was never a demand that we achieve more than we'd achieved already with less money. They were happy where they were.

I was happy where I was as well. Doncaster, being a mining area, is very much like south Wales. The first house I rented up there was on the site of the old miners' club. Every time I left the house there were two old boys waiting for me and they shouted out, "You wouldn't be living there if they'd left the club alone." Then I moved to another new house built on the site of the Markham pit itself. That was ironic, as probably many of the boys from Maerdy had been there on picket duty during the miners' strike, as it was one of the sites where major clashes took place between the pickets and the authorities. There was one night, when I wasn't feeling too sensible, when I got taken into the pit officials' club. If my father and grandfather had known I was in the pit officials' club there would have been hell to play. Edinburgh was a city, and you could go out one day and see something happening which the next day had gone. Doncaster was like a big version of Maerdy. Little changed. It was a mining town. The people there are very much like Valleys people. Their values are the same, and the clubs are still open, although of course the numbers going into them dwindle every year as the old miners die off. Before Jeromin moved up, I was never left on my own – the local people saw to that. As much as I liked Edinburgh, if you went to the checkout at the supermarket they just ran your goods through and took your money. In Doncaster they chatted to you.

I have now worked under four different governing bodies in Wales, Italy, Scotland and finally England. They all have one thing in common, their priorities are the success of the national team and making money. That I can quite understand as they have to make money, and the only way to do it is through the national team, so that they can push that money back into the grass roots of the game and the running of the game. How much money came from the Italian union into Leonessa I have no idea. Nothing came to Edinburgh, and at one point £3m. came from the RFU to Doncaster, but that was to run the club, not to pay wages.

I absolutely loved my four years at Doncaster. Jeromin loved it up there. My daughter and her children came up quite often, and Dale, who was by now eleven, would come to training and got on well with the players. Kian enjoyed the Knight mascot role but Caitlin found the whole rugby thing boring. The people up there were good, the people who ran the club were good, and the players were superb. I really enjoyed it. Frank Sinatra sang the song 'My Kind of Town' and for me that was Doncaster. The problems up there lay outside the hands of the club and away from Doncaster. I don't think the structure of the Championship season is right. I can't see that anyone who knows anything about the modern game can expect players to play week after week after week without a break. There is no thought for the players, and it isn't good for the standard of rugby or the players' welfare.

So why did I finish? Well, for the good of the club. They needed fresh legs and they needed fresh ideas. It would have been easy for me to stay and sign another two-year contract, but it needed someone new coming in to take it on again. That is why I told them at the start of the 2010–11 season that I was going to finish. I didn't wait until Christmas, because I wanted a smooth transition to the next era.

I left a good man in charge. I had brought in Brett Davey from Cornish Pirates to be my number two with a view to him becoming the new director of rugby. I thought two years ahead because I thought it was the right thing to do. Brett had played for me at Pontypridd, he should have been capped by Wales, and I knew he would be ideal for Doncaster when I finished. He has learnt his trade, and I doubt if much of me will remain in Doncaster as Brett is his own man, and sometimes thinks way outside the square. I wish him luck.

As for me, it was home to Maerdy. I fancied one more crack at it as I was not ready yet to retire and sit around the house – not that my grandchildren were ever likely to allow me that luxury. Jeromin soon had me painting the house and doing the garden, but I was frustrated. I needed to be involved in rugby.

I did go on a trip to meet with the officials of Padova rugby club back in Italy, and I did some work with level four coaches assessing their skills for the WRU. I enjoyed that challenge and it was good to be talking to and interacting with fellow coaches. I would go and meet the coach on a Monday prior to his Tuesday session with the players. Then I'd watch the coach on a Tuesday and a Thursday, and again to see what he did and how he did it on a game day the following Saturday. I would then do an assessment on what I had seen, all the sessions would be videoed, and then we would have a meeting when everything that happened was discussed. Finally I would go back to the WRU and suggest that the coach was good enough to be classed as level four or needs more work.

It was a good learning experience for me as well. It's not an exact science so after we had seen the session we would sit down and discuss why things were done or how they were done and suggest how they might have been done differently, but the coach might well turn around and say that this is the way they had wanted to get information over or practice a particular skill. I would look at the use of IT and how that was being relayed back to the player on an individual basis, how they handled one-to-ones, how they used the coaches under them, how they did their analysis. I found it fascinating, but I was also learning. It took me back to the two evenings a week training sessions when, for years, I was lucky enough to have the players in my squads all day every day. These guys had to make the most of the time they had and they had to be clever, more so than when we were just doing two evenings a week. There are some good young coaches out there and you just have to give them time, and as much help as possible. Several people have suggested that my problem is that I am too old school. He was good in his time, they say. But others would say that is exactly what they are looking for.

I must admit I was not too active in trying to find the next task. It was good to do some jobs around the house, recharge the batteries and take the grandchildren here there and everywhere in 'Granddad's taxi'. But then the phone rang again.

The call came one Friday morning in October. The voice at the end of the telephone asked if I would like to coach the Barbarians? There was no pause, I had said yes before my lips had moved! When you are a player you play for your team, and your ambition must be to play for your country. Another is to play for the Barbarians. From what we have seen from my playing career, I was probably never high on the invitation list to wear the famous black and white shirt. But being asked to coach them was yet another of those punch-the-air-and-leap-around-the-room moments. It was an honour to be asked to coach the Barbarians and another coaching achievement for me.

There were just one or two things I had to sort out. My mother was unwell and with Jeromin working I had to make sure I could take time away from the family. Then there was my coaching work with the WRU. I had been asked to assess some of the level four coaches and I was due to watch a session on the night of the Barbarians' game. If they had said it was a problem then I wouldn't have gone and coached the Barbarians because it is important not to mess a young coach about, and he might have done a certain amount of preparation and planning and it would have been unfair to let him down. As it turned out it wasn't a problem for the WRU.

It was also an important opportunity for me to take personal stock of where I was at and where I was going. It had been good to have a couple of months off and to take a step back. It had been good to assess what I wanted to do, and there was no guarantee that I wanted to go back into coaching full time if I am honest. So to have the chance to go and coach someone, even though it was only for a one-off game, re-enforced several things. I realised I had missed the preparation for a game, I missed the adrenalin flow, and I certainly missed the battle at the end of it.

There wasn't too much time to think about things, because my call-up had been a last minute affair as Brian Ashton, the original choice for the game, had been forced to pull out. The call came on the Friday; the game was on the Tuesday, against the South of Scotland at Hawick. It was a game to offer support for the Bill McLaren Foundation. Hawick had been the hometown of the famous television commentator, and his grandson Jim Thompson was captain of the Barbarians.

I flew up to Scotland on the Monday and we all met up in the afternoon. We had a meeting and a chat about how we might approach the game and after that there was a surreal moment and a step back in time. I came around the corner in the hotel bar to see the president of the Barbarians, Micky Steele-Bodger, buying everyone a drink. It was just like the old days, and he bought the coach a beer as well, but it was good that it brought everyone together.

We had players from the USA, Georgia, Ireland, Romania, England, Wales, Scotland and even Jersey in the Channel Islands. It was a real Barbarians mixture. There was no real time to prepare for the match. We had one training session on the Tuesday morning, and I tried to put a bit of a structure in place, but it was a case of relying on the ability of the players to see you through. It wasn't enough, we lost 22–15. But the experience of coaching the Barbarians is something I will always remember. The problem was that it wetted my appetite again, and I needed to be back in rugby.

One thing often leads to another and when I was coaching the Barbarians, an old buddy of mine, Richie Dixon, came along to watch. I knew Richie from his days with the Scottish Rugby Union and the Borders. He is now looking after the second tier nations for the International Rugby Board and one of the countries under his wing is Romania.

Back in the Eighties Romania was in with a very good chance of becoming the sixth nation before the emergence of Italy, but after the fall of Nicolae Ceausescu and communism, the rugby fell apart. The majority of their players in those days came from the armed services and police, so they could spend many hours training for their sport way before world rugby became professional. But after the revolution all that changed, and Romanian rugby drifted backwards at a rate of knots. At the moment they are way off the standard of the team which came to Britain in the Eighties.

The IRB see them as one of the tier two countries with a chance of improving and making an impact on the international scene, but work needs to be done before that happens. Richie inquired whether I would be interested in going over there for a period and working with the national squad. The offer came with a warning that I would have to be careful as there might be a danger that the local coaches might think the IRB were trying to impose outside help on them, rather than recognising that this was an initiative to help their development. There was a need to appoint a Romanian national as head coach for the development of the game, so I would have to be given a job title that would not offend anybody and therefore would be called technical director rather than coach. They could have called me a kipper fillet for all I cared!

I obviously needed to discuss the job with Jeromin and the family and, as always, they were totally supportive of the idea.

It wasn't the travelling which made me think twice about the offer, it was the time away from home. It's only three-and-a-half hours from Cardiff to Bucharest, which compared very well with Leonessa, and from what I was told it wasn't a requirement for me to be out there for month after month at a time. With the family's blessing, I realised it was too good an opportunity to miss and so off I went into possibly more of an unknown venture than the one to Italy back in 2005. I took a flight from Cardiff to Amsterdam, then from Amsterdam to Bucharest, and ran into the coldest weather I'd ever been in in all my life!

They take the mickey out of Maerdy and how cold it is up the Valleys; believe me, the Rhondda is tropical compared with Romania. One training session stands out in particular. We had three inches of snow on the ground, and the temperature was $-13°$c. I ran out of coats and had so many layers on I must have looked like the Michelin man. Fair play to the guys, though, the temperature and the depth of snow wasn't an issue. Back home the players wouldn't have walked out of the door to train in such conditions, but over there they just get on with it.

The first thought I suppose people have about working abroad is the language difficulty. Strangely, I find it easier than in Italy. In Romania they teach English in schools as a second language, so most people have a relatively good grasp of it, good enough at least to make themselves understood. I find the people themselves pretty honest and upfront, but they don't like the thought that someone is undermining them. I think this harks back to the days of communism, when they looked at strangers coming into their world as a threat and coming to take their jobs.

All in all everything was very positive. I was very happy with the rugby side of things, especially with the national coach, Hari Dumitraş, who has become a very good friend. Hari is a good coach. He has coached in France for a number of years, and he knows the game. Here though I had to be very careful how I approached the job. Richie suggested that I didn't appear to be seen as leading Romanian rugby and that suited me fine. It was a delicate political situation.

I have a part to play when I want a part to play. Hari, as I say, knows what he's doing, but with some of the other coaches I have to coach the coaches, who then go onto the field and coach the players. The difficulty for Hari lies in recognising the difference between club rugby and international rugby. I think Hari now recognises this and that is why he has started to accept more readily the suggestions I make to him. I influence rather than direct, which is a subtle difference from what I have done in the past. I am on the field during the sessions, but if I see something which is wrong or needs changing, I don't step in and speak to the players, I do it through the coach and he then puts the suggestion into practice. So everything appears to come from the coaches rather than from me.

Hari plans everything. We have a weekly meeting where he sets out his programme for the week, but by the time we all meet up I will already have spoken to him and put forward the best way I think we should be moving. After the discussion he then sets that out as his agenda and again it all appears to come from him; the politically correct way. As I have said it doesn't worry me in the slightest that I don't appear to be the one driving the operation. As long as they take on board my suggestions then I am happy with the way things have gone.

The game out there is dominated by the forwards. I believe the Romanian national team would probably give an English Championship, or Welsh Premiership team a decent game. With the forwards, though, you could probably put them into a regional team or even a top English team without causing them too much distress. There are plenty of forwards out there whom British clubs should be looking at; Romania is definitely an untapped source of talent.

The backs, I'm afraid, are a different matter. The old story about their tactics is true: the backs get the ball when the forwards have finished with it. As a result their back play is way behind anything in the UK and this is the weakness in the Romanian game. The number ten stands fifteen yards back from a ruck or maul because he knows that if he gets the ball – and it's a big if – his only option will be to kick it. The scrum half gets the ball, he takes two steps backwards, has a look around to see what options he has and if nothing is on then he shovels it back to the stand off. By now the side is at least fifteen yards behind where they won the ball, so going forward and gaining ground is difficult. All this said, the rugby is of good standard and there is a very good work ethic. The biggest improvement to be made is with the coaching and the Romanian Rugby Federation which is in the process of change. I feel that with the help of the IRB, Romanian rugby will improve immensely over the next couple of years.

Hari Dumitraş has been totally on board with everything I have suggested to him; he has used it and it has moved them forward, there is no doubt about that. The first two games which I was involved in were against Portugal and Russia, and we won them both. It was especially nice to beat Russia who had played in the 2011 World Cup, and also they were coached by a mate of mine and fellow Welshman, Kingsley Jones. We did lose to Georgia and that ended any chance we had of winning the Nations Cup. This competition is the European version of the Six Nations, but it goes on over two seasons. So having no chance of winning and with one game remaining against Spain, we decided to plan ahead and introduce a group of younger players. We only lost by a single point which was very encouraging. Following that Romania played Ukraine and won 71–0, so things are looking good. In the 2012–13 season the competition also starts as a qualification for the 2015 World Cup so there is an extra incentive to finish in the top two places; otherwise you have to go through the qualifying rounds.

Just after I arrived I noticed that a lot of work was needed on defence, so I suggested that we got a defensive coach involved. They were very happy with the idea and asked whether I knew anyone. I did, as it happened, and he was available.

Neil Kelly had been working as a defensive coach with me at Doncaster and had also been the defensive coach with Namibia during the World Cup in New Zealand. After I had ribbed him about his side shipping 80-odd points to Wales in New Plymouth, I asked if he fancied coming to Romania. The advantage as well was that his position with Namibia had been an IRB appointment, so they wouldn't raise any eyebrows about him joining me. That has worked well because in all games in the competition since Neil arrived we have only conceded three tries.

The Romanian Federation has made a conscious decision that if the team was going to progress at international level then the best players were going to have to play abroad. An interesting decision when you get some of the top nations discouraging their players from going outside their country. As a result of this policy a large number of the international squad played in France with the captain Marius Tincu, for example, at Perpignan, and one of the props at London Irish in the Premiership, so they were getting good experience of the game at a high level. I have also recommended a couple of players to the Welsh regions.

When I was first approached by Richie, the Romanian job was only being funded by the IRB until March of 2012. At the end of that period I was offered a contract for eighteen months and, providing the IRB come up with the money, that could be extended until the 2015 World Cup. I must admit that I would obviously rather have been coaching nearer to home, but as people said to me at the time, it is not often you get the chance to be involved with a side at international level. Also to be involved in another World Cup would be fantastic. More recently they have named me as the director of rugby, though what difference the name makes I have no idea.

*

Early in this book I wrote that after my experience with the Warriors, I wanted to get as far away as possible from Welsh rugby. Now, there is a completely new body of people involved, and I think they are making a genuine attempt to get the rugby right and realise its best potential.

But, I still believe that there is a big hole at the moment and that is at the development stage. I wonder what's happening at the academies, which is where our next generation of international players will come from. There has to be something in place which pushes these youngsters to the limit so that they can become better players.

The national team is young. Players like Toby Faletau, Sam Warburton, Rhys Priestland etc., who made such an impact in the 2011 World Cup, will be around for a long time, but we cannot afford to relax. We should be thinking now about the next squad, and the one after that.

My thoughts are that we should have a development team in Wales, and where better to put it than in the Valleys? We should have the best young players from the academies alongside some of our players who are coming to the twilight of their careers. Ireland put Eric Elwood and Matt Mostyn and others into Connacht; players like Stephen Jones, Martyn Williams and Shane Williams would be ideal to bring on Welsh youngsters and coach them through matches.

The development team could play in the British & Irish Cup, the Celtic League and the second level of competition in Europe, but not in the Heineken Cup. There would be no regional loyalties, so if one of the regions needed a player they could pull one from the development squad. If they then wanted to keep that player then the development team had done its job.

I am encouraged to see that a group has come together to form 'Valleys Rugby'; it shows the outside world that there is still an appetite for decent rugby in the Valleys of south Wales.

I question whether the introduction of the regions has helped to achieve any more success than we had with the clubs. Since the regions came about, at the time of writing, Scarlets and Blues have reached one semi-final each, and none of the four regions have made a final. For three years we didn't have any Welsh representation in the knockout stages at all. So how can it be said that our rugby now is more competitive? The success Wales had in New Zealand in 2011 shows that something must be going in the right direction, but I certainly don't think it's down to regional rugby.

On the downside several of those players are not playing their rugby in Wales anymore. Many have gone for the big contracts in France. No one can blame a professional sportsman for going after the money and I don't blame them for looking abroad. The problem is there isn't sufficient money in the regional game in Wales. The answer must be a centralised contract. Welsh rugby fans want to see the top players in action at their grounds and, after all, the whole idea of regional rugby was to bring the best players together. These days our best players are not even playing in the same country – let alone the same regional sides.

Romania has given me a buzz again and being involved in another World Cup would be beyond my wildest dreams. The fact that it might see me return to Wales with the Romanian team would be doubly sweet. It would be another opportunity for people to see what they might have missed with Lynn Howells.